VARIETIES OF
AMERICAN RELIGION

VARIETIES OF
AMERICAN RELIGION

THE GOAL OF RELIGION AS INTERPRETED
BY REPRESENTATIVE EXPONENTS
OF SEVENTEEN DISTINCTIVE TYPES OF
RELIGIOUS THOUGHT

EDITED BY
CHARLES SAMUEL BRADEN

Essay Index Reprint Series

 BOOKS FOR LIBRARIES PRESS
FREEPORT, NEW YORK

INTERNATIONAL STANDARD BOOK NUMBER:
0-8369-2307-3

LIBRARY OF CONGRESS CATALOG CARD NUMBER:
76-156616

PRINTED IN THE UNITED STATES OF AMERICA

To

MY MOTHER

ACKNOWLEDGMENTS

THE editor desires to acknowledge with deep appreciation the hearty co-operation of the contributors to this volume. He is grateful, first of all, that, working as all of them are under a heavy burden of responsibility, they were willing to employ the considerable time and effort necessary to prepare the material presented here; and second, for the fine courtesy, promptness and patience with which they have given attention to such detailed matters as it was necessary to bring to their notice. The editor has been impressed at every turn by the humility in which these recognized leaders have submitted their material and the readiness with which they have accepted editorial suggestions. It has been a joy to work with them.

Thanks and appreciation are due also to that small group of my students upon whom I " tried out " each chapter, and whose response proved helpful in evaluating and editing the various contributions.

CHARLES S. BRADEN

NORTHWESTERN UNIVERSITY
Evanston, Illinois
October, 1935

CONTENTS

CONTENTS

Part Three
The Goal of Religion as Conceived within Judaism
in America

VARIETIES OF
AMERICAN RELIGION

FOREWORD

THE purpose behind *Varieties of American Religion* is twofold. It arose first of all out of a definite need on the part of the writer as a teacher of the History of Religions for a brief, consistent statement of the wide variety of points of view in religion in America to which students could be referred. However, a second purpose, perhaps more important in its influence on the project, was that simply of an historian of religion desiring to present a cross-section of the present-day thought of the living religious leaders of America.

The author might have chosen quite another type of contributor. He might have gone to the theological seminaries and enlisted various writers from among the theologians. There are three reasons why this was not done. First, because a systematic theologian might reasonably object to so serious a limitation of space for the expression of his thought; second, the language, like the point of view, of certain representatives might prove to be more or less academic; and third, the result might in some cases represent the cloistered aspect of religion rather than that which actually directs and influences the lives of the masses of men. Instead of going to the theological seminaries, therefore, the editor went to present-day distinguished leaders and preachers who are in the midst of a vigorous ministry and asked them to say just what it is that they are offering in the name of religion and how those values can be secured.

There are obviously some serious objections to such a plan. One is, and it has been voiced to the editor in personal conversation, that one would not get a closely reasoned, carefully worked out, clear-cut statement. But why? he wonders. Certainly if any men in the United States in the active ministry could be found who would qualify on the intellectual side, the men who have written here would surely do so. If it be true, and the author believes that it is not true, that even our most distinguished leadership is not itself clear or cannot express itself systematically and clearly, is not that really the measure of the actual status of religion and religious thinking within the country? Obviously these men have studied in the seminaries or universities. They of course read the books written by the academic professors of religion, but after all it is they who represent in themselves — more effectively perhaps than in any other way that could be found — just how religion is understood and interpreted at the present time.

It will be noted that in the list of contributors there are but two men who stand in academic positions, but both of these men are at the same time preachers who every week speak to greater or smaller congregations and interpret religion to the people. The book must, therefore, be judged strictly on this basis, not as a scholarly contribution to systematic theology but as a cross-section of the thought of distinguished living leaders in the various religious groups in America.

In the selection of writers for the symposium, the editor was guided by his own personal acquaintance with some of them, by acquaintance with the writings and work of others, and in a few cases, by the suggestion of one or several representatives of a given point of view. The men who have written do not represent the particular denominations to which they belong as such, but a point of view. It is partly accident and only partly by design that no two writers belong to the same denomination. The Fundamentalist Protestant is a Baptist. Certainly a Presbyterian or a Methodist might have been found who could worthily, though not better, have represented that position. The Orthodox Protestant is a Presbyterian; he might have been Lutheran, Congregationalist, or Disciple of Christ. The Liberal representative is Methodist; a Baptist Liberal or a Congregationalist or a Presbyterian could have been chosen. The point is that each man stands for something larger and more inclusive than a denomination — a point of view which cuts squarely across lines of denominational demarcation. Bishop Stewart speaks for the Sacramentarian emphasis, to which, while differing of course in some details, many members of other churches, including the Greek Orthodox, would gladly subscribe.

The seventeen contributors to this symposium represent seventeen distinctive points of view in religion. It is possible that another editor might have included more — or less. Why just seventeen? Well, first of all, space made it necessary to place a limit both on the number of writers and the length of their contributions. It would be easy to enumerate other groups which in point of numbers of adherents might claim the right to consideration. In the last analysis the choice was a personal one for which the editor alone must assume responsibility. One definite criterion might be mentioned which at once excluded some points of view, namely this, only movements American in origin have been included among the more modern movements outside the traditional Protestant-Catholic-Jewish groups.

A careful student will observe that within Protestantism — or perhaps better, non-Roman Catholic Christianity — there are distinguished six points of view. Although the editor does not himself like labels in religion, it seems almost necessary for purposes of comparison within Protestantism to use them here. He has, accordingly, adopted such labels as are commonly used, and without, so far as he himself is concerned, wishing thereby to pass judgment either adverse or favorable upon any writer or his point of view, Dr. Riley is classed as Fundamentalist, Dr. Foulkes as Orthodox, Dr. Tittle as Liberal, and Dr. Ames as a Radical. The Fundamentalist, Orthodox, Liberal and Radical are differentiated mainly on general theological grounds; the Sacramentarian on the method of attaining the goal. The Barthian point of view is not to be accounted for as different wholly on the basis of either of these criteria, but is, nevertheless, significantly different.

Are there just six points of view, or are there indeed six? Again it is the arbitrary choice of the editor, supported however, it may be said, by not a few with whom he has counseled in planning the book. The one omission which may be noted is that of the Eastern Orthodox Catholic. But after all, is there a really significant difference between that and the thorough-going Anglo-Catholic or High Church point of view, always considering it of course for our present purpose, with respect to the goal of religion and its method of achievement? It was originally planned to include a representative of the mystic point of view and Dr. Rufus M. Jones was invited to contribute the chapter. Unfortunately he was unable to do so.

What of such new movements as the Oxford Group movement or Buchmanism? Is it, for example, not different? But in what way does it differ materially from Orthodox Evangelicalism, save perhaps in the detail of its technique for attaining its end, individual salvation through Christ? In that there is nothing novel or unusual.

Is one representative of Roman Catholicism enough? Some will think not. But on the basis of the Roman Catholic claim to unity of faith " semper ubique eadem " would it not be impossible to discover significantly different answers to the questions proposed? A difference there might be as to the relative emphasis upon the individual and the social aspects of the church's mission, but after all, has not the church laid down in very definite terms its definition of salvation and its mode of achievement?

The points of view thus far indicated stand within the orbit of traditional trinitarian Christianity which embraces, of course, the vast majority of religious people. But there are important minority points of view which attract no inconsiderable number of people, and some of them, if not large in point of numbers, do nevertheless exercise a profound influence upon American life by reason of the people who adhere to them. This group includes Mormonism, which, while generally regarded by Orthodox Christians as heterodox is, nevertheless, trinitarian in its beliefs. Nor does Unity hesitate in its use of the language of trinitarian Christianity. Save for its emphasis upon healing and prosperity or wellbeing, it does not differ significantly from conservative Christianity.

Christian Science by its very name, of course, associates itself directly with the Christian tradition. It likewise is definitely Trinitarian, although in its interpretation of the Trinity as well as in many other theological beliefs it differs markedly from traditional Christianity. Like Unity it places strong but not exclusive emphasis upon healing, though their respective philosophies underlying healing differ widely. Certainly Christian Science represents a distinctive point of view and an increasingly influential one.

Humanism, at least sheer naturalistic Humanism, is of course no longer to be identified exclusively with Christianity. Their basic philosophies are diametrically opposed, Christianity being theistic, Humanism nontheistic. Yet Humanism in America does derive directly from Christianity and in its general aims and its ethics is recognizably Christian. The leaders of the Humanist movement are or were almost all Unitarian clergymen. That is, they really represent one further step in the graded Protestant shades of difference: Fundamentalism, Orthodoxy, Liberalism, Radicalism, then Humanism. One thing this symposium seems to show is that there is precisely this gradation, not so much in the ends sought after, as in the degree of dependence upon other than human aid in the attainment of the goal.

The question may then arise, what of the point of view of those Unitarians who have not become naturalistic Humanists? The answer is that they do not differ significantly enough from those farther out toward the radical wing of the general Protestant groups to make it necessary to include them. At least that is the opinion of the editor.

Closely similar to Humanism, especially in its ethical emphasis and its strong sense of human values, is the Ethical Culture point of view. It would be easy to confuse the two and it is likely that there is a zone between them in which it would be difficult if not impossible to distinguish one from the other. Yet there is in the two papers representing these two groups a very real difference of view.

Spiritualism and Theosophy stand farther from the traditional groups than any of the former. Spiritualism in its supreme emphasis on the possibility of communication with the departed through mediums is unique among the various religious groups. The specifically religious complexion of

Spiritualism is largely determined by the religious backgrounds of the individual Spiritualists. In a Christian community its coloring is distinctly Christian. Officially defined
as a religion, it lacks the warmth and personal quality of
traditional Christianity. In its religious services, however,
that warmth is by no means always lacking. Theosophy is,
of all, the most definitely foreign of the points of view, being
very largely influenced by Hinduism. Yet even this, in the
paper included in this collection, is brought into some kind
of relationship with traditional Christian concepts. There
is no denying that its view is distinctive.

Finally Judaism, the faith of the Jews of America, expresses itself in three rather distinctive forms. Orthodoxy, or
traditional Judaism, Reform Judaism, the liberal group, and
the so-called Conservative. The difference between the two
extremes is easily recognizable. The position of the in-
between group, never closely defined, is much more difficult
to represent. It embraces every shading of difference from
Orthodoxy to Reform. The paper of Rabbi Goldman, who
is technically a Conservative, does not, therefore, represent
strictly this viewpoint. Where to have turned, and whom to
have asked to contribute what would have satisfied every-
body, the author does not know. At all events, here are three
fairly well defined positions within Judaism.

In preparing his chapter each writer had before him a
definite list of questions which he was asked to consider and
answer somewhere within the limits of his contribution.
Each was asked specifically not to answer them in one-two-
three order, but each in his own way to include them where
and how he pleased. Missing a reply to some of the questions the editor wrote asking about it. Sometimes the reply
was in effect: " My silence at that point represents faithfully

my attitude toward it." The ultimate aim of the book was to get in clearly stated form the answer to what the editor considers the most fundamental questions that can be asked about religion, namely: What is it that religion offers man, and how are these values mediated to him? or in still other words, What is the goal of religion, and how may it be attained? Where the various writers have answered these questions clearly, little insistence has been placed upon detailed answers to the detailed questions asked them. In the appendix is included the list of questions and suggestions each writer was given.

Each contributor is alone responsible for his own chapter. The editor obviously could not agree with all of them. His function as he conceives it has been to set the questions to be discussed, and then accept what the writer offered, limiting himself to attempting to see (1) that the main questions were really dealt with, (2) that the viewpoint was stated in clear and understandable terms, (3) that it did not go over a certain limited length, and (4) that its literary style was up to standard.

Obviously, contradiction between writers as to facts had to be adjusted. Some quite obvious misstatements of fact had to be corrected, but other statements, supposedly of facts which the editor does not regard as facts at all, have been allowed to stand. Some references to various phases of the history of religion on which the editor holds a totally different view have been allowed to go unquestioned. In some cases the conclusion of the writer depended upon his particular statement of the supposed facts. Each chapter is the writer's own; for any errors he is responsible; for any conclusion based upon error he must be held to account.

Ordinarily within a given book spelling and capitalization

would be made uniform. Here, the editor has allowed certain variations from standard style. Both Christian Science and Unity uniformly capitalize certain words, thereby giving them a special significance. Great care has been taken to follow the original manuscripts in this regard.

Here then is the answer to man's most fundamental question about religion. Seventeen men have sincerely tried to express as simply as possible their answers to the question. Fifty years ago the answers would not have been the same. Fifty years hence what will they be? What they were in 1935 we now know. It is to be hoped that this book will serve for many years as a landmark, and in the future as a basis for comparison with that which the unfolding years bring to pass in the ongoing development of religion.

If any who seek the satisfaction of deep needs through religion find in any or all these chapters the answer to their questions about what religion can do, and thus reach the solution of their problems, it will be a source of profound satisfaction to the editor and the contributors.

WILLIAM BELL RILEY

William Bell Riley, pastor of the First Baptist Church, Minneapolis, a Hoosier by birth, was ordained to the Baptist ministry in 1883. He was graduated from Hanover College in 1885, from which he also received his Master of Arts degree in 1888, and was the same year graduated from the Southern Baptist Theological Seminary. After holding pastorates successively in Carrollton, Kentucky, New Albany and Lafayette, Indiana, Bloomington and Chicago, Illinois, he was called in 1897 to his present pastorate, where he has ministered for thirty-eight years. In 1902 he founded the Northwestern Bible Training School and has ever since served as its president.

Dr. Riley has become widely known, not alone throughout his own denomination but the entire church, as a defender of the conservative point of view in theology. Editor of *The Christian Fundamentalist* and executive secretary of the World's Christian Fundamentals Association, he has been a militant leader in the Fundamentalist-Modernist controversy. The titles of some of his books indicate the author's general point of view:

The Finality of the Higher Criticism, 1909; *The Perennial Revival,* 1913; *The Evolution of the Kingdom,* 1913; *Crisis of the Church,* 1914; *Menace of Modernism,* 1917; *Daniel vs. Darwin,* 1918; *Inspiration or Evolution?* 1923; *Christ the Incomparable,* 1924; *Fundamentalism vs. Liberalism,* 1925; *The Blight of Unitarianism,* 1926; and *Ten Burning Questions,* 1930. In 1933 he completed a series of forty volumes under the title *The Bible of the Expositor and the Evangelist.*

With such a record of active leadership in the Fundamentalist movement, it was logical that Dr. Riley should be asked to present in this symposium the goal of religion as conceived by the more conservative leaders of the church.

I

FUNDAMENTALISM

By WILLIAM B. RILEY

RELIGION is the permanent feature of human life. The claim that no tribe of men has been discovered whose savagery was so low that they had no religion, and that no society has yet attained to such heights of civilization as to dispense safely with all religion, is hardly to be doubted.

As, in Nathaniel Hawthorne's story *Main Street,* the hardy American pioneers, " accustomed as they had been to stand under the big arches of vast cathedrals, . . . with carved altar work, with pictured windows where the light of common day was hallowed by being transmitted through the glorified figures of saints, where the rich peal of the solemn organ rolled along wide and lengthened aisles," created for themselves in the American woods a rough-hewn log hut and, crowding into it on the Lord's Day, confidently expected to find God there, so in all the stages of civilization, and under all the conceivable circumstances of human existence, men have sought both to see His face and to secure His favor. These fears and faiths, these spiritual aspirations and endeavors we call religion. This is transcendently the permanent quality in human existence. It is not our purpose to speak of the varied forms religion takes, nor yet of the shifting sentiments of religionists, but rather of religion's goal, as requested by the editor of this volume.

Incidentally we shall strive to answer certain questions propounded in connection with that request. Primary among these is the main question: " What is it that religion offers to men individually and socially? "

The answer to that question is capable of being reduced to a single statement, but the statement will, in its elucidation, demand more than the limitations of this chapter. Our answer is in the language of Christian orthodoxy, and yet we shall contend that it is applicable to the whole subject of religion. It is — *The Salvation of the Soul.*

This five-word statement is, beyond question, religion's quest; but, though brief in statement, it is as comprehensive as the temporal and eternal interests of immortal man. " The salvation of the soul " is a pregnant statement. *It involves a search for God!*

It is doubtful if we have a better definition of the chief end of man than that provided in the Presbyterian catechism — " To glorify God and to enjoy Him forever." " Where there is no vision the people perish." (Proverbs 29:18).

The prophets of every civilization determine the civilization itself. To know them and their views of God would be to know, without the necessity of seeing it, the civilization of which they are the leaders. If that view of God is a debased one, a debased civilization follows. If lofty, a high state of civilization is not only to be expected — it will be discovered.

There are those who imagine that the God even of Christian conception is destined to be lost in the immensity of new discoveries. The measurements of modern science in light years, they tell us, stagger the imagination, and faith is in danger of being lost " in the dark void of a cosmic order in which light itself grows old in its journey from star to star." But the exact opposite result is, for the intelligent, still more likely.

As we read Jeans's *Mysterious Universe* and again his *Stars in their Courses,* the Person of God grows to the immeasurable, His power to omnipotence, and His wisdom to infinity. In other words, modern science — where it is a science and not a speculation — instead of taking God from us, increases Him for us. " The heavens declare the glory of God; and the firmament sheweth his handiwork." (Psalm 19:1).

Religion, therefore, holds no innate antagonism to science; and Christianity, the noblest of all religions, is and has always been its friend and patron. In this remark, let it be understood that we insist upon a clean distinction between science and speculation.

Religion also requires a medium of God's manifestation. The highest form of religion is doubtless that which accepts " one perfect ethical spirit as the ground and lawgiver of the universe and the founder and redeemer of mankind." Jesus is reported to have said to the woman at the well: " God is a Spirit, and they that worship Him must worship Him in spirit and in truth." But man, in his physical and mental limitations, has found it difficult to approach a pure spirit; and so, from the lowest form of religion to the highest, an incarnation has been demanded by searching man and, when not found, has been appointed or created.

This remark is true in all stages from animism through idolatry to the worship of one God. Christianity contends that that desire on the part of man for an embodiment of God finally found its realization in Jesus of Nazareth, who was " God manifest in the flesh."

The advanced thinker of the present day who proposes to repudiate the Incarnate Christ, but who in the next breath supplants Him with either a doctrine of " humanism " or a promise of " the superman," manifestly leaves the heights in religion and starts again on the downward trail to idolatry. If salvation depends upon seeing God, in the sense of coming into a knowledge of Him as both Creator and Divine Redeemer, then certainly Christianity holds the supreme place among the religions of the world of all ages. He is the only Incarnation that hinted a God of infinite power, infinite wisdom, and yet of infinite grace and infinite love.

Dr. J. H. Jowett sanely remarks: "The biggest thing with which the mind can cope is the infinite love of God; and all our sanctified powers, and all the ministries of holy fellowship, and all the explorations of eternity will never reach a limit in its unsearchable wealth. The biggest thing you and I will ever know is the love of God in Jesus Christ our Lord. There will always be 'a region beyond,' and for the already wondering eyes there will always be a new surprise: 'The height, and depth, and length, and breadth, and to know the love of God, which passeth knowledge.'"[1]

But the salvation of the soul involves sins forgiven. The pioneer reason for a search after God is found in the sense of sin. This also obtains with all people of all places and times. Paul's statements — " they are all under sin "; " there is none righteous, no, not one "; " they are all gone out of the way " — are true of the whole human race, and in varying degrees people are realizing that fact and seeking redemption's way.

It is said of Confucianism that " it involves no confession of sin," no seeking of forgiveness; but, if so, that could only be in consequence of the fact that it demands no communion with God, and on that account it can scarcely be called a religion. However, since it is a system of ethics, and since Confucius himself confessed that he had failed to practice all that he preached, that definition of sin which involves " the missing of the mark " applies to its advocates as surely as it

[1] *Things That Matter Most*, p. 10.

does to those who believe that sin is "a transgression of the law" of God.

Buddhism frankly admits sin and places its hope for redemption in Nirvana. Mohammedanism accompanied its command that we worship one God with the demand that we cease from idolatries. But the record of Mohammed's life involves the charges of boastfulness, cunning, cowardice, vengeance, and finally sensuality and murder.

Gaius Glenn Atkins says: "In one form or another every religion has staged a drama of the soul in its quest for deliverance. . . . Religion began with just that, and one may gravely wonder whether, if that motive should permanently disappear, religion itself will permanently endure." [2]

Whether or not we ever find a basis of agreement as to the origin of sin, there is an overwhelming conviction of its existence and the consequent sense that the soul for redemption needs God. It was Jowett again who, referring to having recently crossed the spot in the Atlantic where the Titanic sank, spoke of it as having gone too far down for man ever to reach and recover its treasures; but he added: "And I thought of all the human wreckage engulfed and sunk in oceanic depths of nameless sin — but not too far down for the love of God. 'He descended into hell'; He got down to our sin and beneath it, and there is no human wreckage lying in the ooze of the deepest sea of iniquity that His love cannot reach and redeem." [3]

> Stronger His love than death or hell,
> Its riches are unsearchable:
> The first-born sons of light
> Desire in vain its depths to see,
> They cannot tell the mystery,
> The length, and breadth, and height!

[2] *Religion in Our Times*, p. 13.   [3] *Things That Matter Most*, p. 18.

The problem of *Religion,* then, is the problem of salvation. If Christians are right, and certainly history stands in their favor, that problem was solved on Calvary's Cross when God Himself, in human form, hung there dying — " the just for the unjust," "bearing our sins in His own body on the tree " — and followed the sacrifice with the proffer of pardon, the gift of peace, and the promise of an eternal felicity with Him!

That which favors Christianity above all other religions is the multiplied demonstration of its ability to make good, in the sense of sins forgiven, peace enjoyed, and the exhilaration of a promised heaven. These could bring their witnesses to the Court of Inquiry by the multiplied millions; and in that single respect Christianity tops the religions of the centuries and takes its place at the pinnacle of human experience.

Christ seems to have been able to actualize His departing promise — " Peace I leave with you; my peace I give unto you " (John 14:27) — and His apostles went forth, daring to preach peace by Jesus Christ and promised, through His Name: " Whosoever believeth on Him shall receive remission of sins."

But, as we suggested when we used the phrase " The Salvation of the Soul," there are directly related interests involved in every religion but finding their acme of expression in the Christian religion. These we might call *The Spiritual Products.*

As the salvation of the soul follows a search for God, so the success of that endeavor produces definite results. These we may express in three sentences: The Divinely indwelt man is a better man; the Divinely guided man is a happier man; the Divinely inspired man is a greater man.

The Divinely indwelt man is a better man. Irrespective of the teaching of so-called sacred books, and without reference to the claim of inspiration for the Sacred Scriptures, there is a fair degree of agreement in the world concerning at least the latter half of the decalogue as a basis for morals and conscience. The thing that we call conscience, though found in but slight form with some men, seems sufficiently to assert itself on the subjects of " murder," " adultery," " theft," " false witness " and " covetousness " to effect a fair degree of conviction; and history illustrates that the men who claim an experience of God strive to resist these temptations, and in the endeavor discover ethical superiority.

Chauncey Depew, the brilliant New York attorney, was not ignorant of history nor lacking in keen observation upon the conduct and destinies of his fellow men. When his ninety-second birthday was being celebrated in New York, the reporters interviewed him (as had been their custom for twenty-two years), to draw from his lips some message that might profit the public; and on that memorable day he said: " No young man starting out in life can afford to ignore religion, unless he wishes to be a failure."

Modern unbelief has signally failed to provide religion's competitor in character-building. The ethics and morals of Russia, instead of improving on the substitution of atheism for religion, have so sadly declined that, on the testimony of the best informed, wrongs have abolished rights, lust has displaced love, and murder has obliterated mercy. Harold Begbie's *Twice Born Men* is a clinic of changed and improved characters, and his claim that these moral marvels were wrought by an incoming of God in Christ is difficult to disprove. " By their fruits ye shall know them."

Howe'er it be, it seems to me,
　'Tis only noble to be good,
Kind hearts are more than coronets,
　And simple faith than Norman blood.

The Divinely guided man is a happier man. If multiplied
testimonies can put any question past dispute, this statement
seems justified, and the remark would apply to practically
every form of religion that includes a belief in God. We
may not consent to the teachings of either Zoroaster or Mohammed, but we must admit that each of them attained a
degree of soul-contentment in the continued contemplation
of Him, for Zoroaster sought to escape evil by coming into
His presence and Mohammed by surrendering the will completely to Him.

But again, the religion of Christ shows fruits more satisfactory, for while Zoroaster fretted over the conflict between
good and evil, and while Mohammed sought a complete
surrender of self, neither of them knew aught of the exultant
joy of living for God or the glory of dying for Him, as have
the Christian laborers and martyrs of many centuries. Without asking what he meant by it — which means putting
our own interpretation upon it — we approve heartily the
statement of the late Dr. Briggs: "Divine authority is the
only authority on which man can rest in loving certainty and
build with joyous confidence."

As an elixir of joy, no sentiment exceeds or even equals
this certainty — God is with us! Oliver Cromwell once said
— "I have been inured to difficulties; I never found God
failing when I trusted in Him." It was of such men that
Robertson Nicoll was thinking when he wrote: "Such lives
must draw, not from the shallow streams of earth, but from
the deep fountains that flow out of the throne."

The Divinely inspired man is a greater man. We would not contend that all the great men of earth have been God's men, or even good men. The mental brilliance of certain bad men is not to be denied, nor the greatness of some godless men called into question. But that God in the life of a man is an energizing force, the fruits of which are unmeasured and immeasurable, history abundantly illustrates. John Watson in *The Mind of the Master* remarks: "Christianity is in religion what steam is in mechanics — the power which drives."

Edgar Guest was not necessarily wrong, therefore, when he said: "Without my religion I should have gone down, where I have climbed up; I should have been sordid, where I have found joy in being sentimental; I should have been shunned, where I have been welcomed. . . . I am sure that I should have done many things which would have been to me a shame and a regret. . . . I would rather die leaving nothing to my boy but his religion, than to die leaving him a fortune, with no religion."

It will not be forgotten that when Mr. Gladstone was Premier in England, fifty of his Cabinet of fifty-five were professed Christians and the others religionists of other forms; nor should it be ignored that in our own government — in which, we trust, there is at least a slight advancement over the average intelligence — five-sixths of our representatives profess some form of the Christian faith.

But a wider sweep of history will bring to the fore more important illustrations. To call the names of the outstanding figures of the past two thousand years would be well-nigh like providing a Christian catalogue. Such an attempt, therefore, is out of order in a limited chapter.

But, to touch a few of the spots, let it be remembered that

Thomas Aquinas and Bacon, Leibnitz and Locke, Faraday and Newton, Dante and Milton, Michelangelo and Raphael, Wilberforce and Robert Raikes, John Howard and Florence Nightingale, and a few thousand others worthy to be mentioned with these, were men and women of deep Christian conviction.

If one picks up a volume like Herrick's *Some Heretics of Yesterday* one faces afresh this illustration, for into it are written Tauler, Wyclif, Hus, Savonarola, Latimer, Cranmer, Melancthon, Knox, Calvin, Coligny, William Brewster and Wesley — and yet, instead of completing his roster, he has named only a few. And that which is true in the profession of preaching is almost equally true of the greater scientists, philosophers and statesmen of the past.

Henry van Dyke, after showing how the ideals that men had set before them revealed such defects that Stoicism and Epicureanism became corruption and frivolity, that militarism hardened into intolerable cruelty and tyranny, art into luxury and self-indulgence, and socialism into the ugly shapes of anarchy and nihilism, concludes by saying that men and women who have built upon faith's foundation, involving faith in Christ, " have been the best men and women, and have left behind them the most enduring and glorious work." [4]

This all leads naturally to our last division in this discussion of religion, namely, *The Social Implications*. In fact, we have anticipated that subject to some degree already, but there remains an abundance that can be said, and as one approaches it one longs for a volume instead of a chapter in which to express oneself.

It produces and makes purer domestic relations. The

[4] *Sermons to Young Men*, p. 250.

home is a religious institution; the family is the product of some sort of faith. If a tribe could be found that had no religion of any sort it would pretty surely follow that no marriage relation would be regarded and no domestic morality practiced. The proof of this position is discoverable now in the Bolshevik State, in which marriage is a mere matter of mutual consent and divorce is accomplished at the will of either party at any moment, and in which children are no longer the responsibility of parents but are wards of the state.

Irreligion, therefore, supplants love with lust, parental affection with growing indifference, and the home with a sleeping place where the sexes pig together, where the laws that claim Divine ordination as well as the customs that higher civilization has approved are alike despised. Up to the present time no high state of civilization has been attained without attention to domestic relations, nor have satisfying domestic relations existed apart from some form of religion.

Here again Christianity surpasses all else. Its laws are concise and unchangeable. According to Christ, a man shall " leave father and mother, and shall cleave to his wife: and they twain shall be one flesh." (Matthew 19:5). According to Paul, Christ's chief apostle, children must " obey their parents in the Lord," " honoring father and mother." Fathers are " not to provoke their children to wrath " but " bring them up in the nurture and admonition of the Lord." (Ephesians 6:1, 2, 4). According to the same apostle, " If any provide not for his own, and specially for those of his own house, he hath denied the faith, and is worse than an infidel." (I Timothy 5:8).

The marriage relation and the consequent home — the *sine qua non* of civilization — is one of the social products of

Christianity. Most religions retain some fragment of domestic philosophy — doubtless an inheritance from the Divine arrangement as recorded in Genesis 2:18 — and Chrisianity is the one religion which has recovererd to mankind most fully this social necessity.

Religion also eventuates in social amelioration and improvement. Some time ago an apostate from evangelical Christianity, defending the American Association for the Advancement of Atheism, said: "Let that religious opinion survive and prosper which can best commend itself by the intelligence, upright character and moral enthusiasm of its adherents." That is exactly what has already occurred, and that accounts for the growth of Christianity.

Walter Rauschenbusch quotes those who ask concerning Christianity: "Has it not lifted woman to equality and companionship with man, secured the sanctity and stability of marriage, changed parental despotism to parental service, and eliminated unnatural vice, the abandonment of children, blood revenge, and the robbery of the shipwrecked from the customs of Christian nations? Has it not abolished slavery, mitigated war, covered all lands with a network of charities to uplift the poor and the fallen, fostered the institutions of education, aided the progress of civil liberty and social justice, and diffused a softening tenderness throughout human life?" And he replies:

"It has done all that, and vastly more. The influence of Christianity in taming selfishness and stimulating the sympathetic affections, in creating a resolute sense of duty, a staunch love of liberty and independence, an irrepressible hunger for justice and a belief in the rights of the poor, has been so subtle and penetrating that no one can possibly trace its effects. We might as well try to count up the effect in our organism of all the oxygen we have inhaled since our first gasp for breath. In so far as humanity has yet been redeemed, Christianity has been its redemption. Many of us have made test of that regenerating power in our personal lives. Many, too, have marked the palpable difference in the taste of life between some social circle really affected by Christian kindliness and a similar circle untouched by Christian motives and affections."

Some years ago, when the Inter-Church Movement was at its height, those men who placed as much confidence in unregenerated humanity as they did in the members of the Christian church conceived the idea that in this great world-movement the purses of the godless could be touched with the rod of religious appeal, and from them would flow a financial flood to enrich and quicken the earth. But that abortive endeavor was an effective illustration of the fact that humane sentiments flow only from persons of deep religious conviction, and most freely from those moved by the Spirit of Christ.

It is probably true that Buddhism inspires a degree of humaneness, but Frances Power Cobbe is responsible for the claim that " not till the age of the Gospels did philanthropy thrive," and only when the religion of Jesus was held in highest affection did we produce " a Howard, a Fry, a Joseph Tuckerman, a Florence Nightingale, an Octavia Hill, a Louisa Schuyler, a Miss Dix, a Miss Carpenter, a Charles Loring Brace, and a Lord Shaftesbury."

Finally, religion promises a personal and social perfection. This statement is substantially true of all the higher forms of religion. Hinduism hopes to accomplish both by the transmigration of souls. The followers of Zoroaster are promised a final passage over the narrow bridge into an unending happiness, the wicked having signally failed to cross. Confucius, while holding forth slight promise of a life in the hereafter, advises his advocates to practice industry, modesty, sobriety and thoughtfulness — virtues which, of course, would tend in the same direction. Buddhism holds Nirvana, or a practical annihilation of personal existence, as the solution of all individual and social problems. Mohammedanism holds before its devotees the prospect of improvement here and a paradise hereafter, by the practice of multiplied prayers and fastings, almsgivings and pilgrimages.

Here again the religion of Christ provides the zenith of hope! Personal salvation is accomplished by a regenerative work of the Holy Ghost, the third Person of the Godhead, and sanctification of the spirit is won by the study and practice of Sacred Scripture. Even perfection for the body, and as a result eventually for the whole man, is to be accomplished by a physical resurrection — attended by physical, mental and spiritual perfection. (I Corinthians 15).

Albert E. Wiggam, in *The New Decalogue of Science,* joins the present-day popular writers in an attempt to solve our social problem by the creation of a " national culture " and " national loyalty," to be coupled with " cooperative internationality," and so far as we can make out from his line of argument, this is to be a biological rather than a religious procedure. "The abounding development of humanism amid the free air of individualistic, distinctive, undisturbed nationality " is " to create for all mankind a true world-wisdom through the friendly fraternity of nations that will give this blood-drenched, but still 'moonlit and dream-visited planet,' a virile, virtuous and adventurous peace."

This thesis, like the philosophies of Norman Thomas and

John Haynes Holmes, is born of that idealistic dreaming which imagines that men and nations are not sinful by nature but only through unfavorable circumstances and, consequently, need only correct adjustment in order to end all inhumanities and produce a millennium.

Strangely enough, it is such philosophies that have eventuated in the orgies of lust, war, murder, and every other conceivable form of iniquity known to the mind of man. They have no kinship with the Christian religion.

The Bible presents no utopia as the product of mere human endeavor, but only dire judgments upon the mistakes, the sins, the wars, the world-wreck that human endeavor has wrought and will work.

Paul, writing to Timothy, said: ". . . In the last days perilous times shall come. For men shall be lovers of their own selves, covetous, boasters, proud, blasphemers, disobedient to parents, unthankful, unholy, without natural affection, trucebreakers, false accusers, incontinent, fierce, despisers of those that are good, traitors, heady, highminded, lovers of pleasures more than lovers of God; having a form of godliness, but denying the power thereof: from such turn away." (II Timothy 3:1–5). While Jesus, speaking on the same subject, said: " And ye shall hear of wars and rumors of wars: see that ye be not troubled: for all these things must come to pass, but the end is not yet. For nation shall rise against nation, and kingdom against kingdom: and there shall be famines, and pestilences, and earthquakes, in divers places. All these are the beginning of sorrows." (Matthew 24:6–8).

This much at least must be admitted by the observing: that at this present moment the prophecies of Christ and His apostle are finding literal fulfillment.

And yet, the Christian religion does not leave the world without hope. It has its utopia — its blessed " millennium " — portrayed in all of its prophetic books, but most fully in its apocalyptic writings. Revelation assures a social state from which want, worry and war will be banished and over which God, in the Person of His Son, shall preside for a thousand years, dispensing perfect justice, providing perfect environments, and securing perfect social results.

But this is not the end of promise for the Christian religion. It pictures a final state of felicity to be spent under the direct supervision of God Himself, in the palace that exhausts human speech in descriptive endeavor, in a state that knows " no tears, no death, no sorrow, no pain," and a society never touched by aught that " defileth or worketh abomination, or maketh a lie." (Revelation 21, 22).

Christianity, then, is to the world and lower religions what the torch in the hand of the Statue of Liberty is to contiguous city, land, wharf and sea — the Light that shineth over all!

WILLIAM HIRAM FOULKES

William Hiram Foulkes is pastor of the Old First Presbyterian Church, Newark, New Jersey. Born in the manse at Quincy, Michigan, he took his Bachelor of Arts degree from the College of Emporia, Kansas, in 1897. His alma mater honored him successively with the Master of Arts degree in 1901, Doctor of Divinity in 1907, and Doctor of Laws in 1915. His theological work was done at McCormick Theological Seminary, whence he was graduated in 1901. Following this he held a fellowship at New College, Edinburgh. In 1901 he was ordained to the Presbyterian ministry. His pastorates have been at Elmira, Illinois, Clinton, Iowa, Portland, Oregon, New York City, Cleveland, Ohio, and Newark, New Jersey, where he has served since 1926. However, Dr. Foulkes has spent at least a third of his ministry in the service of the entire church, first as general secretary of Ministerial Relief and Sustentation of the Presbyterian church, 1913–18, and as general secretary of the New Era Movement of his denomination, 1918–24. He has been deeply interested in work with young people. Since 1925 he has been vice-president of the International Society of Christian Endeavor. He has likewise been active in the direction of the missionary work of the church, and as a member of the Board of Foreign Missions.

His writings include *Living Bread from the Fourth Gospel*, 1914; *Sunset by the Lakeside*, 1917; *Youth: Ways to Life*, 1927. He is also contributing editor of *The Christian Herald*. In 1933 he conducted the Friendly Hour over the National Broadcasting Company's radio network, and in 1934–5 for over a year conducted their program called " Homespun." Neither a Fundamentalist nor a theological liberal, he represents admirably in his ministry and in the following chapter what the editor ventures to call orthodox Protestantism.

28

II

ORTHODOX PROTESTANTISM

By WILLIAM HIRAM FOULKES

THE foremost Christian of all the centuries, by almost universal consent, is Paul of Tarsus. By every test and token he stands unrivaled. Some go so far as to say that he created Christianity. In any event, the paradox of his intimacy with Christ and the consciousness of the utter supremacy of his Master gave him the right to speak authoritatively to his day and generation. In so far as he is qualified to become the contemporary of our age, in understanding and spirit, his recorded words are valid and even vital. "We preach not ourselves," he said to his fellow disciples at Corinth, "but Christ Jesus the Lord; and ourselves your servants for Jesus' sake. For God who commanded light to shine out of darkness, hath shined in our hearts to give the light of the knowledge of the glory of God in the face of Jesus Christ" (II Corinthians 4:5, 6). Herein is expressed the true goal of religion.

"For God," and so we start with God. Christianity, like Judaism in which its traditions are historically rooted, begins "in the beginning" with "God" not to prove his existence but to exhibit those characteristics that set him apart, the things that make God really God!

Judaism starts with God. Granted that increasing ethical content was given to the conception of deity and recognizing that the picture of God revealed, for instance, in the book of Judges is quite unlike that disclosed in the writings of the ethical prophets, still the fact remains that Judaism postulates God — does not prove God, does not find him at the end of a long quest, but starts out with him. This gives a religious cast to the old philosophic aphorism *Ex nihilo nihil fit* by substituting the words *Ex Deo omnium fit*. So all through the pages of the Old Testament the Creator is walking in the midst of his creation. Strong and mighty, sovereign and holy, transcendent and infinite, yet he walks in the midst of his world. Marc Connelly's moving drama, *Green Pastures*, wherein the late Richard Berry Harrison, of humble soul and lofty mien, becomes " de Lawd," is only a reverently attuned echo of the pastoral simplicity of early Jewish conceptions of God, at once tangible and ineffable. Christian faith, as it was bound to do, appropriated bodily the Hebraic idea of God. Religion to the Jew and to the Christian cannot be essentially the quest of man for God. It may be that secondarily. In essence it is God's search for man. " In the beginning, God " (Genesis 1:1), begins the Torah of Judaism. " In the beginning was the Word, and the Word was with God and the Word was God " (John 1:1), says the Johannine prologue to the Christian Gospel. To the Christian, therefore, as to the Jew, God is the source and the satisfaction of religious faith and experience. He is what the metaphysicians have called First Cause. To start with God does not mean that religion begs the question. It means only that it begins with an adequate beginning for what is to follow. This does not assume either that to begin one's religion as the Christian does, with the assumption of God, is to invalidate confirmatory revelations, or even to render culpable the full exercise of one's powers of mind. To the Jew and to the Christian, God was and is essentially cosmic. Even though at first, in certain sections of the Old Testament, he is portrayed in more parochial forms, there is always an implication of his sovereign universality. It is a tribute to the majestic significance of the Hebraic conceptions of the transcendent glory of God that even those of us who are Christians continue to find spiritual food in the Psalter of ancient Israel and for the most part have found nothing better, and little as good, for the antiphonal services of public worship.

"For God who . . ." To the Christian as well as the Jew, God is " who " and not " what." There is all the difference in the world between the two conceptions. We who have been living through these recent spiritually precarious years, with the clamor and din of mechanistic assertions in our ears (as sheerly dogmatic as any theological assumptions ever were), find it difficult to think of God as "who." It has been contagiously popular to begin with a " what." That is why all the mechanistic, materialistic schemes have scant room for religion. They provided no room for it in their first principles. Starting with "what" they never arrive at " who." How refreshing it is to a Christian when a master scientist like the late Michael Pupin, with no charge of ignorance justly to be laid at his door, proudly asserts his supreme and sublime confidence in a " God who . . . " There are today stimulating movements in the intellectual borderland between science and philosophy which presage a better understanding between devout theologians and sincere scientists — a rapport that is as rationally justifiable as it is religiously satisfying. While this is gratifyingly true, it does not alter the basic fact that, from its beginning, rooted in the Jewish religion and springing forth in the person of its Founder, Christianity has been the religion of the " God who . . ." Let the scientists speak as they may — and, as it would seem today, they must — of " cosmic energy," " moral purpose," " the creative mind,"

" universal intelligence "; let the seers with their imaginative insights descant upon "the power not ourselves," " the power at the heart of things," " the spirit of wisdom and truth "; in both cases they are only faintly echoing what Judaism and Christianity have postulated all along, that God is not a " what " but a " who." The supreme goal of religion, then, to the Christian, is to find the reality of the universe, by finding the God who, at the beginning, through all the processes of existence and at the end of the way, is the real *raison d'etre* of human life and of the universe itself.

In other words, Christianity is rooted in its conception of the character of God. That is why the humanistic portrayals of life, with many confessedly beautiful and even necessary elements, are basically unsound and inadequate. Humanism, like its ancient prototypes, is once again trying to build its Babel to the sky. Christianity, like its ancient forerunner, finds life revealed from above. "Ye must be born from above." (John 3:7, Revised Version, margin; Moffatt, Goodspeed). Upon so strong and secure a philosophical base the Christian religion has built its conception of God, and consequently its conception of man. God, to the Christian, is all that reverent modern science has declared him to be, upon the assured reality of what prophets and apostles, saints and martyrs have found him to be in their own experience.

"For God who commanded." The Christian religion has been spared the snare of at least one great ethnic religion. God, in the Christian conception, is not lost in his world. He is its Commander-in-Chief. His hand is upon the helm. He controls the throttle and he moves the levers. He commands! It is a bold assumption, but it is vital to a rationale of existence. Even those who deny his right to command

have to invent some "deus ex machina," some blind per-
turbation of force, some fortuitous concourse of atoms, some
mysterious emanation of protons or electrons to take the
place of a God who commands. It is entirely possible that
Christian theologians may have squeezed the vitality out of
the idea of divine transcendence. They may have rendered
it as mechanical and abstract as certain scientists have made
life itself through their use of scalpel and forceps; yet, at its
roots, the idea of divine sovereignty is vital and full of personal value. To the Christian "who lives his creed" God is
contemporaneous in his transcendence. He did not fashion
the world and fling it off into space — and then withdraw to
some Olympian height to watch it spin, until it slowed down
and finally stopped or crashed.

It may have been that a bare score of years ago, under the
tutelage of the intelligentsia, we felt no need of any power
higher than merely human. Were we not well on our way
up from the jungle and the pit? Was not the cave-man
steadily disintegrating and the superman rapidly developing? Had not scientific skill annihilated the time and space
barriers that had so long divided mankind, and did not
glorified self-interest assure us that the end of all internecine
strife was just around the corner? Then suddenly (so it then
seemed) the most devastating war in human history was let
loose upon the human race, and we are still eating its ashes
and drinking its wormwood and gall! The sophisticate
may nevertheless contend that he needs no commander for
his craft. He may even strut to and fro upon the bridge of
his little bark, slapping himself upon the chest and crying
out to the winds and the waves, "I am the captain of my
soul!" But he deludes only himself.

Many of our contemporaries, we have a right to believe,

who are not ready to avow a full-orbed Christian faith, are at least casting wistful eyes in its direction. While they may decline to declare that " the eternal God is [their] refuge and underneath are the everlasting arms " (Deuteronomy 33: 27), they are nevertheless seeking, if they are sincere, for a foundation that standeth sure, for at least a solid foothold in life. Christianity, not copyrighted by the label of some sect or falsely claimed as private property by some cult, but standing upon its own inalienable, historic rights, offers to every sincere seeker after truth a rockribbed universe, with the structural steel framework of truth, and with a divine architect and artificer both behind the scenes and eternally at work in his own creative enterprise. What higher goal could a religion offer to struggling mankind today than that of conscious contact with reality in terms of a God who commands?

" For God who commanded light to shine." The symbolism of light is so matchless that it is easy to lose oneself in its poetic interpretation. Half a hundred similes and metaphors come trooping by in the livery of light. Essentially, light stands for the outshining of the truth. It has reality at its core and revelation as its circumference. " God is light," is the assertion of Christian faith, " and in him is no darkness at all! " (I John 1:5).

As God is one to the Christian, so is truth one. The unfolding of truth must therefore be in harmony with the character of God. It may be progressive; it must be consistent. The function of light is to shine. Once again, the essential idea of Christianity that God is seeking man is implicit in the conception of revelation. Man is not a blind worm groping a sightless way to the light and by itching for it bringing it into being. God is ever causing light to

shine into the darkness and opening man's blind eyes in
order that he may see. The Christian conception of revelation revolves around the central fact of a self-revealing God.
The Scriptures of the Old Testament as a historic base and
the Scriptures of the New Testament as a historic norm are
illuminated from within, by the outshining of a light which
God himself has commanded. That is to say, Christianity
turns to its historic sources in the Holy Scriptures not under
the compulsion of courts and sees, but impelled by a spiritual
apprehension of the direction from which light comes, and it
is met by the unfolding of that light, which makes the New
Testament inescapably contemporaneous after nineteen hundred years. From the Christian point of view God also continues to make his light shine. While there is such a uniqueness in the scriptural revelation of the Word of God that the
Bible becomes to the Christian the very Word of God, it is so
because the historic sources of the divine revelation are recorded there, not because the revelation itself has been
finished. More light is always expected to break forth, not
independent of the Holy Scriptures, but reflected from their
pages and ranging the whole compass of reality. The Christian religion offers the seeker after truth the assurance of an
unfolding revelation, with many rays and hues, not only in
syllogistic form, not always in prosaic annals, but sometimes
in lyric and dramatic guise, often in parable and poem —
and, whatever its form, always supreme and self-consistent.
God commanded light to shine and, for the Christian, still
causes it to shine, cosmic in its sweep and significance and
yet personal enough to be " a lamp unto [one's] feet and a
light unto [one's] path." (Psalm 119:105).

" Out of darkness." Christianity is essentially a religion of
deliverance. What light does to darkness is a parable of the

way in which divine truth overcomes evil. The stern realism of the Christian religion accounts, in part, for the opposition which has always confronted it. Men do not desire to be called sinners. Even today, under the staggering burden of human suspicion and lust, hatred and greed, humanity — individually and collectively — is striving to walk as jauntily as though there were no such realities as sin and guilt. New labels have been invented for old experiences. Drift, estrangement and tension have taken the places of sin, guilt and iniquity. No offense need be taken, however, over a changed nomenclature so long as the reality is recognized and reckoned with. The Christian conception of redemption, arising out of the New Testament record of the life, death and resurrection of Jesus, would be meaningless if man did not need a deliverer. The initial goal of Christian faith is the consciousness of divine forgiveness. The New Testament Scriptures and the history of the Christian Church through the centuries are ablaze with the record of redemptive experiences in which men have been delivered from the darkness of sin and evil and made partakers of moral and spiritual light. The Christian, not less than the Hindu devotee who impales himself perpetually upon a bed of spikes in order to be rid of the curse of evil, seeks divine deliverance. The essential difference is that the Christian finds deliverance proceeding freely out of the divine nature, while the Hindu seeks by self-torture to merit and to procure it. Redemption to the Christian is the moral passion of God, the driving, dynamic urge of the universe, God's love burning at white heat for unworthy man.

The Cross of Christ, which is confessedly central in Christianity, holds its unique and supreme place because it presents in factual form the paradox of the divine passion —

light once being swallowed up of darkness in order that darkness might be finally and forever swallowed up in light. In bold relief, the Cross presents the utter identification of the light of God with the darkness of sin. Jesus without his Cross might have had the vogue of a prophet or seer, but he never would have drawn all mankind to himself. To the Christian that Cross has not yet fully triumphed, for it has yet to win its way until the uttermost stronghold of evil shall be overthrown. The Cross on Calvary is the Eternal Cross. Not merely individual but social redemption is truly involved when the light of God shines out of the darkness. The divine purpose in redemption according to the New Testament is universal — a new heaven and a new earth, the immortality of individuality and the permanent establishment of a perfect social order " wherein dwelleth righteousness."

" God — hath shined." Once again the essential historicity of the Christian revelation is proclaimed. The fires of critical research may have burned away some of the appurtenances of Christianity but they have not touched the validity of its central figure, his birth, life, death and resurrection. His living words, his deathless deeds and, at the center, he himself, are basic to Christian faith. This does not mean that intellectual assent to a historic fact is equivalent to faith. Yet it does involve the necessity of confidence in such facts. " According to the Scriptures," was a first century norm. It is still authoritative. The New Testament records, made fresh and vivid by translation and retranslation and by all the sidelights of competent scholarship, are to the Christian source materials of the first magnitude. That is why careless unconcern as to what the records really are offends the sensitive Christian consciousness. It is not because he must believe that every word and phrase has in it the magic of absolute accuracy, but because he knows that the essential historicity of the New Testament is vital to his faith. When such competent modern scholars as Edwin Lewis in his startling volume *A Christian Manifesto* and Ernest F. Scott in his remarkable book *The New Testament Idea of Revelation* are calling the church back to a fresh and assured confidence in the New Testament records and revelation, the plain Christian may well be emboldened to pin his faith firmly upon the fact that " God — hath shined! "

" In our hearts." In nothing does the Christian religion permit such an unparalleled approach as in its conception of the continuing contemporaneity of the light that shone historically so many centuries ago. Indeed, just as theistic philosophy presents a creative mind who is contemporaneous as well as eternal, so does Christianity rest upon a Christ who lived and died and who as truly lives today " in our hearts." The blending of the historical and the contemporary, the theoretical and the experimental, the theological and the mystical elements of Christianity gives it continuing power. The Christian religion presents, as one of its goals, a continuing and contemporaneous experience of reality identified with the person of Jesus Christ and known as the Holy Spirit, the living God at work in his world, preserver and governor, teacher, comforter and guide unto all truth. It is impossible, however, to expect that every man's conception of Christ, historic and experimental, shall be identical with that of every other man. We do not require Hoffman and Tissot to paint identical likenesses of Jesus. We do not require Handel and Bach to provide the same musical setting for the Christian motif. We have not demanded of Luke and John, Paul and Peter, the same records or the identical interpretation of the life of the Master. We only require as the one basic necessity that the light which "hath shined" in the New Testament Scriptures shall be the same light which still shines "in our hearts." Instead of crowding out fresh insights, Christianity is hospitable to all such disclosures so long as they are consistent with "the faith which was once delivered unto the saints."

"Light . . . of the knowledge of the glory of God." (Exodus 33:18, 19). Christianity's ultimate goal is so transcendent as to appear beyond the pale of realization — to achieve a full and satisfying knowledge of the glory of God. The word "glory" has fallen upon evil days, in part because it has been permitted to sink into desuetude or has been employed to convey an inadequate and even unworthy idea. In popular parlance, glory is the chaplet that is fastened upon one's brow; it is the badge that bedecks one's breast; it is the acclaim that greets one's appearance. One's glory is the acquisition of something that has not hitherto belonged to him. In the New Testament, the glory of God is always conceived as the lustrous outshining of what God essentially is. It is the luminous unfolding of the divine nature. The glory of God, instead of being the trappings of a potentate on parade, is the disclosure of the essential moral nature of the Infinite and Eternal One. In the days of his earthly life, Jesus was always striving to show his contemporaries what kind of a God his Father was. Further, he was seeking to demonstrate by every word and deed that his Father's highest glory was man's greatest good. The "good life" to him was not a mediocre existence upon some middle ground, but a high adventure characterized by fellowship with God.

It is also a *knowledge* of divine glory that constitutes the goal of Christian faith. In contrast with those views of knowledge which make it only available as the end of logical processes of thought, or as the direct result of some sense impression, Christianity presents a doctrine of " gnosis " in which man's capacity to know is not limited by the processes of sense or by speculative reflection. The validity of an inner insight by means of which man knows reality is so conclusive to the Christian that he builds his life upon it. Nor is he deluded by the sophistry that says that since his knowledge is not absolute, therefore he cannot know the absolute. As well say that since his knowledge is not absolutely true he cannot know the truth. " We speak that we do know " (John 3:11) is the confession of Christian faith. And " this is life eternal that they might know thee the only true God and Jesus Christ whom thou hast sent." (John 17:3).

Through the Christian centuries this knowledge of God, through Jesus Christ, has been set forth in many and varied terms. The question as to how men find this knowledge is vital. Through meditation on the Holy Scriptures, through the processes of daily devotional discipline, through loving obedience to the will of God, as revealed in Jesus Christ, through the exercise of one's whole being in an attitude traditionally called faith — involving confidence, trust and committal — through prayer and worship, both public and private, through the fellowship of a Christian community and, not least, in continuing ministries of human service motivated by the spirit of Christ, the Christian has found the way to the enrichment of this knowledge which is his ultimate goal. What John Stuart Mill suggested as a fair test for life — " so to live that Jesus of Nazareth would approve " — might well be claimed by the Christian.

And so the first century Christian came for his climax to

that same reality to which the twentieth century Christian and the Christian of every century must come, and he found it where we must find it — " in the face of Jesus Christ." Christianity is Christ. He is not alone the center but the circumference; he is the issue as well as the source. Behind the symbolical imagery of the conception of a face abides the reality for which it appears;

> . . . it shall be
> A Face like my face that receives thee;
> a man like to me,
> Thou shalt love and be loved by forever;
> a Hand like this hand
> Shall throw open the gates of new life to thee!
> See the Christ stand.
> (" Saul," Robert Browning.)

In the face of Christ the apostle found the full authentication for the historic basis of the gospel. It is implied in the historic record that he had seen that face as he had heard that voice on the Damascus way. That Voice was henceforth authoritative and that Face ultimate. In the face of Christ he saw what we may see — the full disclosure of all the divine attitudes toward life. In that face he saw, as we may, " God — manifest in the flesh." (I Timothy 3:16). It was there that he became fully conscious of sin, and also supremely assured of redemption. In the light of that face he found the norm and test of all his activities. Before the searching light of that face all the schemes of mankind passed in swift procession for commendation or for judgment. Let no one say that in such a conception as the face of Christ there is no room for a broad social content. Truth is that the ultimate test of every economic theory, every social plan, every human enterprise, every ethical act, is the light of that face. The economic and social injustices of the present order, its lust and greed, its suspicion and hatred, its mad glorification of war, and its espousal of the causes which inevitably produce war, have already been judged in the light of Christ's face. The slowly but surely emerging purposes and plans for a better world, for economic justice and racial understanding, for righteousness, peace and good will, have not alone received the approval of his countenance but have their deepest motives in his gospel. It is no mere poetic fancy that conceives the light of the face to be determinative in its judgment of moral conduct and character. Even on lower and merely human levels we set the greatest store by the light of the face, by what it approves and what it condemns, whether in parenthood, in filial or conjugal relationships, in the realm of friendship or in legal judgments. It is what we see in the faces of those with whom we have to do that marks and determines our crises. In the face of Jesus Christ the apostolic church found a satisfying symbol of the full revelation of God. It was the divine fullness that shone in his face, hatred of sin, love of the sinner; impeccable righteousness, accessible compassion; divinity, humanity — all indissolubly blended. The fact of death and the reality of immortality, the shameful cross and the open tomb, are all mirrored in that face. In such a light, the great first century Christian went on his troublous but victorious way, meeting every trial and overcoming every obstacle until at last the hour of his departure was at hand.

In the sharpest contrast with the Apostle Paul, the truly Christian gnostic of all the centuries, stands out the great nineteenth century agnostic, that man of monumental mind, transparently honest and irrevocably thoroughgoing, Herbert Spencer. When the hour of his departure was at hand, he looked out upon life with wistful regret over what he must soon lose and leave. " The volume herewith issued I can say with certainty will be my last," [1] he declares in the Preface to this curious collection of miscellany, published posthumously. In it he discusses such matters as " The Origin of Music," " The Pursuit of Prettiness," " Weather Forecasts," " Gymnastics," " Euthanasia," " Grammar " and " Ultimate Questions." With the latter, Herbert Spencer closes his last book, and at the outset of this concluding chapter he writes: " Old people have many reflections in common. Doubtless, one which I now have in mind is very familiar. For years past, when watching the unfolding buds in spring, there has arisen the thought — Shall I ever again see the buds unfold? Shall I ever again be awakened at dawn by the song of the thrush? Now that the end is not likely to be long postponed, there results an increasing tendency to meditate upon ultimate questions." (P. 300). In this final chapter the great agnostic comes at length to the problem of Space. With his penetrating and masterful mind he ranges all the known theories of Space, subjective, objective and in-between. He finds them all wanting, and, as he closes the record of his earthly pilgrimage, he inscribes a graphic, tragic " Finis," as he plucks and tastes the bitter fruit of his philosophy. " Of late years, the consciousness that, without origin or cause, infinite Space has ever existed and must ever exist, produces in me a feeling from which I shrink." (P. 304).

The Apostle Paul, too, had come to his journey's end. It was all over except the dying, and the sentence of martyrdom had already been pronounced. He too looked back upon the pathway over which he had been traveling, but with no

[1] *Facts and Comments,* Herbert Spencer, Preface, page v. Appleton.

misgivings or regrets. " I have fought a good fight," he said, " I have finished my course, I have kept the faith." (II Timothy 4:7). Then with rapt and burning eyes he looked out upon the unknown future and he saw a face, " the face of Jesus Christ." " I know whom I have believed," triumphantly he cried, " and am persuaded that he is able to keep that which I have committed unto him against that day! " (II Timothy 1:2). He, too, went out — not into the night, but into the light! Not " shrinking " with fear, but shouting in victorious faith. So shall those who wait for his appearing. " We shall be like him, for we shall see him as he is. And every man that hath this hope in him purifieth himself even as he is pure." (I John 3:2, 3). Christlikeness — the goal of Christianity!

ERNEST FREMONT TITTLE

Ernest Fremont Tittle, pastor of the First Methodist Episcopal Church, Evanston, Illinois, was graduated from Ohio Wesleyan University in 1906, and from Drew Theological Seminary in 1908. Ordained to the Methodist ministry in 1910, his early pastorates were in Christiansburg, Dayton, and Delaware, Ohio, seat of his Alma Mater, where he became noted for his ministry to students. Transferred thence to Broad Street Church, Columbus, which serves the campus group of Ohio State University, he remained two years. Finally he was called to the famous First Church, Evanston, where he has ministered for the past seventeen years.

Yearly preacher at Yale, Harvard and the University of Chicago, he is in frequent demand as occasional preacher in many schools. In 1932 he gave the Lyman Beecher Foundation Lectures on Preaching, published under the title *Jesus after Nineteen Centuries*. His other books are *What Must the Church Do to be Saved?*, 1921; *The Religion of the Spirit*, 1928; *We Need Religion*, 1931; *The Foolishness of Preaching*, 1932; and *A World That Cannot be Shaken*, 1933. In 1934 he gave the Earl Lectures at the Pacific School of Religion, the Gates Memorial Lectures at Grinnell College, and the Russell Lectures at the Auburn Theological Seminary, and in 1935 the Ayer Lectures at Colgate-Rochester Theological Seminary.

Dr. Tittle saw Y. M. C. A. service in France during the war. He has since been one of the most implacable foes of the war system. His ministry has been notable for its liberal theological outlook and for its intense social passion, yet he has found much time for individual students and members of his great church who have sought his aid and counsel. Dr. Tittle has been awarded honorary degrees by Ohio Wesleyan University, Garrett Biblical Institute, Yale University and Wittenberg College.

III

LIBERAL PROTESTANTISM

By ERNEST FREMONT TITTLE

LONG ago, a Philippian jailor, terrified by an earthquake which flung open the doors of his prison and threatened the escape of his prisoners, cried out, "What must I do to be saved?" He, no doubt, is a historic figure. But as he utters on a night of terror that earnest, appealing cry, is he not also an arresting symbol of mankind? Throughout his whole pilgrimage on this agitated planet man has been asking, What must I do to be saved?

His first concern was nature, before whose manifold and mysterious forces he stood in fear and awe. How to secure food and shelter, how to escape a gruesome death from the claws or fangs of savage beasts, how to propitiate those ghosts and demons with which his dark imagination peopled the world? That was his problem and the burden of his cry when he asked, What must I do to be saved? But to this primitive problem a slowly developing communal life added another which in time became no less formidable. The human heart, with its strange capacity for greed and cruelty, produced situations quite as difficult as any to which raw nature gave birth. Not only occasional floods and famines but also such human inventions as war, tyranny and slavery forced from man's lips the anxious cry, What must I do to be saved? Finally, the human individual, as he developed a conscience, discovered that he had still another problem on his hands: how to avoid the condemnation and secure the approval of this strange, imperious voice in his own soul, how to live at peace with himself. And this of all his problems proved to be, if not the worst, certainly the most intimate and persistent. The saying is Saint Paul's but the experience is universal: " The good which I would I do not, but the evil which I would not, that I practice." The division which appears in society between the best and the worst of men appears also in the individual life, and bitter indeed is the ensuing conflict between the best and worst in oneself. Here, probably, is the deepest meaning of man's cry when he asks, What must I do to be saved?

This ancient question man is still asking, as well he may in view of the chaos which he finds in his society and in his own soul. Indeed, with a growing realization that what is at stake is nothing less than the existence of civilization itself, man is now asking, What must I do to be saved? In the world we now have, millions of people are doomed. They are doomed to poverty, unemployment and war — to poverty notwithstanding the fact that we are now in a position to produce all that is needed to maintain vast populations in physical health and comfort. In an age of science and machine production we might be fed, we who are hungry; we might be clothed, we who are naked; we might be educated, we who are ignorant. But we are living in want in a world of plenty because we are unable to buy what nature, harnessed to machinery and driven by science, is now able to produce. We lack purchasing power, and we lack it because, in a world which tolerates reckless competition for private gain, it is impossible to secure any just or intelligent distribution of the product of man's toil. In such a world there is bound to be poverty and unemployment, inasmuch as there is no way of maintaining the balance between production and consumption. Furthermore, in a world where men recklessly compete for private gain, both individual and national, there is bound also to be war. In such a world strife is inherent. And we now have a type of civilization to which war is fatal, inasmuch as international strife profoundly unsettles and threatens to destroy the whole structure of industry, commerce and finance on which modern society depends for its very existence. Today, therefore, man has abundant reason to ask, What must I do to be saved?

What is the answer to this ancient question as it appears on modern lips?

There are those who believe that all we now need to do is to alter the attitudes of individuals; the salvation of society will then follow as a matter of course. And there are those who believe that we have only to alter the political and economic structure of society; the salvation of individuals will then follow as a matter of course.

It may be said, and it is probably true, that few persons, if any, fully subscribe to the Marxian doctrine of economic determinism. Even in present-day Russia there appears to be a lively recognition of the fact that if there is ever to be a new world there must be a new motivation in individual lives; and in Russia today a deliberate attempt is being made to create in individuals a new motivation. Almost every conceivable agency of propaganda, excepting only the church, is being employed to create a public opinion which will encourage if not compel the individual to think of others besides himself, to seek first and passionately the success of the Russian experiment, not his own private pleasure or material gain. Is there anyone who fully subscribes to the proposition that human individuals are completely molded by the environing order in which their lives are lived? No doubt we must qualify the statement made above that there are those who believe we have only to alter the structure of society;

the salvation of individuals will then follow as a matter of course. But this statement may serve to point out the fact that many people do *not* believe that a good world will ever come of a purely educational or conversional process. They have come to the conclusion that the structure of society must be deliberately changed, and they are inclined to believe that the reconstruction of the social order is now of greater importance than the redemption of individual lives.

Opposed to them is the group first mentioned — persons who hold strenuously the view that it is men who make social orders, not social orders that make men, and who, therefore, believe that all we now need to do is to redeem the lives of individuals; the redemption of society will then follow as a matter of course. In a sermon recently delivered from an evangelical pulpit the preacher has before him the chaotic condition of the world, the terrific suffering, confusion and near-despair of millions of men. He clearly recognizes the need of an improved social order in which such want and worry as men now know shall be no more. Yet he appears to deplore any appeal from a Christian pulpit for the reconstruction of the existing order of society. "Our need," he says, "is not for new systems, new programs. Systems and programs will not transform the world. Our need is for a new mind and a new heart." That, commonly, has been the contention of evangelical religion. Redeem individuals and these redeemed individuals will presently redeem the world. Create in individuals a new soul and the old world cannot remain; the new soul will inevitably create a new world.

Let us thoughtfully examine these divergent views. And first, the view that today the reconstruction of society is more imperative than the redemption of individual lives. In his monumental study of modern democracies, Lord Bryce has a chapter on "Theoretical Foundations" in which he describes the hopes that were once entertained for political democracy. "Toward the end of the eighteenth century," he says, " the spirit of reforming change was everywhere in the air. Reforms were long overdue, for the world had been full of tyranny, inequality and injustice. . . . Inequality and repression had engendered one set of vices in rulers and another in their subjects — selfishness and violence, hatred, perfidy and revenge. Under good government . . . human nature . . . would return to the pristine virtues the Creator had meant to implant. Under Liberty and Equality the naturally good instincts would spring up into the flower of rectitude and bear the fruit of brotherly affection. Men would work for the community, rejoicing not merely in their own freedom but because they desired the welfare of others also. These beliefs were the motive power which for a time made faith in democracy almost a religion." [1] How very painful it is to read that today! The reconstruction of the political system, the substitution of democracy for autocracy, the rule of the people for the rule of a king — it was once fondly hoped that that would be the achievement of good government and that, given good government, men themselves would become good. What a contrast between hope and history!

Lord Bryce himself found comfort in looking back from the world of today to the world of the sixteenth century. He finally says: " If democracy has not brought all the blessings that were once expected, it has in some countries destroyed, in others materially diminished, many of the cruelties, terrors, injustices and oppressions that had darkened the

[1] See Bryce: *Modern Democracies*, Vol. I, p. 46. The Macmillan Company.

souls of men." We also may find comfort in that. Nevertheless, we are compelled to acknowledge that the mere transfer of power from king to people has not given us good government — a fact which may well give pause to anyone who supposes that a reconstruction of the economic order is now all that is needed to usher in the millennium.

Is it true, then, that our need is " not for new systems, new programs," but only for " a new mind and a new heart "? One fact ought at once to engage our attention. Ever since the Protestant Reformation, that is, during the past four hundred years, evangelical religion has been working on the inner lives of individuals, seeking to save men from folly and sin. Yet the social order remains unredeemed. The world is still a place where millions of people, night after night, go hungry to bed. It is still a place where men live in awful dread of poverty, of unemployment, and of war. What then? Are we to conclude that evangelical religion has completely failed in what it has conceived to be its redemptive task, or are we to conclude that it needs to be given more time in which to do its redemptive work on individual lives? If so, how much more? The question is imperative, for it is now completely evident that western society cannot wait many more hundreds of years (or many more years) for something radically redemptive to occur.

Moreover, it may be seriously questioned whether evangelical religion, even though it should be given another four hundred years, would produce a kind of new mind that could be counted upon to produce a new world. What happens when you take the position that our need is not for new systems, new programs, but only for a new mind and a new heart? When that position is taken in a pulpit there is great rejoicing in every reactionary pew. There is nothing really wrong, then, with the world. The social structure is all right. There is no need to change it, no occasion to try to improve it. So one remains morally comfortable in the presence of systems and programs that before one's very eyes are spelling out disaster for millions of men. One does not question the validity of existing political and economic arrangements. One supposes that they belong to the nature of things. Nor does one seriously question one's own conduct, the program of one's life. Is not one honest, chaste, industrious, thrifty, kindly disposed? Does not one support the church and various benevolent and missionary enterprises? What more should a Christian do? Evangelical religion, with its sanction of the existing order, its refusal to cry out against social injustice, can hardly hope to produce in its converts a type of mind that will be greatly concerned to improve the world.

However, for the sake of the argument, let us suppose that evangelical religion may produce an intelligent and sensitive conscience. It will, then, be proper to observe that anyone who has such a conscience is likely to have a tough time of it in a society which is organized not on a basis of co-operation for the common good of all but rather on a basis of (more or less) selfish competition for private gain, both individual and national. Nor is this all or the worst that requires to be said. Consider the extremes of present-day society. And first its slums. Our need, we are told, is only for a new mind, a new heart. But what hope is there of producing fine character, or a significant culture, in the environment of a slum? I do not say it cannot be done. It has been done in the case of a few superior individuals. But the odds against its being done are simply terrific, as the proponents of evangelical piety ought clearly to recognize. How many of them would be willing to have their children grow up in the environment of a slum? How many of them would themselves be willing to live all their lives in a slum — even as the head resident of a social settlement? Is there not something suggestive of self-righteousness and hypocrisy in this complacent view of the favorably situated that all that is needed is a new mind and a new heart? And the Gold Coast! Does that provide an environment in which it is possible to develop and maintain an ethical outlook on life? We have been condemning " a certain rich man " who during terrible years, when millions of people were living on the dizzy edge of starvation, consented to receive in salaries and bonuses one and a half million dollars. We have been condemning him, we middle-class people who have known neither the moral dullness that comes of dire poverty nor the moral blindness that comes of great wealth!

Of course it is true that a world which contains vast numbers of unredeemed individuals, men and women who are thoroughly selfish, is likely to be a bad world, irrespective of its political and economic arrangements. But what hope is there of producing vast numbers of high-minded, unselfish individuals in a world which tolerates greed, sanctions selfishness, permits an unregulated individualism — a world whose bottom is an abyss of poverty in which human souls have no more chance to develop than has a bulb in a basement and whose top is an absurd and cruel wealth which corrupts those who possess it and places their children in moral jeopardy? In order to redeem the lives of individuals you must create a social order in which the potential goodness of human nature has a fair chance to flower.

Is it possible to build a society in which the human spirit, no longer thwarted by war and want, would have a chance to develop its latent powers? Who with cool and intelligent deliberation can face that question without raising, also, certain others? What is the meaning of life? *Has* life meaning; or is it "a tale told by an idiot, full of sound and fury, signifying nothing"? What is man — a beloved son of God; or merely a cosmic accident, "the product of forces which had no pre-vision of the ends they were achieving"? What of the human adventure? May we dare to hope for some magnificent outcome which will justify the travail and pain of a slow-moving and long-continued evolutionary process; or must we, with Oswald Spengler, suppose that historical cultures are social organisms which, like physical organisms, are destined to run a certain course and then to die, so that all we may look for is an endless cycle of fruitless events? Here *are* questions which thoughtful people are now asking. Indeed, even the man on the street has uncomfortable moments when he finds himself wondering what it is all about, this persistent and often hectic striving that is life. And surely one may risk the observation that men will hardly be able to put forth the vast and continued effort required to build a great age unless they have some assurance that life is meaningful and that, despite occasional setbacks and tragedies, it is moving toward some great end: unless, that is, they can believe in God.

For my own part I find significance in the fact that even in this world evil has no security. Nearly one hundred years ago William Ellery Channing wrote: "I am not sure that dark and desolating storms are not even now gathering over the world. When we look back upon the mysterious history of the human race we see that Providence has made use of fearful revolutions as the means of sweeping away the abuses of the ages. . . . Whether such revolutions may be in store for our times I know not. The present civilization of the Christian world presents much to awaken doubt and apprehension. It stands in direct hostility to the great ideas of Christianity. It is selfish, mercenary, sensual. Such a civilization cannot forever endure. How it is to be supplanted I know not. I hope, however, that it is not doomed like the old Roman civilization to be quenched in blood. I trust the existing social state contains in its bosom something better than has yet unfolded." [2] A prophecy on which, today, verbal comment is quite unnecessary, comment of a far more eloquent nature being supplied by the whole contemporary situation!

The mills of the gods grind slowly, but they grind exceeding small. Even in this world evil has no security. Even when it is intrenched, organized and fully determined, at whatever public cost, to maintain its own existence, evil is unstable. And, as Professor Whitehead has said, " The fact of the instability of evil is the moral order in the world." [3] There *is* a moral order which slowly but surely spells out the doom of evil. True, " this instability of evil does not necessarily lead to progress "; but it is a fact that on the plane of history there has been progress — what astonishing progress! — since man first turned his face from the clod. And is it not possible for intelligence to surmise that the source of this amazing progress has been not simply the vision and will of men but also the purpose and power of God? Today, how significant the fact that we are being compelled, willy-nilly, to think of others, not only of ourselves, to have some regard for their welfare as well as our own! Unless they are able to

---

[2] See Channing's Works, New Edition Complete (1892). American Unitarian Association.

[3] Whitehead, *Religion in the Making*, p. 95. The Macmillan Company.

buy, we are unable to sell. Those of us who have much cannot hope to retain much unless we see to it that our underprivileged fellows receive more. Today, moreover, we are being compelled to think in world terms and to develop a decent regard for the welfare of all mankind! We have reached a stage in human evolution where no people can have prosperity unless other peoples have it too, no nation can enjoy security unless the whole world is made secure. What has led us to this place? As a race we began in the jungle, "plunged in blackest ignorance, preyed upon by hideous and grotesque superstitions," muttering incoherently, fighting like dogs over a bone. What has led us to a place where, as a race, in order to survive we are obliged to develop a vision, an imagination, an understanding, a sympathy, an enlightened *un*selfishness which hitherto have appeared only in a few outstanding individuals?

There is much to be said in support of the Christian interpretation of the world and life. Christianity does not attempt to explain everything. Albert Schweitzer tells us that for ten years before he went to Africa, he prepared boys in the parish of Saint Nicholai, in Strassburg, for the confirmation; and that after the war some of them thanked him for having taught them so definitely that religion is not a formula for explaining everything. It was this teaching, they said, which kept them from discarding Christianity when they experienced the horrors of the trenches.[4] Christianity does not attempt to account for all that is evil in the world. What it does attempt to account for is all that is good in the world *and making for good*.

According to Christianity, good is not simply a human

---

[4] Albert Schweitzer, *Christianity and the Religions of the World*, p. 89. Doubleday, Doran.

achievement; it is also a cosmic reality. Indeed, all we ourselves know of good is but a partial revelation in time of an
eternal reality whose own goodness far transcends any historical achievement. Furthermore, Christianity, which does
not deny either the fact or the power of evil, holds fast the
faith that this cosmic reality which is transcendent good is
also transcendent power — power greater than man's and
sufficiently great to secure an eventual triumph of truth and
right and love.

Of this cosmic reality which is at once transcendent good
and transcendent power Christianity finds a glorious symbol
in that sublime figure of a man hanging on a cross for the
sake of an ideal *and conquering as he dies.* Concerning
Jesus it is written: "In him life lay, and this life was the
Light of men." This writing may be found in the New
Testament — and not only there. It may be found in all the
history of man upon the earth: in the death of empires which
took the sword and perished with the sword; in the collapse
of civilizations which failed to achieve justice and co-operation; and in the survival and continued growth of institutions
such as the home, the school, and the church, in which violence has given way to persuasion and private interest has
been subordinated to the common good. Indeed, all we now
know about the drama of life points to the conclusion that
even before man appeared upon the stage the chief cause of
extinction of species was failure to co-operate, the great secret
of survival was mutual aid; so that it might also be said that
this writing concerning Jesus appears in the order of nature,
the constitution of the world. In the universe there *is* a
power, Christlike in character, which, in the midst of chaos
and of night, is striving evermore to secure the triumph of
truth and right and love and which, a reasonable faith may

dare to believe, will eventually prevail; so that today, even in the face of odds undeniably great, men of intelligence and good will, striving to build a great age, a glorious and enduring civilization, may carry on in the assurance that their labor is "not vain in the Lord."

What must man do to be saved? My own conviction is that the answer which today we are eagerly seeking, knowing that we must find it or witness the collapse of our civilization, is just the answer which was given to that Philippian jailor long ago: "Believe on the Lord Jesus and thou shalt be saved, thou and thy house." To be sure, this ancient answer may be so interpreted as to make it of no avail. It has been so interpreted times without number. It has been made to appear that belief "on the Lord Jesus" involves nothing more than bare assent to Christological dogmas which carry the label of orthodoxy. But that, of course, is a travesty on the New Testament. That is what happens when Christianity loses its vitality, when it ceases to be a religion — an affair of the whole man — and becomes merely a philosophy, or an institution, or a hollow if not hypocritical convention. Genuine belief "on the Lord Jesus" would produce at once the motivation and the faith needed to build on earth a great and enduring society, in the building of which human individuals would achieve in their own souls unity, nobility and peace.

It may be true that some measure of frustration is inherent in a time process which must carry the heavy weight of egoism and fallibility. It may even be true that the whole material world is steadily and irrevocably running down like a clock, as some astronomers now believe; or it may rather be true that some other force as yet unknown or but partially known is working to counteract the "second law of thermodynamics." But in any case, Christian hope is not tethered to the earth or, indeed, to anything material. It travels beyond " our bourne of time and place." Earth and sky may wax old as a garment, they may one day dissolve and be no more; but the kingdom of truth, of beauty, and of love — the Kingdom of God — will endure. And the immortality of God means the immortality of all those his servants who have greatly incarnated these enduring values.

EDWARD SCRIBNER AMES

Edward Scribner Ames, pastor of the University Church of Disciples of Christ, Chicago, Illinois, and professor emeritus of philosophy in the University of Chicago, was born in Eau Claire, Wisconsin. He took his Bachelor's degree from Drake University in 1889, his Master of Arts in 1891, and from Yale Divinity School he received the B.D. degree in 1892. After a further period of study in philosophy at Yale he went to the then new University of Chicago as a fellow in philosophy. In 1895 he was awarded the Ph.D degree. His early work lay in the field of teaching, first at the Disciples' Divinity House, then at Butler University. In 1900 he returned to the University of Chicago as instructor in philosophy, where he has remained for thirty-five years. In 1931 he became head of the department. Since 1927 he has also been dean of the Disciples' Divinity House. In 1900 he became pastor of the University Church of Disciples of Christ, where his unbroken ministry has attracted and continues to attract a large following from among the university community and the intellectuals of the city.

From his seminary days Dr. Ames was deeply interested in the psychology of religion, then a new field. His first book was *The Psychology of Religious Experience,* 1910. It is still widely used by students of religion. Other books are *The Divinity of Christ,* 1911; *The Higher Individualism,* 1915; *The New Orthodoxy,* 1919, *Religion,* 1929, and a book of sermons *Letters to God and the Devil,* 1933, concerning the soul and God.

Some men are easy to classify; Dr. Ames is not. By many he is regarded as a humanist. His position seems to be somewhere between more extreme liberalism and thoroughgoing naturalistic humanism, a position still within the bounds of Protestant Christianity.

IV

RADICAL PROTESTANTISM

By EDWARD SCRIBNER AMES

My first confession of faith, in the form of a sermon, was given from the pulpit of the University Church of Disciples of Christ in 1902. I was then just about half as old as now. The whole of the latter half of my life has been entirely devoted to study and reflection upon religious problems and tasks. As a teacher of philosophy I have had the opportunity of specializing in the psychology and the philosophy of religion. When that first confession of faith was published I was only a few years from my student days, and I was full of the enthusiasm engendered by the new knowledge brought forth so recently by scholars in religious and scientific fields. Higher criticism had made a new book of the Bible; church history had thrown revealing light upon the life and teaching of Jesus, upon the thought and work of Paul and the other Apostles, and upon the course of Christian history. The doctrine of evolution, published by Darwin only thirty years before I graduated from college, had already revolutionized old patterns of thought in every subject, and opened wider vistas of the possibilities of human development. All this fitted easily into the religious training of my denomination, which sprang from the teaching of John Locke, the father of the Eighteenth Century Enlightenment in England. One of his books was entitled *The Reasonableness of Christianity as Delivered in the Scriptures.* This, with his *Essay on the Human Understanding,* furnished the intellectual background of the religious thinking of Alexander Campbell, who discarded all creedal theology and promoted a common-sense, practical, reasonable interpretation of Christianity. Campbell, like Locke, rejected speculative, metaphysical theology as nonessential to religion, and turned away from traditional forms of mysticism and of emotionalism. Their understanding of religious conversion illustrates their religious reasonableness. They held that the terms of salvation are plainly given in the New Testament, and that whoever accepts those terms becomes a Christian by that acceptance. That acceptance may be the occasion of a sense of relief and of deep satisfaction, but the emotional experience is secondary and not itself the evidence of conversion. Doctrines like that of the trinity, the virgin birth, and the future life, were not insisted upon but were left to private opinion. Greatest emphasis was put upon the moral ideals and example of Jesus, and upon the practice of natural piety.

With this inheritance it was not difficult to respond to the new ideas taught in the theological seminaries and universities of the late nineteenth century. I was undoubtedly greatly excited and stimulated by the critical remaking of the Scriptures, and filled with wonder over the marvelous perspectives which the idea of evolution gave to the world of nature and of human history and to dreams of the future of man. But there was no such emotional upheaval and tragic sense of spiritual disaster for religion and for personal experience as some students underwent. I have always been thankful for the inheritance which spared me that poignant struggle.

It is not strange, therefore, that my first confession of faith reflected this new knowledge in the statement of my beliefs about God, Christ, the Bible, salvation, the church and its ordinances, Christian missions, social idealism, and religious progress. It was a statement of modernism with all the characteristics which have been ascribed to it either with approval or in criticism. It was optimistic, reasonable, humanistic, evolutionary, idealistic, democratic, romantic. I frankly accept all these characterizations of my present beliefs too, though I admit that they are now tempered with the qualifying influence of longer experience and more maturity.

Since the war a dark sea of pessimism has swept over the world. In literature and theology it seldom boldly adopts the name of pessimism, but it appropriates to itself the word "realism." The novelists, the poets, the artists, and certain theologians talk about realism as if the only real experiences were drab and bitter. They seem to take no account of the fact that sugar is sweet, that the sunshine is warm and healing, that love is comforting and inspiring as well as exacting and jealous. Their favorite jibe about planning and expecting happy events is that this is romantic thinking. It never seems to occur to them that there may be romantic pessimism, but certainly it is possible to color one's view of life by subjective moods of gloom and distrust until the interpretation made is just as distorted as if one chose only the rosy tints. A genuinely realistic impression of the world, if it is true to the facts, must see the high lights as well as the shadows, the pleasures and the pains, the successes as much as the failures.

While these pessimists, parading themselves as realists, think of themselves as tough-minded heroes facing gallantly the stark facts of experience, I have come to think of them as very tender-minded, if not cowardly souls. They are extremely fearful of being deceived by any claim of good or worth-while values in life, and therefore they take a wholly negative attitude and refuse to act upon their better impulses. Their contention is that if we hope for nothing we cannot be disappointed. Or they say, if a man sleeps on the floor he cannot fall out of bed. I think this saying reveals the timidity and squeamishness of these self-styled realists. In this world of so many nice, comfortable beds, from which probably not one person in a million ever falls out, it is as absurd as it is amusing to hear of a man priding himself on being so realistic that he thinks it is more in keeping with the real nature of things to choose the discomfort of sleeping on the hard, cold floor, in preference to the satisfaction of reposing in an ordinary bed. As a matter of fact, these realists talk one thing and live another. They seek good jobs, they plan for good food and drink, they strive for recognition among their fellows even if they have to write shocking novels, risqué poems, and pessimistic philosophy to get it. They are really the court jesters of modern life, dressing themselves in fantastic mental garb and making jokes out of the serious affairs of sober people. They create nothing and only laugh at those who are courageous enough to venture some effort for achieving better things.

Perhaps the theologians are more responsible for this pessimistic unrealism than is commonly recognized. Early Christians despaired of the present world because they were misunderstood and persecuted by it. It was not the teaching of Jesus, but that of Paul and Augustine and Calvin and Luther, that gave us the doctrine of human sinfulness and the final word of hopelessness about this present world. Dante, John Milton, and John Bunyan painted the picture into the mind and imagination with unforgettable vividness.

A more wholesome and truer view of human nature and society was developing before the world war. What William James called a religion of healthy-mindedness was making rapid headway in various New Thought cults, and was softening the old theological austerities of Protestant churches, when the war plunged the world back into suffering, tragedy and hysteria of fear, and revealed in the roar of blazing cannon and falling bombs the possibilities of human ferocity and brutality. Ah! said the theologians, here is proof again of what our masters, Calvin and Luther, taught years ago — the natural man is an animal and incapable of any substantial good within himself. He needs the miracle of Divine Grace to regenerate his soul and to make him capable of any good deed or destiny. Karl Barth is the spokesman of this revival of the old doctrine that God is wholly Other, that man is on earth and God is in Heaven, and that there is no way from man to God. Only from God to man is there a way, and this way is entirely in God's hands. It is the way of a supernatural revelation and of the act of an inscrutable, divine will. This pessimism concerning human nature is the first principle of the traditional theology and of its present revival under the name of religious realism. This realism still holds on to the idea of a remote and ghostly deity, but the realism of the novelists and poets takes over the pessimism of the theologians and completely dismisses any God from the scene. The literary realists of our day are therefore the old theologians of despair without even the compensation of a remote Divinity remaining. They are just atheistic, irreligious theologians!

In contrast to all this I believe we must seek for an understanding of religion in human experience itself. We must face it with a genuine realism that has due regard for all the facts — the outreaching idealism, the forward striving, the appreciation of the good and the beautiful, as well as the weakness, the blindness, the cruelty, of human beings. War, the inhumanity of man to man, the selfishness, the tragedy of life, are part of the reality, but they are not the whole of it nor the most significant part. Jesus recognized the innocence of little children and said, " Of such is the kingdom of heaven." He observed the natural love of parents for their children and conceived God in terms of this love. He believed that even the Gentiles exhibited love for one another and was convinced that this love of friend for friend could be extended into wider relations, to strangers and to enemies. He proclaimed to men, " The kingdom of heaven is within you." He challenged unrighteous men with their own discrimination of good and evil and said to them, " Why do ye not of your own selves judge righteous judgment ? " He held that men could know the truth and declared, " Ye shall know the truth and the truth shall make you free." " Wisdom is justified of her children." Wisdom needs no other sanction than its own insight and its fruits.

Men have a natural love of life. They seek to save their life, though they may not always choose the proper way to do so. They at least realize that life is of supreme value and have but one answer when asked, " What does it profit a man to gain the whole world and lose his own soul ? " There are those who hunger and thirst after righteousness, and they are blessed. Human beings differ in the talents they possess, and in their capacity to appreciate and utilize truth and wisdom. Some are like rocky soil without depth, some are like thorny ground where good seed is choked, and some are like good ground where seed grows an abundant harvest. Some people listen when teachers speak, while some are deaf. Some persons have foresight and thoughtfulness like the wise virgins who filled and trimmed their lamps, but some are careless and are likely to be caught without oil — or gas. I interpret Jesus as a teacher of practical,

matter-of-fact wisdom about successful living. He seems to
me to have believed in the natural man's capacity to distinguish between love and hate, between selfishness and generosity, between the transient, material goods of life and the
more enduring things of the mind and heart. He does not
appear to have claimed any peculiar authority for the words
he spoke beyond their validity in ordinary experience. He
was willing to submit his teaching to the test of life itself,
and to stand or fall by the practical consequences of his principles, as he thought every man must do. By their fruits ye
shall know prophets of religion just as surely as a farmer
knows trees or vines by the fruits they produce.

I think it is a pity that this sane, simple, appealing religion
of Jesus was distorted and obscured by those who followed
him. They made a magical deity of him, attributed to him
an unnatural birth, ascribed to him impossible miracles,
founded a church and tried to give it a monopoly of his
power so that no one could become a Christian unless he
believed its creeds, submitted to its ordinances, and uttered
the prayers it prescribed. Protestantism tried to free itself
from these assumptions of the Roman Catholic church, but
the Protestant churches set themselves up immediately with
the same claims to final authority and failed to recover the
original gospel at which they aimed. No one of them has
ever really succeeded in adopting the simple, natural religion of Jesus, with his deep human sympathy, his lofty
idealism, his generous patience with sinners, his confidence
in love and wisdom, and his trust in the divine quality of
man's aspiring life. This naturalistic interpretation of the
religion of Jesus is found in many of the most scholarly
studies of his life, but no organized movement has ever
consciously and heartily adopted it without compromising

it by alien elements of supernaturalism or external authority. If it were adopted it would provide a basis for a truly universal religion in harmony with the experience of all mankind and integral with the vital and enduring elements of all the great religions of the world. Men of all races and nations know in their own experience what love is, the love of parents for children, and of friend for friend. They know and appreciate various goods and evils, and they seek well-being and cherish in all the great cultures the higher, " spiritual " values of life. Men everywhere respond to Christian missions whenever the missionary activity promotes education, health, kindliness, and the better fruits of civilization. It is mainly Christian dogmas and formal Christian practices which raise difficulties and arouse opposition. The same is true of nonchurch people in Christian lands. Very few enlightened persons in our country reject the spirit or the ideals of the natural religion of Jesus. What they object to in the prevailing Christian religion does not properly belong to it — for example, miraculous conversions, prescribed rites based upon irrational dogmas, opposition to the teaching of science, and blindness to the spiritual value of the arts and recreations of refined society.

The religion of Jesus as I conceive it is identical with the natural idealism of mankind, and this idealism which springs from human nature itself is capable of cultivation and development to the highest levels of the noblest religious experience. It may be seen and understood in the normal unfolding and maturing of ordinary men and women of our daily acquaintance. It may even be more sensitively felt in our own individual growth. The child, in his first years, lives within the encompassing shelter and warmth of an intimate circle of persons — his family, the school, and the environing neighborhood — very much as he lived before birth in the body of his mother. This human group mediates life to him, supplies him with means for growth through play and work, through the language society gives him ready made and through the customs of respectable behavior. It leads him, reproves him, hails him with acclaim for what it feels to be good conduct, and disciplines him when he gets out of bounds or rebels against its ways. By its nods and frowns it shapes his habits and sets the patterns of his imagination. Modern psychologists, in their studies of the development of personality, have discovered that the influences of these earliest years are much more persistent throughout life than formerly has been believed. Great importance is now attached to the environment and conditions of infancy and later childhood. Did the child have a happy home, with one or both parents, with brothers and sisters or none, with congenial playmates or only with older, unresponsive companions so that he was mentally unaroused, or being sensitively alive indulged in fantasies and dreams? Was he pampered or cowed, indulged or repressed, put forward or kept apart? Did he encounter some shock of fear, or illness, or accident, or misfortune? Any of these things may have given a set to his mind and emotions.

In any case, some time after his tenth year a change began in him. He matured physically and mentally, and especially he came to be more and more conscious of himself in relation to the people and the world about him. His games he played with team-mates and he saw himself as a member of a group of his equals. He had a voice in making the rules, and when he played a game like baseball he had to play all the other positions in imagination in order to play his particular part successfully. He learned to see himself from the point of view of others, and to judge himself as they judged him. There was a common mind in all the boys of the team and this common mind, built up by the demands of the play, became the standard and conscience for each one. It was a kind of watchful eye which all the time noted how well or how ill he did his part. To have the approval of that eye was his fullest joy and to have its disapproval was his deepest humiliation. Praise and blame of one's group are the most compelling forces of human life. They register the emergence and expression of natural idealism, or what I also call natural piety. They are forms of reverence, of aspiration, of devotion. By them the self is integrated, and challenged again by new situations toward further and more adequate reintegration.

This experience of playing a game as a member of a team has been used by social psychologists to describe one of the profoundest of all human experiences. Life is largely a matter of living in relation to other people, as neighbors, citizens, and members of business, social and religious organizations. Every group has its customs and purposes, and these are gathered up in the common will of the members. An active, participating member is sensitive to this common will. It is embodied in the written constitution, in the character and thought of the leaders, and it quickly makes itself felt in the approval of actions which harmonize with the spirit of the whole and in the disapproval of misconduct or indifference. This common will may strive forward toward new experiences, toward enlargement, toward enrichment of the individual members and of the whole. It is in this experience of the individual in relation to this larger whole of which he is a part that is to be found the meaning of what religion calls the relation of the individual and God. God is the Other, the higher will, in which the soul shares, yet which also at times stands over against the soul and judges its worth with praise or condemnation. The law of the sea requires the captain of the ship to remain at his post in the storm and in a fatal tragedy to go down with his ship. The honor of the business man exacts his last dollar when the notes are called. The code of the scientist holds him rigorously to an impartial report of the facts regardless of his wish or preconception. These are ways in which the divine appears within the human realm and works its will not apart from, but in and through, individuals. It is only a false conception of the utter sinfulness of human nature that makes it difficult to recognize the reality and validity of this living relation of God and man. Theologians have exalted God so much and debased man so far that it has become almost impossible for them to believe that men are truly the children of God, sons of God. No wonder it seems to them that only a miracle of conversion and of mysterious rebirth could bring men into this relation. We have become familiar with the idea that God is to be identified with "the personality-evolving activities of the cosmos." This conception is more acceptable, for it includes those activities of self-criticism and imagination within man himself by which he strives for the realization of ideals. We are workers together with God in the processes of redemption. In very real ways we must work out our own salvation. But this does not lessen the reality of God. It rather gives to the divine all the reality of the living process of growth in the discovery and realization of our better selves in both our individual life and our concrete social life.

In these terms is to be understood the nature and function

of churches. They are groups of persons consciously seeking to discover and cultivate ways of developing for themselves and for the world of mankind a richer, fuller and happier life. Religion is the quest of the good life in its fullest and widest meaning — nothing is foreign to it. Religion, through churches and manifold agencies, must concern itself with philosophies of life, with social problems, with the sciences and with the arts. It cultivates all the real values of life — health, work, knowledge, beauty and love in their complex interrelation. The chief end of man is to *grow,* to achieve abundant life for all.

It is the pursuit of such a realistic ideal that gives greatest meaning and worth to human life here and now, and it is this which makes significant any conception of immortality — the great question concerning life in the future, as in the present, is not so much whether it is a sheer fact as whether it is worth while, and this at last is a question of how it is lived. Likewise, other terms receive new meaning when religion is identified with the quest for satisfying life. Evil, sin, atonement and redemption gain functional meaning.

Herein lies also the significance of the mystical quality of all meaningful human experience. In the elevated moments of appreciation of the harmonies and beauty of nature and of understanding love the soul feels itself at one with a greater life. It is the function of religious symbols, as of all true works of art, to open to the imagination the wider vistas of the possibilities of growth and satisfaction. What we call worship is the dramatic representation to the mind and heart of those ways of life which make for greater fulfillment and enjoyment of the ideals prompted by wisdom, love and beauty. In imagination, stirred by examples of heroism, by songs of aspiration, by prayers of reverence and questing hope, by all the symbols of light and sacrifice upon our altars, the soul is disciplined and inspired to share the larger life of the divine, and to find comfort and assurance in the midst of its partial and imperfect attainments.

Natural piety is sensitive regard for the ideal tendencies in the common heart of man. It is responsiveness to the light of the imagination within us — the light that lighteth every man that cometh into the world. The great sin is neglect or disobedience of this light, for if the light that is in thee be darkness, how great is that darkness! This is the Hound of Heaven, of which Francis Thompson wrote:

> I fled Him, down the nights and down the days;
> I fled Him, down the arches of the years;
> I fled Him, down the labyrinthine ways
> Of my own mind; and in the midst of tears
> I hid from Him, and under running laughter.
> Up vistaed hopes I sped;
> And shot, precipitated
> Adown titanic glooms of chasmed fears,
> From those strong Feet that followed after.
> But with unhurrying chase
> And unperturbèd pace,
> Deliberate speed, majestic instancy,
> They beat, and a Voice beat
> More instant than the Feet —
> " All things betray thee, who betrayest Me."

GEORGE CRAIG STEWART

The Right Reverend George Craig Stewart, bishop of the Episcopal diocese of Chicago, Illinois, began his ministry in the Methodist Episcopal church, to which he was ordained in 1900, while still a student in Northwestern University, where he took the Bachelor of Arts degree in 1902. His further training took him to the Western Theological Seminary (Episcopal), from which he graduated in 1903. He was ordained deacon and priest of the Episcopal church in 1903 and became rector in Glencoe, Illinois. A year later he went to Saint Luke's parish, Evanston, to which he gave twenty-six years of effective leadership and left one of the outstanding churches of his denomination. On his election as coadjutor-bishop of the Chicago diocese in 1930, and as bishop a few months later, he was made rector emeritus of St. Luke's, which became the pro-cathedral of the diocese.

Six times he was a delegate to the General Convention of the Episcopal Church, before being elevated to the bishopric. He is a trustee of Northwestern University and of Seabury-Western Theological Seminary, and is a member of the National Council of the church. Among his publications are *Evolution, a Witness to God*, 1921; *Spanish Summer*, 1928; *Six Altars*, 1929; *The Call of Christ*, 1931; *The Face of Christ*, 1932; and *The Victory of Faith*, 1935. Bishop Stewart has been honored with degrees by Kenyon College, Northwestern University, and the Western Theological Seminary.

Long recognized as one of the outstanding leaders of the Anglo-Catholic movement within the Episcopal church, he is unusually well qualified to represent the definitely sacramentarian point of view of those outside the Roman Catholic church.

76

V

SACRAMENTARIANISM

By GEORGE CRAIG STEWART

IT is hard to define Religion. Like Poetry, it haunts us but defies definition. It is not mere ethics, and yet it is the dynamic behind all great moral codes. It is not a mere project of moral reformation, and yet it is the most potent of all forces in transforming moral ideas and practices. It is not mere philosophy. "The primary assurances of Religion are the ultimate questions of Philosophy."[1] Nor is it a rival of science, whose appraisals of the universe are in terms of measure and are therefore quantitative; and yet it gives to the findings of science their ultimate significance in qualitative terms of the imperishable values of religion, of truth and beauty and goodness. Nor is it mere art, although in the moment of deep appreciation of beauty there is discovered something religious —

> The moment eternal, just that and no more,
> When ecstasy's utmost we catch at the core.
>
> ("Asolando," by Robert Browning)

Nor is Religion a vague humanitarianism, though it furnishes the driving motive and power for multifarious movements against oppressive social evils, and holds men's hopes up forever to a new heaven and earth in which shall dwell righteousness. In a word, as Professor Hocking has said, "Religion is not so much an actor as a parent. We speak not so much of its utility as its fertility." It is not a segment

---

[1] William Temple, *Nature, Man and God*, p. 35.

77

of life. It *is* Life. It is a vision of the whole, and Communion with the very heart of Reality.

> Religion's all or nothing,
> It's no mere smile of contentment,
> It's no mere sigh of aspiration, Sir,
> No mere quality of the finelier tempered clay,
> As its whiteness or its lightness,
> But stuff of the very stuff —,
> Life of life, self of self.
>
> ("Sludge the Medium," by Robert Browning)

"It is," as Professor Whitehead writes in a memorable passage, "the reaction of human nature to its search for God, the vision of something which stands beyond, behind and within the passing flux of immediate things. . . . Apart from it human life is a flash of occasional enjoyments lighting up a mass of pain and misery, a bagatelle of transient experience."[2]

And then he adds: "The immediate reaction of human nature to the religious vision is worship; and worship is a surrender to the claim for assimilation urged with the motive force of mutual love. The power of God is the worship He inspires."

Now the Christian religion is based upon a living experience of God. The Christian creed is not a dead dogma, but the expression of a living pragma. It is warm with the repeated and renewed experience of a living and contemporary body of believers. God is conceived and experienced as personal, as both immanent within the created and creative process and transcendent as well. He is not a vast, impersonal, unconscious "cosmic environment" or "cosmic urge." He is not what the old Yankee farmer, when asked what he

[2] Alfred North Whitehead, *Science and the Modern World*, pp. 266–268.

meant by God, described as "a big oblong blur"; or what Matthew Arnold in accents more refined called "a power *outside ourselves* that makes for righteousness." He is, as Lord Balfour said, "A God whom men can love, to whom men can pray, who takes sides, who has purposes and preferences, whose attributes, however conceived, leave unimpaired the possibility of a personal relation between Himself and those he has created." [3]   He is not only without us, but within us.

All truth from whatsoever quarter it comes is His thought partially apprehended by us; all beauty is a reflection of His glory, but seen by us as in a glass darkly; and all goodness is none other than His character.

And He, the Eternal God, has revealed Himself in time; He, the infinite, has revealed Himself to us in space; He who is spirit, who has neither hands nor feet, nor place nor passions nor parts, has in love, by a continuous self-limitation, incarnated Himself in a human life known in history as Jesus of Nazareth. This is the astounding central claim of Christianity. It is today, as it was in St. Paul's day, "to the Jews a stumbling block, and to the Greeks foolishness." But to the Christian participant in His life it is the realest of all experiences. The heart of the Christian religion is to be found on Christmas Day. Not in the mere foregrounds of the beautiful pictures of the Nativity given by the Synoptics — the infant in the manger, the Virgin-mother, Saint Joseph, the shepherds, and the cattle in the stall — but in the vast eternal backgrounds of that scene presented by the writer of the Fourth Gospel in the Golden Prologue, in the Gospel of the Feast of the Nativity, which is read by the priest at the

[3] Arthur Balfour, *Theism and Humanism*, p. 21.

altar as the "Last Gospel" after every Eucharist on every other day of the year: "The Word was made flesh and dwelt among us and we beheld His glory, the glory as of the only begotten of the Father full of grace and truth." (John 1:14).

This central note is repeated by Saint John in his letter: "That which was from the beginning, which we have heard, which we have seen with our eyes, which we have looked upon, and our hands have handled of the word of life, for the life was manifested and we have seen it and bear witness and show unto you that Eternal life which was with the Father and was manifested unto us." (I John 1:1).

That apostolic experience of communion with God through the Incarnate Logos or Word of God is a normal constant central experience of Christian discipleship. All a Christian's faith centers there — all his standards of personal character and all his social passion for the Kingdom of God are based upon the Incarnation.

"There is one thing necessary," says Amiel, "and that is to possess God." "There is one thing necessary," agrees the Christian, "and that is to possess Christ and to be possessed by Him."

The Christian, then, thinks of God, believes in God, worships God, and achieves conscious communion with God in terms of Christ, *sub specie Christi, and the supreme goal of the Christian religion is identification with Him.* "I am come," He said, "that they might have life and that they might have it more abundantly." (John 10:10). To share that more abundant life, and to make it available for all people who will share it — this is the aim of the Catholic religion, and this is its supreme goal upon earth. Some people confuse the prize and the goal. They seek the prize of salvation rather than the goal of their high calling in Christ Jesus.

But a wise runner keeps his eye on the goal and lets the prize take care of itself. The aim of the disciple of Christ is not to adopt His words as a legal code of ethics, not to copy the accents of His Jewish milieu, not to sentimentalize over Him as a great human hero, not to worship Him as a demigod, certainly not to try to exploit Him as a magical Savior from a Dantean or Fra Angelican hell — which, by the way, He did not teach — but to possess Him, to be incorporated into Him, to have the mind of Christ, the spirit of Christ, and to share His own divine valor for the redemption of a world of men. This is after His own injunction: " Abide in me and I in you. As the branch cannot bear fruit of itself except it abide in the vine, no more can ye except ye abide in Me! " (John 15:4). The classical and typical example of such discipleship, the very echo of these words in a life which transformed Europe, is to be found in St. Paul's affirmation: " I am crucified with Christ; nevertheless I live; yet not I but Christ liveth in me; and the life which I now live in the flesh I live by the faith of the Son of God who loved me and gave himself for me." (Galatians 2:20).

Once this fundamental goal is grasped, the sacramental life of the Church becomes clear. She is not a mere organization of religious people seeking to find God. She has found Him in whom her soul delighteth. She does not crown the towers of her places of worship with a pathetic question-mark, but with a great exclamation-point in the form of a cross. Her doors are thronged not with wistful Jobs crying, " Oh that I knew where I might find Him, that I might come even to his seat," but with joyful people who have found Him, " who are not only worshipers of the divine Being but sharers in the divine abundant life, whose self-discipline rises from His control, whose lives are radiant with His indwelling, whose " bodies are made clean by His body and whose souls are washed with His most precious blood so that they may dwell *in* Him and He *in* them." [4]

Now how does all this come about? How is this vital, spiritually biological incorporation accomplished? How does one " put on Christ " (to use the Pauline phrase)? Well, St. Paul describes the Church as none other than the mystical Body of Christ, the extension of His incarnation in this space-time world, the social expresssion of His loving will to incorporate human lives with His own divine life. " We are members," says St. Paul, " of His body." (Ephesians 5:30).

The goal is perfectly clear to the apostle — " Till we all come in the unity of the faith and of the knowledge of the Son of God unto a perfect man unto the measure of the stature of the fullness of Christ." (Ephesians 4:13). The means to that goal is equally clear to him — participation in the life of the mystical Body, the Church.

If anyone goes into a Catholic Church, Roman or Anglican, the first thing he sees is the font. It stands at the entrance of the Church building because it represents the sacrament of initiation into the Church. " As many of you as have been baptized into Christ have put on Christ." (Galatians 3:27).

Our Lord seems to teach baptismal regeneration; at least the author of the Fourth Gospel so represents Him. " Verily, verily, I say unto thee, except a man be born of water and of the Spirit he cannot enter the Kingdom of God." (John 3:3–5). And St. Mark, the oldest of the Gospels, records the words of the risen Lord, " He that believeth and is bap-

[4] *Book of Common Prayer*, Communion Office.

tized shall be saved." (Mark 16:16). St. Peter, according
to the Acts of the Apostles, (Acts 2:38-39) seems to lay great
emphasis upon baptism in his famous sermon on the day of
Pentecost. St. Paul says: "We are buried with Him in baptism into death, that like as Christ was raised up from the
dead by the glory of the Father, even so we also should walk
in newness of life." (Romans 6:1-4). From St. John and
St. Paul forward to the Reformation, for at least fourteen
hundred years, there was no serious question of the sacramental character of the Church, nor of baptism as the gate
to the new life in Christ.

After all, what is birth? It isn't magic, and it isn't the
beginning of life. Life is in the womb, "through all the
months of ante-natal gloom." Birth is, rather, the emergence of a life already there into a new environment, into
new relationships, into citizenship, into a family, into a body,
a corpus of society. And the new birth, regeneration of a life
by baptism, is not magic, nor is it the original conveyance of
the spiritual germ, for " He lighteth every one coming into
the world," but it is a birth — the new birth of a life into the
Divine Society, a society with its own atmosphere, its
own disciplines and pressures, its own standards of behavior,
its own spiritual articulation of members, its own biological
oneness with the divine Head. It is the sacrament " wherein
we are made members of Christ, children of God, and in-
heritors of the Kingdom of Heaven." [5] A Christian, therefore, is clearly one who has been Christianed (or " chris-
tened "). The baptismal vows [6] are three: " To renounce
the devil and all his works, the pomps and vanities of this
wicked world; to believe the Christian faith as contained in

[5] *Book of Common Prayer*, Church Catechism.
[6] These are taken by adults as sponsors for infants.

the Apostles' Creed; to keep God's holy will and commandments, and walk in the same all the days of one's life." Baptism in itself is no more an assurance of goodness or virtue
or sanctity or salvation than birth in America, which constitutes American citizenship, is a guarantee that the citizens
will never go to jail or will of necessity escape hanging. It
is, however, a fact that the person in one case is a member
of the Christian Church and in the other is a citizen of the
Republic. And no protestations upon the part of an alien
that he admires America, loves " all her rocks and rills, her
woods and templed hills," will be accepted as a substitute
for his naturalization. Nor will any degree of sentimental-
izing about Christianity make a man a Christian who has
not " as a little child " put off the old man and put on the
new in baptism and become a sharer of the life of the Christian fellowship. Moreover, the initiated Christian, even as
an infant, is thereafter treated as an insider, not as an outsider; not as one who must experience a psychological upheaval known as "conversion" before he can "join the
Church," but as a child who shall learn in the family how
to talk the Christian way in prayer, walk the Christian way
in obedience, feed upon the Christian food in Holy Communion, and by the assistance of divine grace fight the Christian fight against sin, the world and the devil.

The Church after all is not a club of saints; it is a hospital
for sinners. It is not a society one joins; it is a family into
which one is born. It is not a field free of weeds, but a field
in which wheat and tares " grow together unto the harvest."
It is indeed the Body of Christ, but a human body, and therefore a constant reminder to us and a tragic illustration of the
depths of His loving condescension " who for us men and
for our salvation came down from Heaven and was made

man " — a phrase, by the way, which in the public services of the Church brings the congregation to its knees.

If entering the Church one sees the font at the door, he is also certain to look up and see that the one dominant note in the Church is the Altar. Not the pulpit. That is likely to be at one side. And why? Because worshipers do not come primarily to hear a preacher, however eloquent, but to offer a sacrifice of praise and thanksgiving to God. They come not to get something, but to offer themselves. The sermon is not the *piece de resistance* of the service. The act of wo. ship is. The preacher does not hold the center of the stage. The crucified Son of God does. It is not broken rays of dim religious light that bring the worshipers here, but the broken Body of the Lord; not the strains of lovely music poured out, but the Precious Blood of the Redeemer poured out. As all Catholics say, " It is the Mass that matters."

And at the altar, in mystical vestments designed to wrap him round and indicate his ministry as that of the great High Priest from whom alone his priesthood in the Body is derived, the priest, a differentiated organ of the Body, is heard — or rather through him is heard the voice of One — saying again: " This is My Body, This is My Blood."

To eat and drink the life of God sacramentally, to share in that life abundant, to be strengthened with the Bread that cometh down from heaven, to pour out to the Redeemer in penitence one's sins, to hear once more the great Absolver say, " Thy sins be forgiven thee, go and sin no more," to lift up one's heart in a great Sursum Corda, to join with angels and archangels and all the company of heaven in the great Trisagion, Holy — Holy — Holy, to offer oneself with his fellows, and above all with Christ, " ourselves, our souls and bodies to be a reasonable holy and living sacrifice," and then to go forward and kneel down at the common communion rail, rich and poor, high and low, savant and ignoramus alike, in one great democracy of spiritual hunger and thirst for God, to share in the one bread and to drink of the one cup — this is the high and holy and mystical experience of the Christian, a mystical experience, a shared experience, a social experience, a vital, dynamic, controlling, revolutionary experience which accounts for the centrality of the Altar and the Mass in every branch of the Catholic church, a stubborn fact which no doubt must ever seem to the outsider a strange and unaccountable phenomenon. Sacraments are not physical or non-ethical; they are spiritually vital and effective symbols.

Today as never before, however, we have been made aware by science of the sacramental character of the whole universe. Materialism is dead as a dodo. "The old contradictory notion of *dead* matter as the vehicle of life disappears in the light of our new knowledge." [7] Matter is discovered not to be dead, but to be very much alive, if energy be life. In his recent book, *New Pathways in Science,* Sir Arthur Eddington answers the questions whether the nature of reality is material or spiritual or a combination of both. [8] And he answers it by asking another question: "Is the ocean composed of water or waves or both? Is it aqueous or undulatory?" Then he goes on to assert that "the nature of all reality is spiritual, not material. The putting together of the adjective ' material ' and the noun ' nature ' does not make sense."

Each of us is a sacrament; the body, our shape and physical

[7] J. C. Smuts, *Holiness and Evolution,* p. 51.
[8] Sir Arthur Eddington, *New Pathways in Science,* p. 319.

substance of body, constitute but the outward and visible sign of an inward spiritual reality known as a person. Animals no doubt we are, but not just animals. The house is the house of a brute, but the spirit transcends and transforms the outward and visible sign. In the Holy Communion, spirit with spirit meet in the only way they ever meet in this world of sense, of Space-Time — sacramentally. The bread and wine are vehicles of the divine Life because He chooses through the simplest food to meet the hunger for spiritual refreshment presented to Him through sacraments of human body and blood. It is idle to charge Catholics with materialism or anything approaching cannibalism. They repudiate all gross and carnal theories of the Presence in the Blessed Sacrament. Our Lord is present after the manner of a spirit: objectively, yes; really, yes — but carnally or chemically, no!

Now if the goal of the Christian religion be identification of the individual human life with the Incarnate Son of God, it is no less true that this goal is a social goal, for Christ claims Kingship over all human life and all of human life.

No religion based upon the Incarnation could be individualistic. Because God became Man, every man is recognized as of infinite worth, as infinitely precious to God. And because our life is hid with Christ in God, it is fully integrated only as it ceases to be self-centered and becomes God-centered, Christ-centered, socialized. The Church which is His Body is itself a correction to self-centered individualism. It is international, interracial, universal, Catholic, in which " there is neither Greek nor Jew, circumcision nor uncircumcision, barbarian, Scythian, bond nor free, but Christ is all in all." (Colossians 3:11). The Church is the one and only true "International." And its sphere is the world of sinful, bewildered, weak, discouraged men.

The Church is not itself the goal, but it is both the type of the goal and the divine social instrument of the goal. It is, as St. Augustine called it, the *Civitas Dei,* the Commonwealth of God, a city that hath foundations and whose maker and builder is God. Its existence stands not in an ideal of human construction, but in God's self-giving; it is never perfected in time, but is always being built. The true sacramentarian is bound to be filled with social passion. If he is a priest he anoints the sick with the Church's oil as well as prays for them; and he prays for the dead, not merely buries them; he is an intercessor daily, not weekly, and a constant confessor to the sinful, a director to the bewildered, an absolver, in the name of Christ through his Body, of the penitent, a ministrant to the discouraged; he is at the wedding feast of Cana, and beside the widow of Nain, and always a friend of publicans and sinners. And the faithful layman is a brother to all men.

How could he be otherwise? The broken bodies of his brothers and the poured-out blood of the sons of men cry to him from the streets; they are victims, like his Lord, of the ruthless selfishness of men and the brutal force of a worldly and anti-Christian order; and his Lord has told him plainly, "Inasmuch as ye do it unto one of the least of these my brethren, ye do it unto me!" It is significant that the so-called Catholic revival in the Anglican Communion has been marked throughout by an enormous emphasis upon this social passion: as witness for example the work of the late Bishop Gore; of Father Dolling of the Portsmouth slums; of Father Stanton of St. Alban's, Holborn; of the great Chris-

tian social leaders today in England — men like Maurice
Reckitt and Dr. W. G. Peck and Dr. Carlyle and Father Bull
of the Mirfield community and the great Archbishop of
York. It is equally true in America, as witness such Anglo-
Catholic leaders in social movements as Canon B. I. Bell,
Professor Niles Carpenter, Vida Scudder, Father St. John
Tucker, Canon David Gibson of Chicago, Secretary Wallace
and a host of others.

But the goal of the Christian religion, after all, is not a
Kingdom of this world. The Church, as Dean Inge has so
repeatedly pointed out, has no faith in " a delusive millennium on earth." She has no illusive hope in the inevitability
of human progress. She does not look to see the world of
men carried steadily forward on the back of an amiable
monster called Evolution. She is not persuaded that every
man may work out his own salvation alone if he will. She
does not believe that man can lift himself up by his boot-
straps. Our Lord instituted His Church because men, it is
pretty certain, will destroy themselves without a sanctuary,
be bewildered and lost without a guide, and find themselves
without strength for the climb to sanctity without the aid of
supernatural grace.

" My Kingdom is not of this world," said Christ. " My
Kingdom," he also said, " is like leaven hid in three measures
of meal till the whole was leavened."

Christianity does not seek to dominate the kingdoms of
this world, but to permeate them with the spirit, the motive,
the presence and the power of Jesus Christ. And if, after
nineteen hundred years, the word " Failure " is hurled at
her, she does not forget that, judged by the world's standards

of success and failure, the cross at Calvary marked Jesus Himself as the supreme and most tragic failure.

Jesus Christ rose from the dead the third day. And the Church like her Lord is ever bursting her cerements, rolling back the stone from the door of the tomb where she has been safely and finally buried, and greeting the astonished world with a risen life, still bearing upon her body the prints of the nails in hands and feet, but moving with power and authority which cannot be denied.

The Christian today, moved by the vision of the Eternal, throws himself into life without haste and without rest to make the perdurable values of eternal life real not only in his own life but in the life of his generation. He seeks not heaven; he fears not hell. He only loves God and fears Him, and therefore loves his neighbor as himself. He is willing to lose his life to save it. He knows that he must here and now breathe the air of eternal values if he is to live forever. He knows his weaknesses, his own unworthiness, his own incapacity, but his is a life surrendered to Another who is mighty to save. He is not a slave of circumstances nor a coward full of fears, but signed with the sign of the cross in token that he " shall not be ashamed to confess the faith of Christ crucified and manfully to fight under His banner against sin, the world, and the devil, and to continue Christ's faithful soldier and servant unto his life's end."

And his goal and the goal of humanity is ever before him! What is it? Oneness with Christ! To that goal he presses forward, forgetting the things that are behind. " Beloved, now are we the sons of God and it doth not yet appear what we shall be, but we know that when He is made manifest we shall be like Him, for we shall see Him as He is." (I John 3:2).

The Kingdoms of this world go by
 In purple and in gold;
They rise, they flourish, and they die,
 And all their tale is told;
One kingdom only is divine,
 One banner triumphs still;
Its King — a servant, and its sign
 A gibbet on a hill!

E. G. HOMRIGHAUSEN

An Iowan by birth, Dr. E. G. Homrighausen was educated in various schools and colleges in Iowa, Wisconsin, New Jersey, Indiana and Illinois. He is a graduate of Princeton Theological Seminary, a Doctor of Theology of Dubuque University, and has studied at Butler University, Iowa State University, and the University of Chicago. Dr. Homrighausen was for a time minister of the First English Reformed Church of Freeport, Illinois, and is at present minister at the Carrollton Avenue (Evangelical and Reformed) Church at Indianapolis. To the duties of his pastorate he adds the responsibility of teaching church history in Butler University.

Though he is still a young man, honors have already come to Dr. Homrighausen. He has lectured at the University of Geneva in Switzerland for the Ecumenical Seminar, was delegate to the Pan-Presbyterian Assembly, Belfast, 1933, and to the International Council Committee on Life and Work in Denmark in 1934. He has recently been appointed a delegate of his denomination to the proposed 1937 World Conference on Christian Life and Work.

He has contributed to various religious journals, including *The Christian Century, Religion in Life, The Congregational Quarterly* (London) and *Union Seminary Review* (Richmond). He assisted in the translation of two volumes of sermons of Karl Barth and Dr. Thurneysen published under the titles *Come Holy Spirit* and *God's Search for Man,* and is assisting in the preparation of another volume of essays. Much interested from the first by the Barthian movement in Germany, Dr. Homrighausen has applied himself diligently to its study and, while not a one hundred per cent Barthian, has come to be regarded as one of the leading exponents of the general Barthian point of view in America.

92

VI

BARTHIANISM

By E. G. HOMRIGHAUSEN

THE goal of my life is God. That is the goal of not only personal but social life. I start with God and end with God. Life has no meaning in itself. It must revolve, like a wheel, around something for which it was created. And God is that Reality which exists simply because it exists. God is without proof. God is the cause, the sustainer and the centrum of life, without whom nothing would have an eternal meaning, without whom there would be no sanction or standard for life's actions, no dynamic for goodness, no eternal refuge, no integrating cosmic support in the realm of constantly changing time. This God is self-revealing. In Jesus Christ he has revealed himself, as the sovereign of life and history. In the light of what I apprehend about God in Christ, I am writing the following pages.

My life does not contain its own meaning. Nor can I create an eternal meaning for my life, any more than a sunbeam could create the sun. This is especially true because life somewhere has lost its fulcrum. Something has crept into this world, and into my life, that disrupts my relation with God. It has distorted my capacity to find life's goal. That something is sin, which consists in a selfish independence and autonomy on man's part, which takes the things of God and uses them for egocentric purposes. This sin has created a great discontinuity between God and man, not metaphysically but ethically and personally. God is still God, but man has " fallen " from a former high estate.

Sin is not only individual; it is social as well. The whole

world is enmeshed in this ungodly and unsocial human autonomy. Sin has warped men's minds, perverted their understanding and actions. Therefore, God is "hidden" in the world which he has created. All attempts on man's part to find this God of life and history are tragic and futile. They end in sterility and confusion. That is why we have so many religions. The true God is not to be found as a datum naturally in general history. Nor is he to be found perfectly in the human God-consciousness, nor in human experience. Whatever men call God seems hardly more than their own warped ideas about God projected into space. This true God is not found in any of the religions. Nor is he to be found in any synthetic Religion.

Let me explain this more fully. We must be realistic. Men worship God, but he is an "unknown God." I would agree with John Dewey that there are too many religions. They only confuse the issue. And it is the peculiar "contents" of religions that confuse us. We need a new evaluation of religions and Religion.

There is no hope for finding the goal of life in religions. Nor is there any hope of getting the best of all religion together into a synthetic Religion. Such a synthesis would take the most important elements out of all religions and kill them. Most religions are provincial and local. They cannot be adapted or made universal without destroying their strong points.

Therefore, religions and Religion do not interest me. I must have God, the God that smashes all these little systems and orthodoxies, these mysticisms and ethical codes and provincial religions. I must have a goal for my life that is not utterly dependent upon local history, nor upon man's interpretations. I must have a God who is God, who gives me a religion of his own content; I cannot be content with a man-made god. Besides, there is no such thing as *one* man-made god, common to all religions. I must have *the* God who is not a product of the sin and autonomy and egocentricity of this depraved world. I must have a God who reveals himself, who moves toward me, who confronts and invades me as God. And when he reveals himself, he must reveal himself in a personal way; not in a mystical vagary, a freakish theophany, a geographically limited theology, nor in a hard and cold rule of ethics. No, he must reveal himself unmistakably, personally, decisively, universally, as sovereign, and once-for-all. He must make his appearance in some historical event, and yet transcend in this all historical events and groups, all provincialisms!

Now, this revelation of himself is given; it is emergent and irrupting. It stands out in history as an unavoidable Gibraltar of energy and divine meaning. It transcends the goals of religions. It makes them all pale into insignificance; they all become not only inferior in degree, but actually different in kind from this true revelation. Man by his searching does not find God. God has himself found me. I am not doomed to grope around in my quest for life's chief end in tragic futility. I have found the goal of life in terms of a meaning that is higher, and " other," than *my* best possibilities.

This revelation, or self-movement of God toward me, I have found in the Hebrew-Christian tradition, culminating in the person of Jesus, whom men have called the Christ, the Messiah, the Son of God. It is attested by reliable witnesses whose words I believe. I accept their testimony.

I think that the reality of God in Jesus verifies itself to anyone who faces Jesus seriously, just as the reality of the sun is made manifest to anyone who stands in its rays. Anyone who thus submits himself, scientifically, to Jesus, just as an earnest scientist submits himself in the presence of a bare fact, will know something *in* and *about* Jesus that ordinary people will not see. That serious person will see an *objectivity* in Jesus, as Peter and Paul and millions of others have seen, not by reason of their logical ability, so much as by their downright, simple faith in that object. The truth, therefore, of the goal of religion is not so much in *my* experience of that reality in Jesus as it is in that very sovereign *Reality* itself, in men's witness, as recorded in the Gospels, of that Reality, which I did not create but which I stumbled onto and which invaded me. Christianity is not unique in the things it has in common with other religions; it is unique in its absolutely uncommon, arresting, decisive and universal objective reality in Jesus. It is ultimate. It is personal. I do not give *it* a value. *It evaluates me.* It tells me I am a sinner, a rebel against God, a prodigal. And being a sinner means that I do not have power within myself to redeem myself. And I am a sinner as long as I live, which will always keep me from pride or from that deadly modern sin which is reducing society to atomic human individualism and self-seeking autonomy. The whole New Testament is a witness to what that invading and decisive reality in Jesus did to men. It is there, as surely and as irrevocably as the sun. It meets me as it moves not from my world (from which all my religions and philosophies come), but from another world.

That Reality is ultimate. I can think of nothing higher. I either accept or reject its claims. It places me. It evaluates me and all men realistically. In its presence life stands still. This Reality does not allow me to take my religion as an opiate or a subjective mysticism. It sensitizes my conscience and ethical power of decision. It takes a strong and stern hold upon me — it apprehends me!

It does more. It promises me forgiveness. I cannot forgive myself. No — that forgiveness, too, comes from the "other" side of life, from God. That "grace" and love mysteriously judges and forgives. That forgiveness lifts my head. It restores my lostness. It bridges that discontinuity between the sinner and God, which the sinner cannot bridge by himself. It gives the "power of forgiveness" in life. I, then, give back or restore to God my whole life and he gives it back to me, but from now on I live, not by myself but by him and for him and in him. My whole life then becomes God-centered, deposited in God, even while I am a sinner and a part of this world. I live by faith and grace.

But this new eternal centrum of life does not cause me to escape from this world. It demands that I remain in it, but as a new creature whose life is now hidden with Christ in God. I am no longer a theocentric humanist. I am a humanistic theocentrist! I live my life, then, in a sense of living and personal relationship with God in Christ. I am motivated by a constant living responsibility to my world, to my neighbor and to my generation. I always live in a crisis, in a vortex between two worlds, the world of God and the world of sinful man. This is not mysticism, it is not dogmatism, it is not ethicalism, it is not ecclesiasticism — it is not even "Barthianism." It is God-realism and life-realism. It is not religion. For that reason Christianity is not a religion at all. It is *plain life-realism*. It smashes all *man's* religions. It is a life based upon God's own revelation of himself. It is not a *man's* religion, but it is *God's* religion. It is a realism of life that is done with all illusions. It is not escape from life, but real, everyday life, lived in my place with a new mean-ingfulness and a new hope. It is a life that has had a terrible pronouncement of judgment made upon it by that reality of God in Jesus, and it is a life that has been remarkably re-deemed by the marvelous promise and power of grace and forgiveness and resurrection from God in this present life. Resurrection is the same as revelation, and as forgiveness. It means that we are not left to grope in the arguments about immortality. God has now revealed himself as victor. Res-urrection is not so much an open grave, as it is a victorious energy of God's creative love conditioning everyday life. Resurrection means the *living* God. It means God is alive.

I do not romantically whitewash this sinful world of which I am a part, nor do I tone down the eternal world by which I am apprehended, and to which I am committed. I now live not by philosophy or religion, but I live by God's *revela-tion*.[1] I am not terribly concerned about what Dewey or Whitehead or Jeans may say! (All religions are attempts to rationalize, or in some mystical or ethical fashion to explain — or escape — the very reality of life). In Jesus, I have no more illusions. Here my life is truly evaluated, my illusions are smashed. In Jesus I find that reality which critically and realistically tells me what I am meant to be, what is wrong with me, and also provides God's remedy for me. It kills the old and gives birth to something new.

The Bible is not history, nor science, nor even religious his-tory. It is primarily a witness to that reality which came to full expression in Jesus. It is the story of God's coming to man when man himself could not " give birth " to a God who was real and true. *The God of the Bible is not man's*

---

[1] My idea of revelation would coincide with that of E. F. Scott, described in his book *The New Testament Idea of Revelation*. Charles Scribner's Sons.

idea. He far transcends and exceeds anything man ever dreamed of. Here is the story of a God whom man does not reach by thinking or questing, nor whom he can reach by ethical action or monastic asceticism. Here is a God who presents himself to man as God, not because man can give him birth or prove him, but because he is God. This God is not the object and result of *my* thinking. I am the subject of his thought and love. This God meets me, tells me his will, makes his demands upon me and gives me the gift of his grace and mercy, and promises me life eternal. In faith and humility I accept his judgment, receive his grace freely, and accept my life again from his hands. My security, then, is no longer in my thought, my science, my self, my religion — but in God, the God of revelation.

I do not need to defend this reality in Jesus. I need merely to face it honestly, and as a Christian truly proclaim it. I may speak of this God of revelation as " other," yet not in the sense that he is metaphysically removed from me, but that he confronts me as Lord, as one who comes to me in my " lostness." He breaks into my life and he bursts out of my life in this revelation. I do not care to use the terms transcendent and immanent. They are philosophical terms, and philosophy does not provide me my goal of life. Philosophy is a rationalization. Its chief function is critical.

My goal of life is not a product of my natural self. No, what has happened is that my true self has been grounded and rooted in a different choice and object of life. I have attached myself to the true Vine of life, from whom I expect all things. Salvation is not personal intensification, but a personal commitment to the content of God in Christ. I will never be perfect in this relative world in myself. But a new purpose has now entered my life that has been given me of God, which purpose is nothing less than the work of the Holy Spirit. This gives my life a true derivation. That purpose has already carried me beyond death.

By that I mean that death is not that last tragic incident that shall some day cut off my earthly existence. No! Death is what human life is all the time without this true goal of life. When once I gave up all other life-goals, then I submitted myself to death. Christians have already passed from death to life. They have, for better or worse, thrown their lot in with God's lot, and they trust in him for everything. They have already faced the bitter reality of death. Any life that lives by itself, that gropes around attempting to find life's true God by itself, is still living in the darkness of an earthly life which has no light to point it beyond life's transiency. It is a dead life. Arguments for the immortality of the soul, therefore, do not interest me. They *prove* nothing. They only surmise. But being raised in and with Christ is an experience that gives life the " tone " of an eternal existence, at least in promise, here and now. This is the " power of resurrection " which Paul desired to know and share. I live in a body that will surely decay, and any day may be laid low. But since there is a God who cares, and who has moved toward men in love, why should I fear? *His faithfulness* is greater than all the arguments for the possibility of the survival of personality through death. Such is resurrection-life.

This revelation does not offer me a detailed cosmology, nor a minute political or economic philosophy. It does not promise a magical existence in this life! It offers no hedonistic happiness. It offers blessedness, and a person may be blessedly unhappy. It gives me a theology, a God-centeredness and a divine meaningfulness for life that is not based upon intellectual, moral or mystical ingenuity, but upon God's marvelous life and self-giving. It gives me power to affirm life here and now as I meet it day by day. I serve God and my generation with what capacities I have in my place in the world.

This revelation is preserved for me in the living tradition of the Church. The Church is the living witness, and " contemporizer " of the revelation event. And one is a Christian only in fellowship with others who are kindred in mind and heart. This reality in and around Jesus makes me especially conscious of the fact that I am a social being, that I belong always to others, as well as to Another. Not that the Church is a magical institution in its physical structure. It is rather what the Church witnesses to and what its secret life is, that makes it so important. It is a sort of new humanity in the making of life-realists and God-realists. They are not perfect, but they have been apprehended by that reality and have committed themselves to that reality. The Church, then, is a community, an incubator for the hatching of sensitive, brotherly, repentant human beings who ought to create a ferment, a flavor, a germinant in social life for a new society. The Church still is the depository of this revelation in spite of the fact that it is divided into warring and dogmatic churches, and thus sins against its unitive reality. Whenever men lose sight of the reality in Jesus that gave the Church birth and which reality has power to sustain it, then the Church loses its true catholic unity and function, and forfeits its right to be the sacred channel of the Truth. Any attempt to rob that Reality at the heart of the Church of its sovereignty by orthodoxy or by liberalism is a resurgence of the old spirit of man which seeks to make God less than Lord, and which will not walk with him as a child in trust and faith. Church fellowship is a symbol of true society, of true obedience and freedom, and of true individualism.

Now the goal of my faith, socially, is the Kingdom of God. That kingdom is in this world, operating wherever men realistically evaluate themselves in the face of true revelation. But this kingdom cannot be identified with any social program.

I am not so foolish as to believe that this kingdom will come on earth by sheer human effort. Nor do I think that this kingdom will come by an "inherent necessity" in the nature of the universe automatically to produce a perfect world. Even if communism should succeed to a stage where men had all the necessities of life, such a world might be far from the Kingdom of God, in which love would reign and in which there would be no more inequality, or sickness, or premature death. The true kingdom is always beyond humanity. Even communistic projects in the Church have not succeeded.

But for that reason I do not flee from the world. I am a sinner, and as such I am dependent upon God and am not myself God. I am also organically united with the sinfulness of my age. I am bound to man and to God by a sense of responsible mutuality.

To me, the goal of religion socially is not in a code of ethical conduct, nor even in a socially applied "golden rule"! The goal of religion is a true society, which can come only as men acknowledge themselves as sinners toward God and as brothers toward their fellows. Thus the Kingdom of God becomes a working power in the social order, like leaven, like the life of the seed, like salt. It cannot work in pure isolation.

Whenever men forget the true goal of society in God, they become self-sufficient, individualistic and bourgeois. And self-sufficiency may be collective as well as individual. The confusion of modern times is due to this sin.

I would agree with the Marxist in his attack upon the modern bourgeois capitalist. He "atomizes" society. He makes his religion a comfortable opiate and sanction for his pharisaic self-sufficiency, and uses his religion to lift himself to the throne of mastery over his fellows. He makes a true society impossible. It is a method of self-deification. The modern individualist thinks he can live unto himself.

But the communist and the fascist are equally wrong in their conception of a true society. They are, indeed, attempting to regain a true community life. The modern socialist often harbors the same motive. But surely, autocratic collectivism is anything but a true society. It is nothing more than an inverted capitalism and rests upon foundations equally false and egotistic. There is no repentance in these collectivisms. There is no difference between a modern collectivist and a Manchester liberal.

For that reason I am not going to be deluded by the bread which the modern collectivists offer me in these days. It also is stone. It does not bring about a true society. The true community comes when men rightly evaluate themselves, not by a standard of a "classless" society, or a radical nationalism, or an aristocratic and unrealistic socialism, or a rugged individualism. True society, or community, is attained when and where men are evaluated by a standard that places them all in judgment, when men seek a common grace, and are bound to their brothers by a sense of commonness and mutual responsibility, and when they seek to fulfill their calling in life more than they seek to fight for their rights. Modern marriage, church life, community life suffer largely because men ground these collective units in *themselves* individually.

What the modern world needs is not more social coercion and force, not new programs of action, so much as it needs a new dynamic for the creation of a social spirit of community life. For that reason my Christian faith does not foist a cold social code upon me. It does not give me political platforms to foist upon my neighbors. It offers me no Kantian imperative. No, it offers me a moral and personal and dynamic indicative to break down the proud individualism and proud collectivism of my age, which keep the true society from coming into being. The autonomous man is today the real reason for his social maladjustments.

It is not the business of the Church primarily to work for superficial social reform. The Church has to deal with the social problem in its intensest form. That problem is sin. It is a denial of God's lordship! This is the disease from which we are suffering. And many of the programs which men offer for the betterment of the social system do not take seriously the basic reality of sin which makes a true community impossible. The Church must lay bare the main issue. The goal of religion must be nothing less than the inner redemption, not merely the external reorganization, of society. And to achieve this goal, there must be new men.

I am not under the illusion that I can escape my immoral social order. I live in an immoral social order all the time. But while I live in it, I do not inwardly assent to it. In a real sense, I try to reconcile the immoral daily world with the world of the Kingdom. That strategy is plain voluntary suffering. This is the work of reconciliation.

The argument may be brought forward that such love is not enough. We live in a world of immorality, and therefore we must work in the world and with its methods. I know that, intellectually considered, such suffering love may never *eradicate* the evils in the world. It may only offer the wicked man greater opportunity for his selfish pursuits. But while such love cannot coerce the evil man, it can qualify the social struggle. And without that fountain of new social force, the world would soon become a jungle of barbarians. The restraint of love still has power of light and salt and leaven. I do not, and I could not, avoid using the world's methods every day. I am always under obligation to live a life of obedience to God in Christ, which is now the center of my life. But while I must therefore labor for the relief of victims of an unjust social order, it is also my task to labor in the spirit of repentance through regular and constituted means, with all the ingenuity I possess, to make the world a little more tolerable, if not instantly perfect. I must use the best methods I can, although every method I use will be relative and sinful. I must try to mitigate the evils of the world. But I must never forget that the real basis of the world's evils is not in man's intelligence or social organization so much as in his sinful autonomous will, and that no amount of anxious political or social change in the world will make the world any better unless downright health comes to the basic nature of man's sense of God and his neighbor. To add my violence to that already in the world is to make the world worse, and surrender my high calling as a Christian whose life is rooted in God!

Therefore, I am not a passive romanticist. Nor am I an other-worldly realist. My whole Christian ethic is one based not upon a neat code of infallible rules, but upon a life that has been apprehended and called and forgiven by the grace of God in Jesus. This is the fountain out of which my ethical responsibility springs. There are things that men can do and there are things men cannot do. Some social forces are so huge that man cannot affect them. These in his own time God brings low with his righteous judgment. As a Christian my social goal is both to wait and work, both to pray and to labor.

But I am convinced that I cannot follow some modern groups which are set on reforming the world with an activistic program. These movements are clothed in fine idealism, but their spirit is wrong. Their basic motive is not commensurate with what I would conceive the task of the Church to be, nor is their methodology commensurate with realistic social or theological knowledge. Nor will their success make men basically better. The world, at long last, will not remember many of these movements, nor will the world even be made more tolerable by them. Some of these movements are based on inherent hatred or on unrighteous indignation.

There must come a reversal in our attitude toward life and God and man. A new community-mind must be born! As it is, the world is going to ruin by the sheer force of collective and individual egotism. And so long as men seek the goal of individual or social religion in themselves, in the intensification of what they naturally are or want, we will have a world of pure disintegration. This false spirit is the cause of history's tragic failures — and its ruins.

The real cause of our social and personal disease can be plainly seen today. The remedy lies alone in a life of obedience to God, whose we are by sheer grace, in spite of our sins, and in whom we all cohere as brothers of a common, self-revealing Father. This religious basis gives life a fulcrum beyond itself, and it gives society a basis in a true community in which alone individual man can find his true freedom and fulfillment.

FULTON JOHN SHEEN

Monsignor Fulton John Sheen is a member of the faculty of the Catholic University at Washington, D. C., but at the same time he is one of the most widely heard preachers of the Roman Catholic Church in America. Born at El Paso, Illinois, he was educated in Spalding Institute, Peoria, Illinois; St. Viator College, Kankakee, Illinois (A.B., 1917, A.M., 1919); St. Paul (Minnesota) Seminary (S.T.B. and J.C.B., 1919); Catholic University of America (S.T.B. and J.C.B., 1920); and Louvain (Belgium) (Ph.D., 1923), where he was also *Agregé en Philosophie,* 1925, and won the Cardinal Mercier Prize of Philosophy. He has been honored since with degrees of Doctor of Divinity in Rome, Doctor of Laws from Loyola University, Chicago, and St. Viator College, and Doctor of Letters from Marquette. He was ordained to the Roman Catholic priesthood in 1919, taught for a time in St. Edwards College, Ware, England, and joined the faculty of the Catholic University of America in 1925.

He has been several times preacher at summer conferences in the Westminster Cathedral, London, and in 1930–31 was lecturer in the Cambridge University Catholic Summer School. Since 1931 he has been the Lenten preacher at St. Patrick's Cathedral, New York, and since 1930 has been heard regularly as preacher on the Catholic Hour over the National Broadcasting Company's radio network.

Father Sheen's list of books includes the following titles: *God and Intelligence,* 1925; *Religion Without God,* 1928; *The Life of All Living,* 1929; *The Divine Romance,* 1930; *Divine Immanence,* 1931; *Moods and Truth,* 1932; *The Way of the Cross,* 1932; *Seven Last Words,* 1933; *The Eternal Galilean,* 1934; *The Philosophy of Science,* 1934; and *The Mystical Body of Christ,* 1935. It would be difficult to discover one better fitted than Monsignor Sheen to represent the Roman Catholic viewpoint in this discussion.

108

VII

ROMAN CATHOLICISM

By FULTON JOHN SHEEN

THE problem of salvation is studied in this chapter from the Christian point of view: namely, that Christ is the Son of God and the Redeemer of man. It begins with the principle that God made a moral universe. He willed from all eternity to build a stage upon which characters would emerge. He might, of course, have made a world without morality, without virtue, without character — a world in which every one of us would sprout virtues as an acorn sprouts an oak, or a world in which all of us would become saints with the same inexorable necessity with which the chariot of the sun mounts the morning sky, or the rain falls to embrace the earth. God might have made us all like so many sticks and stones controlled by the same rigid necessity that makes fire hot and ice cold. God might have done this, I say, but He did not. And He did not because He willed a moral universe in order that, by the right use of the gift of freedom, characters might emerge.

Suppose, now, it be granted that God chose to make a moral universe, or one in which characters would emerge. What condition would have to be fulfilled in order to make morality possible? If God chose to make a moral universe, then He had to make man free, that is, endow him with the power to say " yes " and " no," and to be captain and master of his own fate and destiny. Morality implies responsibility and duty, but these can exist only on condition of freedom. Stones have no morals, because they are not free. We do not praise iron because it becomes heated by fire, nor do we condemn ice because it is melted by heat. Praise and blame can be bestowed only on those who are masters of their own wills. It is only the man who has the possibility of saying " no " who can have any charm in his heart when he says " yes."

We have said that God chose to make a moral universe and that He could make a moral universe only on condition that He made man free. This being so, we have an answer to the question, Why does God permit evil? The possibility of evil is in some way bound up with the freedom of man. Since man was free to love, he was free to hate; since he was free to obey, he was free to rebel; since he was free enough to be praised for his goodness, he was free enough to be blamed for his badness. Virtue, in this present concrete order, is possible only in those spheres in which it is possible to be vicious; sacrifice is possible only on those levels on which it is possible to be selfish; redemption is possible only in those realms where it is possible to be enslaved. The world has no heroes except in those battles in which every hero might have been a coward; the nation has no patriots except in those causes in which each patriot might have been a traitor; the Church has no saints except in those hearts each of which might have housed a devil.

God in His goodness did not choose simply to make a man moral and then give him merely the moral rewards to which a man is naturally entitled. He willed to do more than this. When a man becomes a father, is he content merely to give his child only that which is necessary? Does he not rather as a loving father give to his son even more than that which is his due? So, in like manner, God willed to give man certain gifts of body and soul which far exceed the nature or the capacity of man. Imagine a wealthy banker who would

form a trust fund for a foundling baby, from which a vast
sum of money was to be paid to the child when he reached
the age of twenty-one, provided that during that time he led
a good moral life. Now God established some such trust
fund. He willed to give to the first man and woman certain
gifts which would be permanently for them and for their
posterity, providing that they proved faithful in their love.
Among these gifts were: immunity from disease and death;
freedom from the rebellion of flesh over reason; above all,
a gift of knowledge which far surpassed reason and enabled
man to grasp divine truths in a far more wonderful way than
that in which a telescope reveals to the eye the distant stars
and planets; and a gift of power or grace which made the
first man and woman not mere creatures of the handiwork
of God, but God's own children, and co-heirs with Him in
the Kingdom of Heaven. These gifts, be it understood, were
even less due to the nature of man than the power of bloom-
ing belongs to marble, or the song of a poet belongs to a
beast.

But these gifts were conditioned, for the universe is moral.
They could be kept on one condition, namely, by loving God,
and loving God means loving what is best for ourselves. But
how try love? The only way to try love is in a test which
forces one to declare it. The only way for Adam and Eve as
free moral beings to prove their love and gratitude to God
was by choosing Him in preference to all else, and admitting
that their added knowledge and their added power or grace
were gifts. A double condition was laid upon them to test
their love. The first part of the condition was obscure; it
gave them an opportunity to admit that the added knowledge was a gift of God. The second part was reserved; it
allowed them to admit that the added power of the will was

a gift of God. Thus they would show that they loved God with their whole mind and their whole will, and preferred Him to all things else. In concrete terms, the trial was that they might enjoy all the riches of the garden of Paradise, but the fruit of one tree — the tree of the knowledge of good and evil — they were not to touch. God did not say why they should not — and that was the obscure point on which their intelligence was tried. Man should believe God on this point as on all others. God did say that they must abstain from the fruits of that tree. That was the reserved point which was the trial of their will. God was imposing a limit to the sovereignty of man, reminding him that if he did the one thing forbidden he would imperil all the things provided, and that, like Pandora later on, if he should open the forbidden box, he would lose his treasures and let loose confusion worse confounded on the world.

The whole trial was perfectly reasonable. Imagine a wealthy man who owns a beautiful estate. He tells his chauffeur and the chauffeur's wife that he will permit them to live in his mansion, ride in his motor-cars, use his servants, enjoy his yacht, play about his spacious gardens, eat at his expense. In a word, they are to enjoy everything provided that they will not touch a certain oil painting that hangs in one of his drawing-rooms. By doing the one thing forbidden, they would lose all the things provided, and who would accuse the master of the house of injustice if he no longer permitted them to enjoy his gifts?

The doctrine, then, of the fall of man is far from the travesty of it by frivolous minds who make the ordinance of God repose solely on an apple, for to do this is to miss the point of the whole story. To speak of the fall does not mean merely a garden and a serpent; to say that it is much more than any garden or any snake is not the same as saying there was no garden and there was no snake. It is simply saying what is of primary and what is of secondary importance; what is primary is the respect due to God, the fruit of the tree being the symbol of that respect. To make light of the fruit of a tree under such circumstances is just as rash as to make light of the flag of our country, as a symbol of our country's sovereignty. A flag stands for a nation, and the hand that carries it would retain it at the cost of a thousand deaths rather than let it be seized and desecrated by the enemy. It may be a small thing to violate a cloth that is red and white and blue, but it is no small thing to desecrate that for which it stands. So likewise in the terrestrial Paradise, the famous tree in which God summarized all the knowledge of good and evil was a symbol, a moral limit which God imposed on the sovereignty of man to prove his obedience and his love. To say it was only a fable is to miss the great truth that things — a handshake or a smile, for example — may not only be, but may also signify.

There are two points that I would make in conclusion concerning the fall of man. The first is that by this act of disobedience, which is called his original sin, man lost nothing which was due to him or to his nature. He lost only gifts, and became, as St. Augustine has said, " just mere man." On Christmas Day when you distribute gifts to your friends, a person with whom you are unacquainted would not dare come to you and argue that you had refused to give him gifts as you had given them to your friends. Your answer would be: " Sir, I have done you no injustice. I have deprived you of nothing which is your due. I have even given to my friends that which was not theirs." And so it is with original sin. In losing the gifts of God, man lost nothing which was due to his nature. He was reduced to a state in which God might possibly have created him, with the difference that the loss of the gifts weakened his intellect and will, but did not make his nature intrinsically corrupt. Imagine a line of soldiers; notice one of these in particular. He resembles all the others in dress, appearance and action, but yesterday he was an officer, thanks to political preferment rather than to meritorious advancement. For a misdemeanor he was degraded and the badge of his office taken from him. He was reduced to the state in which you see him now. Original sin then is not to be in the state we are in, but to have fallen into that state.

Secondly, this sin of Adam was not merely the sin of an individual, it was the sin of all humanity, for Adam was the head of all humanity. If he had been faithful we would have enjoyed all of his gifts, for he acted in our name. Since he was unfaithful we suffer his loss, for he acted in our name. This is not an injustice. All human beings are bound up with one another. In 1917, for example, President Wilson proclaimed war without any explicit declaration on our part. He was our political head and he acted in our name. Adam was our head and he acted in our name. When he declared war against God, we declared war in like manner, without any explicit declaration on our part, because of our oneness with him. And just as in the physical order the infected blood of a father may pass on to a son, so too the stain of the first man has passed on to the whole human race and stained every one but our " tainted nature's solitary boast " — the Blessed Mother of our Lord and Savior Jesus Christ.

How can the human atone to the divine? How can Justice and Mercy be reconciled? If satisfaction is ever to be rendered for the fall of man, the finite and the infinite, the human and the divine, God and man must in some way be linked together. It would not do for God alone to come down and suffer as God alone, for then He would not have anything in common with man; the sin was not God's but man's. It would not do for man alone to suffer or atone, for the merit of his sufferings would be only finite. If the satisfaction were to be complete, two conditions would have to be fulfilled: First, man would have to be man to act as man and to atone. Man would have to be God in order that his sufferings should have an infinite value. But in order that the finite and the infinite should not be acting as two distinct personalities, and in order that infinite merit should result from man's suffering, God and man in some way would have to become one; or, in other words, there would have to be a God-man. If Justice and Mercy were to be reconciled, there would have to be an Incarnation, which means God assuming a human nature in such a way that He would be true God and true man. There would have to be a union of God and man, built upon somewhat the same lines as the union of spirit and matter in man. Man has a double nature, the nature of a body which is material, and the nature of the soul which is spiritual, and yet he is only one person. The Incarnation of God would imply some such union of two natures in the unity of a Person, but quite naturally a far more perfect one.

A link or bond there must be between God and man. Man is sinful, God is holy; and there is nothing common between the two. Man is finite, God is infinite; and there is nothing common between the two. Man is human, God is divine; and there is nothing common between the two. By my own power I am not able to touch the ceiling of my room, but the link of a ladder would effect a union between me and it. In like manner, if there were ever to be a real communion between heaven and earth, between God and man, there would have to be a link between the two. Those who seek the missing link between the man and the animal say that that link must have something common to both. In like manner, we who seek the link between God and man say that that link must be both human and divine.

Where seek that link? In a cave? Yes! The world is right in seeking the Cave Man, but is seeking him in the wrong cave. If we are to find the prototype of man we must seek it not in the cave of Moulin, but in the cave of Bethlehem, and the name of that Cave Man is not Pithecanthropus but Christ; the light shining in his eyes is not the light of a beast coming to the dawn of reason, but the light of a God coming to the darkness of men; the animals in the cave are not wild beasts shrieking at one who came from them, but the ox and the ass bowing down to one who came to them; the companions in the cave are not wild creatures with lifted clubs as a sign of war, but Joseph and Mary with folded hands as a symbol of peace. In a word, Christ is the link between the finite and the infinite, between God and man, because finite in His human nature, infinite in His divine, and one in the unity of His Person; missing, because men have lost Him; Pontiff, because the Bridge-Builder between earth and Heaven, for such is the meaning of Pontiff; Mediator, because the High Ambassador of God among men. All these names are only other ways of saying that which we forget was the life of Christ above all things else — the life of a Priest.

Many of the emasculated lives of Christ today picture Him merely as a moral reformer, a teacher of humanitarian ethics, or a sentimental lover of birds and beasts. Our Lord is primarily none of these things. He is first and foremost a Redeemer. In that He breaks with all reformers and preachers who ever lived. Take any of them: Buddha, Plato, Confucius, Socrates, Lao-tsze — why did they come into the world? Every one of them came into this world to live. But why did Our Lord come into this world? He came into the world to die. It was the supreme business which engaged Him from the day of His birth: " The Son of man," He said of Himself, " is come to seek and to save that which was lost."

Socrates, on the contrary, came into the world to teach. Hence the greatest tragedy of his life was the cup of hemlock juice which interrupted his teaching. Death was his greatest stumbling block. But the Cross was not to Christ what the hemlock juice was to Socrates. It was not the interruption of His life — it was the very beginning. His teaching was not stopped by His death. It was His death that proved His teaching true.

Buddha came into the world to preach the philosophy of renunciation. He was a philosopher and only a philosopher. His supreme business in life was solely and uniquely to explain defeat — in a certain sense fatalism. Death spoiled his preachments about renunciation. But death to Christ was not what death was to Buddha. Both preached renunciation. Death was the end of Buddha's preaching about renunciation. Death to Christ was the renunciation. Death was the end for Buddha. But for Christ it was only the beginning.

Our Lord did not walk about the earth forever telling people platitudes about truth. He was not just explaining truth, defeat, resignation, sacrifice. Everyone else did this. The goal He was seeking was death. From the beginning to the end only one vision was before His eyes — He was going to die. Not die because He could not help it, but die because He willed it. Death was not an incident in His career; it was not an accident in His plan — it was the one business He had to do.

In like manner, if a man is ever to enter into the higher life of Christ — and man has no right to say there is no higher life than his own any more than a rose has a right to say there is no higher life than it — if he is ever to enjoy communion with Him, so as to have the blood of God running in his veins and the spirit of God throbbing in his soul, he must die to the lower life of the flesh. Aye, he must be born again, for unless a man is born to that life of God by a death to the lower life of nature, he cannot enter the Kingdom of Heaven. And hence the law of Calvary is the law of every Christian: unless there is the Cross there will never be the resurrection, unless there is the defeat of Calvary there will never be the victory of Easter, unless there are the nails there will never be the glorious wounds, unless there is the garment of scorn there will never be the robes blazing like the sun, unless there is the crown of thorns there will never be the halo of light, unless there is the descent into the grave there will never be the Ascension; for the law laid down at the beginning of time which shall be effective until time shall be no more is that no one shall be crowned unless he has struggled and overcome, and no one shall enjoy the life of God until he has died to his selfish self. But in this surrender of the lower life, let it not be thought that mortification is a sign of weakness; rather it is a sign of power: it is the will controlling itself, submitting itself to defeat at its own hands, in order to win its finest victory; it is the making of the dead self a steppingstone to better things and the conquest of self the condition of the victory which brings everlasting peace and joy with God.

Wrongly indeed do we think that Our Blessed Lord might

have saved us in some less costly way than in emptying His Precious Blood from the chalice of His Body. Oh, if He were only a teacher of humanitarian ethics, if He were only a moral reformer, then it might have sufficed for Him to show His inimitable tenderness, His heavenly purity and His melting kindness; then He might have sat, like some Greek teachers before Him, in some market place or on some porch, where the great minds of the world might have sought out His wisdom and His counsel. But if He was to be more than a teacher, if He was to be the High Priest Who would not make a new world but invigorate an old one, if He was to force the human conscience to stand face to face with the sternest sides of truth ere He disclosed His Divine Remedy, then, unless the existing conditions of human life were to be altered, He had to die to the ignominy of a Good Friday to live to the life of an Eternal Easter.

The foregoing illustrates that salvation is both something social and something individual. Just as Adam appears in history as the head of fallen humanity, so does Christ appear as the head of regenerated humanity or the Church. The process by which individuals become incorporated to Adam and to Christ is by birth — birth by the flesh makes us members of the society of Adam; birth by the spirit makes us members of the society of Christ. Such was the meaning of Our Lord's words to Nicodemus that he had to be reborn in order to live. Rebirth to Christ implies death to the world, for death to the world is the door to the saving grace of Christ.

Nature settles her account with natural things here and now. But the moral side of the universe has not made its lasting reckoning with every man on this side of the grave: there is too much anguished innocence, too much unpunished wrong, too much suffering of the good, too much prosperity of the evil, too much pain for those who obey God's laws, too much pleasure for those who disobey them, too much good repute for those who sin unseen, too much scorn for those who pray unseen, too many unsung saints, too many glorified sinners, too many Pilates who act as righteous judges, too many Christs who go down to crucifixion, too many proud and vain souls who say, "I have sinned and nothing has happened."

But the reckoning day must come, and just as once a year each business man must balance his accounts, so too that important hour must come when every soul must balance its accounts before God. For life is like a cash register, in that every account, every thought, every deed, like every sale, is registered and recorded. And when the business of life is finally done, then God pulls from out the registry of our souls that slip of our memory on which is recorded our merits and demerits, our virtues and our vices — the basis of the judgment on which shall be decided eternal life or eternal death. We may falsify our accounts until that day of judgment, for God permits the wheat and the cockle to grow unto the harvest, but then, "in the time of the harvest, I will say to the reapers: gather up first the cockle and bind it into bundles to burn, but the wheat gather ye into my barn."

But what is the nature of judgment? In answer to this question we are more concerned with the particular judgment at the moment of death, than with the general judgment when all nations of the earth stand before their God. Judgment is a recognition. Imagine two souls appearing before the sight of God, one in the state of Grace, the other in the state of sin. Grace is a participation in the nature and life of God which Christ restored by His Redemption. Just as a man participates in the nature and life of his parents by being born of his parents, so too a man who is born of the Spirit of God by Baptism participates in the nature of God — the life of God, as it were, flows through his veins, imprinting an unseen but genuine likeness. When, therefore, God looks upon a soul in the state of Grace, He sees in it a likeness of His own nature. Just as a father recognizes his own son because of likeness of nature, so too Christ recognizes the soul in the state of Grace in virtue of resemblance to Him, and says to the soul: " Come ye blessed of My Father: I am the natural Son, you are the adopted son. Come into the Kingdom prepared for you from all eternity." This soul is saved.

God looks into the other soul that is in the state of sin and has not that likeness, and just as a father knows his neighbor's son is not his own, so too God, looking at the sinful soul and failing to see therein the likeness of His own flesh and blood, does not recognize it as His own kind, and says to it as He said in the parable of the bridegroom, " I know you not " — and it is a terrible thing not to be known by God. This soul is lost.

Christ crucified has no redemptive relation with the dead: He has either redeemed them, or they are beyond the reach of redemption. While we yet have life, the pierced hands of Christ are outstretched to beckon us onward to drink the wine of love from the great chalice of His Sacred Heart. But when our soul has passed the gate of eternity, those pierced hands, which all during life we saw outstretched on the Cross, will detach themselves and fold together in judgment.

JOHN A. WIDTSOE

Dr. John A. Widtsoe, member of the Council of Twelve Apostles, Latter-Day Saints (Mormon) church, was a native of the Island of Fröyen, Norway. His family came to America while he was a child, and he received his education for the most part in this country. In 1891 he was graduated from the Normal department of Brigham Young College in Logan, Utah, in 1894 from Harvard University, and he won a Doctor of Philosophy degree from the University of Göttingen in 1899. He was traveling fellow of the graduate school of Harvard in 1898–1900, studying at the Polytechnicum in Zurich in 1900. He was honored with the Doctor of Laws degree by Utah State Agricultural College in 1914 and by the University of Utah in 1921.

His major interest lay in the field of chemistry, which subject he taught for a time in Utah State Agricultural College. He was at one period director of the Utah Experiment Station, and became principal of the agricultural department of the Brigham Young University in 1905; he served as president of the Agricultural College of Utah, 1907–16. Dry farming and irrigation naturally engaged his interest and to the solution of the problems in this field he gave years of study. He was president of the International Dry-Farming Congress in 1912 and three of his books relate to the subject: *Dry Farming,* 1911; *Irrigation Practice,* 1914; and as late as 1927 he wrote *Success on Irrigation Projects.* From 1916 to 1921 he was president of Utah University. Since 1921 he has been a member of the Council of Twelve Apostles of the Church of Jesus Christ of Latter-Day Saints. He served as President of European Missions for his church, 1928–33, and is at present Commissioner of Education for his denomination.

Like many of the lay leaders of the Mormon church, he has written and lectured widely on his faith. Among his best known religious books are *A Rational Theology* and *In Search of Truth.*

Part Two

VIII

MORMONISM

By JOHN A. WIDTSOE

THE welfare or happiness of mankind — the eternal quest of man — is the goal of religion. It cannot be otherwise. Religion exists to supply the needs of man. Indeed, in the words of the Nephite prophet, " Men are that they might have joy." This objective must color and explain every doctrine and activity of religion.

Happiness as the aim of life may be defined as the increasing joy of living that comes from robust health of body, mind and spirit. It is far from the selfish satisfaction of unnatural appetites. It is rather the normal unfolding of the natural, inborn powers of man, together with the recognition and wise use of the immutable laws of progressive existence. It represents man's adjustment to his environment. Complete health — the full possession of our powers, a correct realization of the issues of life, and an unyielding endeavor to obey the laws of life — can alone yield complete happiness. It is the function of religion, which exists for human good, to provide the means for such development.

Happiness must be continuous, else it is incomplete. Religion is as necessary on weekdays as on Sundays. Different days may command different duties, but all must lead to joy in life. Days are holy when devoted to the legitimate needs of man. Now and here is the place of religion. Salvation must be a daily affair.

Such a religion must be more than a lifeless system of ethics, designed for outward human needs. It must provide the sustaining hope and life-giving power which come to him who knows his place in a universe directed by intelligent beings far above him in the scale of progression. "Man does not live by bread alone," for the greatest sorrows and joys are always from within.

Nevertheless, though spiritual concerns are vastly more important than material things, both are necessary in filling man's cup of joy, and neither must be excluded. Man is not wholly satisfied by the promise of heavenly rewards. Provision must be made in an acceptable plan for human welfare for the needs of today on earth, as of tomorrow in another world. Man needs food and shelter today; he needs congenial employment and refreshing recreation today. He can find full enjoyment and make the most of his life, whatever his situation in life, only when temporal as well as spiritual wants are satisfied. Such practical service touching all human needs makes religion real, breathing, alive, and points the way to secure happiness.

The world-wide aim of religion should be to help all men. It is unthinkable under the doctrine that all are children of God that one man can find full happiness in a world where other men and women are unhappy. In religious perspective the individual looms large and is of first importance. Lifting the individual is the best method of lifting the group. The happiness of humanity is attained with greatest certainty by making every man and woman happy. The measure of the success of religion is the small number of unhappy persons, rather than the average condition of the group. Religious activity should be directed toward group contentment through happiness for every person. The ultimate aim of religion is to develop a strong people made up of strong men and women, all of whom are vigorous in body and soul, of righteous desire and disciplined will, temporally prosperous and spiritually enlightened. Religion should project an illimitable, satisfying future for every member of the human race.

To achieve its goal, religion must enter into every concern of human life. It must resolutely set about to serve the many needs of man — physical, economic, social, mental and spiritual. It has too long specialized in spiritual aid and therefore often failed in its dear desire to bring full happiness and comfort to mankind.

The physical welfare of man should be a prime concern of religion. All elements of human happiness lose their savor and value in a condition of physical ill health. Good physical health is a requisite for complete happiness. The great religious leaders from the earliest times have recognized this; and in this day, with its manifold offerings of things injurious to health, physical welfare should be doubly a concern of religion. Every new, tested principle of bodily welfare should, in the interest of the goal of religion, be taught from the pulpit.

Likewise, there must be no hesitancy on the part of religious leaders to attempt a solution of the economic problems of the day. After all, the Gospel of the Lord Jesus Christ provides ample direction for economic prosperity, however difficult it may be to convert people to it. In this day, also, when hand labor has been so largely displaced by machine service, the wise use of leisure time, a modern type of recreation, occupies a new position of importance. The mechanization of our civilization raises social problems closely connected with family life, with courtship, marriage and divorce, with morality and spirituality, in the solution of which religion should and must take the lead.

In this new day of enlightenment, religion must support

and foster all means by which every man may share in the intellectual gains of the age; otherwise an aristocracy of learning will cause unhappiness among the masses of people who desire the satisfactions of the mind that our new knowledge has brought. Education — sane, rational, usable for all — must be included in the goal of religion. In short, as has been said, if human happiness be the goal of religion, then everything that bears upon human welfare must be actively the concern of religion.

A rational comprehension of man's relationship to the universe and its contents is the foundation of happiness. The spirit of man ever sighs for a knowledge of the meaning of life. Freedom from temporal anxieties does not relieve him of this desire. Forever he gazes back into the time before he came on earth and forward into the eternities that shall follow his earthly career. Whence did he come? Why is he here? Where is he going? Competent answers to these questions result in man's spiritual contentment. Religion has often failed of its duty by explaining life hereafter and leaving the past and the present unexplained. There can be no real happiness unless man possesses at least an outline knowledge of life, its meaning and purpose, into which may be fitted the experiences of the day.

Religion must begin its answer to the questions that come from within by declaring its fearless acceptance of the existence of an unseen universe, one greater by far than the visible world; an unseen universe which may be known in part by mortal man if he explore it honestly and intelligently. The reality of the unseen world is a foundation fact in a religion devised for human happiness. There is no real difference between the seen and the unseen worlds except in the states or conditions of the eternal elements from which the universe, visible and invisible, is built. The mind of man finds peace in the unity of nature with respect to the origin of things.

So closely connected are these two worlds, the seen and the unseen, that every law for the guidance of man on earth has a spiritual equivalent or counterpart. The Lord has declared: " Verily I say unto you that all things unto me are spiritual, and not at any time have I given unto you a law which was temporal . . . for my commandments are spiritual; they are not natural nor temporal, neither carnal nor sensual." The humblest task, therefore, may be of value, through divine transmutation, in fulfilling the purposes of man's existence. We live and walk in the midst of spiritual as well as temporal realities. That thought again brings religion into everyday affairs.

There are personal, living beings in the visible earthly world. There are personal, living beings in the invisible spiritual world. From out of the unseen world man comes; into the unseen world he returns. Who shall deny the existence of personal, intelligent beings in the unseen universe? Who can deny that man upon earth may be helped and guided by beings of the unseen world?

In that other world is God, our Father, whose glory is intelligence, a compound of love and wisdom. Him we may approach in supplication, assured of helpful response. Prayer is ever the ready, certain means of securing revelations from the Lord for our help and guidance. There are no ultimate barriers between this and the other world. The joy of such association is unsurpassed. The questions which have always stirred the depths of the human soul can be answered satisfactorily only in terms of the living God. God does not forget his children. As he has communicated with man in the past, he may speak to man today. The assurance of such constant communication between God and man opens the deep springs of secure happiness.

The origin of man is of equal concern in human happiness. Man is one of the eternal realities of the universe. Not only shall he endure after death; he lived as a spiritual, pre-existent being before he came upon earth. He " was in the beginning with God." Men and women of earth are spirit children of God, his very children, therefore brothers and sisters in a divine family. Who shall with convincing evidence deny man's existence before his earth life?

In that spirit world, in the pre-existent state, we were engaged actively, intelligently, in perfecting our powers. The idea of progression was paramount. Increase and development are key principles of the Gospel. In the past, the present or the future, progression with all that it implies has been, is, and will be the primary aim of intelligent beings. Intelligence is not static; it is alive, therefore active and progressive. Even such a glimpse of man's beginning removes the heavy pressure of the unknown.

The time came in our spiritual estate when we had developed sufficiently to enter upon a further education that would come from direct contact with the material things of the universe. Power to conquer and direct surrounding forces makes progress possible. Our Father knew this, and desiring, in his love for us, our further growth, presented a divine plan, known as the Gospel, by which we might secure this earth-education. The purpose of the plan was to provide for man's progressive, eternal happiness. There can be no sense of joy without progression. Rest is but as sleep, a preparation for action. Man must ever strive to progress, to develop, to gain greater power over himself and the forces about him. Life is purposeful; and purpose gives definiteness to life and certainty to happiness.

The conditions of the proposed life on earth seemed severe: Forgetfulness of the happy days of pre-existence; toil and struggle with the new and stubborn elements of earth; obedience to certain requirements; subjection to death, by which the spirit would be separated for a time from its earth-won body. These conditions were really means to happiness, set up to assist us on our progressive path, for they would strengthen our wills, perfect our free agencies, and fit us thereby for greater conquests of truth. It was to be an education of the best kind from within, of doing and achieving. Only as man stands upon his own feet, conquers himself and directs his own powers, can he rise to greatest heights.

Man really earned the right to come on earth. He had fitted himself for the new adventure and accepted for himself the plan for an earth-life proposed by his Father. The plan was not forced upon him; he chose to come upon earth. Man may then amidst his earthly tasks hold his head high in courage and self-confidence. When the chance which seems to envelop the mystery of life disappears, even in part, the path to happiness is made clearer. Mortal man, with a memory closed against the events of the world from which he came, may not understand wholly the coming into earth of human beings in different countries, in riches or poverty, in health or disease, but he knows that all events are parts of a definite plan and that chance plays no real part in the appearance of men on earth. The intervention of man's will may give temporary direction to the plan, often to our confusion, but the end cannot be affected thereby. The supervision of the plan under which man lives on earth has never been surrendered by its Maker. The Lord directs the slow unfolding of his purposes on earth among the children of men. He will see to it that the plan is finally consummated. He is at its head and his authority overshadows his children on earth. The actual operation of the plan, however, is in human hands. Men and women represent the Lord in developing his purposes.

All men live after death. Without that hope the goal of religion could not be happiness. The spirits of men enter after death into the unseen world out of which they came at birth. They return home, into the spirit world, with the powers possessed on earth and perhaps others. The spirit world itself is a place of action, growth and progress for all who care to use their opportunities well, and progression there is unending. Therefore, the destiny of man is infinitely great.

The Father's plan of salvation is for the progressive development of all members of the human family. The joys of salvation — of development and attainment — are intended for all. God is not a partial Father. The Lord said to Moses: " This is my work and my glory, to bring to pass the immortality and eternal life of man." It is doubtful if the Lord's plan can be completed before all his children have won the joys of some degree of salvation.

The conception of an actual relationship among all humanity places upon every human being a family responsibility. To help our neighbor is to help our own. Our hearts must beat toward our neighbor as toward a brother if we are to be truly happy. That is the spiritual meaning of the law of charity. The troubles of the world cannot be overcome until that brotherhood with its attendant obligations and consequences is accepted in practice. It is a false teaching which declares impractical, because of human nature, the attempt to live up to the doctrine of the brotherhood of man. An exaltation of feeling follows the knowledge that every man is indeed a son of God, carries within his soul the elements of divinity, and may look forward into a distant, increasing future, throughout which his divine nature shall continually unfold. Then we look with new respect and love upon our fellow men, sons of God, with possible Godlike destinies before them.

What then would hinder all from winning the joys which the Father's plan provides? The answer is that different individuals use their free agencies unequally. The eternal will of man explains human history. Progress under the Plan requires obedience to several requirements. Some render such obedience fully, some in part, others not at all. It is so in daily life, with respect to mundane affairs.

It is a cardinal principle that as one sows so shall he reap. A person will be judged according to his works. The goodness of the Lord, the Great Judge, will temper the judgment; yet even he cannot ignore our works. Every man by his daily acts shapes his salvation. The principle of cause and effect is operative in the spiritual as in the material domain. Only when put into action does faith become irresistible.

The love of a Father for his children makes it necessary to believe that, despite the varying deserts of men, all shall receive in the life to come full and glorious reward for whatever good they have done. Provision is made in the eternal plan for graded salvation. He who has done best is placed highest — he will receive the highest glory and his power of progress will be the greatest. Those who have not done so well are placed lower, with lesser glories, and with diminished power for progress. The judgments given to men, based upon their acts, shall vary as the sun and the moon and the countless stars in the firmament. "In my Father's house are many mansions." The lowest of these rewards, reserved for the vilest sinner, will be glorious beyond the understanding of man, though infinitely less than that of the highest. There can be no hell in the traditional sense if human happiness is to be preserved. God is love. Intolerable burnings do not comport with the feelings of an affectionate father for his children. The equivalent of hell is the unending regret of him who having had great opportunities finds himself by his own wilfulness in a lower stage of progress than he might have been. That is a heavy but inescapable punishment which can be forgotten only in resolute attempts to move onward in the days to come.

The mystery of God's punishment is not known to man. We can only make conjectures based upon general laws. But we do know that he is most merciful. In response to questions concerning this matter, light was given to the Prophet Joseph Smith: "I am endless, and the punishment which is given from my hand is endless punishment, for Endless is my name. Wherefore — Eternal punishment is God's punishment — Endless punishment is God's punishment." Many things have been withheld from the understanding of man, but our Father's loving gentleness is beyond debate. Looking thus into the future a new joy will follow man's eager struggle for righteousness.

So runs this conception of man's eternal journey. He existed before he came on earth; he was with God "in the beginning"; he accepted the opportunity provided by his Father to come on earth to be tried, refined and educated; he lives on earth under laws and regulations and the authority of the Lord; he shall die, but in time he shall regain his body, and because of his righteous endeavors shall go on forever into eternal, active, progressive exaltation. Man's destiny is divine. Life on earth is but a chapter in an eternal journey. Man is an eternal being. He also is " from everlasting to everlasting."

In this manner of thinking, salvation acquires a definite meaning. Whoever is in process of development or progression is in process of salvation. Increasing knowledge, used in conformity with the plan of the Lord, becomes power to remove all obstacles to progress. In the words of Joseph Smith, to be saved is to be placed " beyond the power of evil." Clearly, then, our salvation began in the dim past, is being worked out by us on earth and will be approached in its greater perfection throughout the endless ages of future life. By that token all men may be saved but in degrees proportionate to their righteous works. Does a man then save himself? From one point of view, yes. However, it is only through the divine plan that salvation may be won; therefore, man is only a partner in the saving process. Salvation is a co-operative enterprise between God and man.

The Lord Jesus Christ, our elder Brother in the pre-existent world, is the Being from out the unseen world to whom the Father delegated the labors connected with the earth and its inhabitants. It was in his role of assigned leadership that he became " the lamb slain before the foundations of the world." He is the Redeemer of man, the central figure in the plan of salvation. Therefore we speak of the plan as the Gospel of Jesus Christ.

It may not be overlooked that a religion the goal of which is happiness, and which strives to supply all needs of man, temporal and spiritual, must require something in return. There would be no personal development or progress if religion gave everything and required nothing. To be effective, any plan for human good must be accepted by those who are to share in its benefits, and they must give evidence of their acceptance by compliance with stated requirements. That is the logical method of winning the gifts of earth or heaven. One cannot at the same time accept a plan and be independent of it. A " free lance " does not belong to a group, accepts no plan, is lawless. Conformity to law is the evidence of the Christian life and the unfailing source of happiness. A religion worth the acceptance of intelligent man must be God-made and its requirements therefore of eternal character and ultimate human value. Such a point of view indeed makes formal ordinances indispensable in a religion with happiness as its goal. Faith and repentance, baptism and confirmation and the other required principles and ordinances of the Christian religion must be accepted in that spirit and with that understanding.

The goal of religion — happiness — can be attained only upon the condition of the love of and correct use of truth. True happiness, the greatest satisfaction, the product of complete health, is derived from the acceptance and practice of the principles of tested truth, and there is no other source. Disease was not under control when people believed that it was caused by the evil eye of a witch. Joseph Smith said, " A man cannot be saved in ignorance," and, also, " Knowledge is the pathway up to the Gods." As knowledge and the proper use of knowledge increase, man's power to win happiness is augmented, in both the physical and the spiritual domains. Religion must recognize and teach the supreme value of truth. It requires also of every man who seeks happiness that when truth is found he discard the clashing untruths that hoary tradition may have foisted upon him.

He must be as willing to forsake old fallacies as to accept new facts. He must feel as Brigham Young declared, "I will trade every error in the world for one truth." Without such an attitude of mind there is no saving grace in truth.

The whole domain of truth, new or old, is accepted and taught by true religion. Every scientific discovery is welcomed. Every new and more correct presentation of the nature of the universe is hailed. No limitations can be placed upon the search for truth. Religion demands of the truth-seeker only that he distinguish carefully between facts of observation and hypotheses of inference. The former, if correctly made, do not vary; the latter are bound to change as facts are multiplied. Since the body of truth is constantly increasing, there must be a continuous seeking and offering of truth within the field of religion. In addition, since the growth of knowledge is continuous, religion, the conservator of truth, though its foundations never change, must ever be enlarging its content and boundaries. Religion is a living thing, therefore always in a state of growth and increase.

There can be no happiness, even when possessing truth, unless it is accepted willingly. Freedom, the right to act for himself, is one of man's fundamental cravings. Slavery and happiness are incompatible. They cannot travel together. Men are not pawns to be moved about irrespective of their desires. Only those who can express themselves freely in thought and action rejoice in life. Free agency, held by true religion to be an inviolable right of man, makes every person accountable for his own acts. He cannot shift the responsibility for life's endeavors to other shoulders. A body of believers must be governed by common consent. This does not mean that men may be lawless. The supremacy of law — natural, human and divine — remains whatever men may do. The whole matter is that those who choose to obey law gain thereby. " Ye shall know the truth, and the truth shall make you free." By the use of his free agency man may move upward to freedom or downward to bondage. To use one's agency within the law is the high ideal set up by religion.

Control of self is a corollary of free agency. While the right to act as one chooses inheres in every human being, yet the desire for happiness requires that every man conform to law. Such conformity is the only method by which full happiness may be obtained. Self-mastery is an essential element of human happiness. People who choose to obey the law are happy. They develop their individual power to shape their own destinies. In modern revelation this thought is formulated as follows: " Men should be anxiously engaged in a good cause, and do many things of their own free will, and bring to pass much righteousness; for the power is in them, wherein they are agents unto themselves." When that is done the goal of religion is within easy reach.

The philosophy sketched briefly above enables the Latter-day Saints to answer many pertinent questions concerning the goal of religion:

What is the object of religion? To make people happy in this life and in the hereafter. It is a truthful and complete compass or chart for life's voyage, and an effective guide for human effort, in every occupation, condition or need. It has common sense and is practical.

When is religion acceptable? When it conforms to the many-sided nature of man — that is, when it is complete and therefore satisfies the physical, economic, social, mental, moral and spiritual needs of man. When it is the guiding philosophy and supporting power of all human actions.

What does religion offer men individually? It offers guidance in every affair of life; it presents the Gospel as a measuring stick by which the virtue of all acts may be determined; it explains measurably the mysteries of life in our vast universe; it holds out the promise of endless achievement, progression, proportioned to the efforts put forth; it gives understanding, contentment, love; it points to a divine destiny; it assures the right of freedom of choice; and declares that man must bear the consequences of the exercise of that free agency.

What does religion offer man socially? It offers to the social group all that it offers to the individual; it explains that men are true brothers, for all of whom the plan of salvation was devised, and that full happiness cannot be won so long as one of our kin fails to tread the road of progress; it declares that society is responsible for every individual.

What is salvation? It is the condition that results when a person is in harmony with truth. Man may ever be on the way to salvation, but in its fullness, salvation is the eternal goal. The law of salvation as of all life is eternal progression. One must grow daily and forever in righteousness and good works. Those who are in a state of salvation are in a constant state of progression; those who are static or who retrograde are "the lost." Even for the latter, the tender mercy of God provides a fitting place in his kingdom, and the opportunity for continuous repentance. Whoever has placed himself by obedience to divine law beyond the power of evil, to that extent is saved.

How may salvation be attained? By accepting the principles and practices of truth issuing from God and constituting the plan of salvation; by the resolute use of the will to obey at any cost the requirements of the Gospel; and by constant appeal in prayer to God for assistance.

Does Christ do something for man which man cannot do for himself? Yes. He is our Redeemer; he leads us along the dim path; his sacrifice will enable us to recover the bodies we lay down in the grave; he is our advocate with the Father; he is our Captain.

Happiness as the goal of religion implies that religion will help provide for all the needs of man, will teach the meaning of life from the dim beginning to the vast future, will set forth the conditions of obedience upon which happiness is wrought, and will help develop in men love of truth, strength of will, love for fellow men and the other personal requisites to travel the way to happiness. Perhaps the greatest and the most difficult duty of religion having happiness as a goal is to help direct the stubborn human will into compliance with the requirements for achieving that happiness.

CHARLES FILLMORE

Charles Fillmore was born in Minnesota. He is self-educated for the most part. In 1889 he and his wife, Myrtle Fillmore, founded the Unity School of Christianity in Kansas City, Missouri, and he has served continuously as president of this school for more than forty-five years. At eighty-one years of age he is still active in its direction, and in addition writes, travels and lectures extensively. He has been an indefatigable teacher, speaker and writer, having published over a hundred booklets and tracts besides his two widely used books, *Christian Healing,* 1912, and *The Twelve Powers of Man,* 1930.

The Unity School of Christianity reports that it has over five hundred allied schools or "centers" and some two million members who follow the course of readings and studies furnished by the school at Kansas City. It is prolific in its publications, maintaining six periodicals, and circulating many books and tracts without number.

In the latter half of the nineteenth century there occurred in New England what is sometimes known, to those who derive from it, as the modern Renaissance of Christianity. Out of this general religious movement there developed several organizations differing not a little in general theological outlook but having certain common points of emphasis, namely: health, well-being and prosperity. They differed widely in the techniques by which these values could be achieved. Some departed notably from the prevailing Christian orthodoxy, others only slightly. Among the several present-day groups arising from this source, Unity is the most closely related to traditional Christianity. No more authoritative exponent of the point of view represented could possibly be found than the original founder of the movement.

IX

UNITY

By CHARLES FILLMORE

ABOVE all else the great goal of religion is to develop in man the glory of Christ. " The mystery which hath been hid for ages and generations: but now hath it been manifested to his saints . . . which is Christ in you, the hope of glory." (Colossians 1:26). Paul goes on to say in the same Scripture: " Whom we proclaim, admonishing every man and teaching every man in all wisdom, that we may present every man perfect in Christ." That this is the fundamental work of religion is plain to anyone who is quickened in the spirit and beholds the universal truth that, as we all have the mind of Christ as the implanted seed of the perfect man created by God, our prime object in living should be to follow the Master in making that ideal real.

God has done His part in imaging His perfection in His Son or Word of promise, described in the Gospel of John as the Logos, in which is implanted all glory and power for man when he complies with the divine law. Let it be emphasized that this glory of man was not the exclusive privilege of Jesus of Nazareth, but is open to all men who follow Him in the regeneration: " Verily I say unto you, that ye who have followed me, in the regeneration when the Son of man shall sit on the throne of his glory, ye also shall sit upon twelve thrones, judging the twelve tribes of Israel." (Matthew 19:28).

To most men the Son of God is still a mystery, although Christianity has been trying to reveal Him for nearly two thousand years. Such revelation by the followers of Jesus has not always been an easy matter, because we have exalted the personality of the Master beyond the range of human companionship; we have made Him all divine and ourselves all human. Yet we are taught, and it appeals to our reason, that God is no respecter of persons. It must therefore be true, as stated in the Scriptures, that we all have the same essential attributes, developed or undeveloped. If Jesus was the Son of God, we also are sons of God, the difference being that Jesus unveiled the mystery of man's inherent glory and found Himself.

This revelation that we all are sons of God on the way to a consciousness of that mighty truth does not belittle Jesus, but it does exalt man. The revelation that all of the divine powers that Jesus expressed exist as potentialities in all of us gives us a new hope and stirs in us the ambition to attain, at least in a measure, the perfection that He attained.

However, if Jesus demonstrated His sonship through suffering, we shall not wholly escape the same soul surgery, although we have faith in His vicarious atonement for our sins. Jesus taught the law and opened the door to the forgiving love of the Father, and we must follow Him. To follow Jesus is to do the works that He did and " even greater works," as was His prophecy. Through His marvelous insight and understanding of divine law, Jesus forged far ahead of our race consciousness; so far in fact that in our limited conception of man and His powers we have looked upon Jesus as very God and men as worms of the dust.

The Jews wanted to stone Jesus because, being a man, He made Himself God. Jesus answered them: " Is it not written in your law, I said, Ye are gods? " (John 10:34). He then explained that those to whom the word of God came were

God's sons and that it was not blasphemy for Him to say,
" I am *the* Son of God." (John 10:36).

The Son of God is God's perfect, ideal pattern of man, to
whom we all have access and through whom we come to the
Father. There is no other way. Whoever tries to climb up
some other way is a thief and a robber. When the Christ in
Jesus made this proclamation He made it not from the standpoint of the personal mind but from that of the universal
Christ mind. So we should make the proper distinction in
reading the Scriptures; sometimes it was Christ the Son of
God talking and sometimes Jesus the Son of man. In the
end, however, the Son of man was swallowed up by the Son
of God.

To understand fully and apply practically the saving grace
of the Lord Jesus Christ, it is very helpful to understand man
in his mind and brain structure. Modern science in philosophy, medicine and psychology is revealing laws in body
structure that shed light upon the teaching of Jesus. Both
John the Baptist and Jesus emphasized a change of mind
as essential to salvation. Their slogan was "Repent ye!
Repent ye!" which means a change of mind. We make
a sharp distinction between the thought processes centering
in the head and those centering in the solar plexus or heart.
Those functioning through the heart are emotional and
much more pronounced in their action upon the nervous
system than those in the head. "And Jesus knowing their
thoughts said, Wherefore think ye evil in your hearts?"
(Matthew 9:4). He indicated that the thoughts of the heart
are virtually equivalent to the overt act. Progressive physicians tell us that our heart thoughts, or emotions, are responsible for about half of our bodily ills.

Dr. William Brady, who conducts a syndicated health

column in the daily press, recently declared: "Worry, anxiety, fear retard or inhibit the digestive process. It doesn't matter much whether you worry about meeting the interest on your mortgage or about the dire effects you will suffer from autointoxication. Anger, hatred, jealousy, malevolence, all have a marked inhibiting action. These unpleasant emotions throw the brakes on the normal processes of digestion. That is how a little flare-up of anger or jealousy just before dinner drives away appetite."

At a gathering of the American College of Physicians, Dr. Edward Weiss of Philadelphia read a paper on diseases of the heart. He cited the journal of John Wesley, written in 1759, in which Wesley told of the case of a certain woman with a continuous pain in her stomach, for which doctors prescribed drugs without avail. Wesley wrote that he found the pain to have resulted "from fretting over the death of her son," and that when she was comforted her physical disorder left. "Why then," asks Wesley, "do not all physicians consider how bodily disorders are caused or influenced by the mind?"

Doctor Weiss replies: "'That is just what we are beginning to do,' is the answer of the doctors of today. After 175 years of medical darkness we are emerging into the light as to the source of about fifty per cent of humanity's ills — a state of mind." The doctor further said that many persons had undergone operations to get rid of pain or discomfort that was entirely due to some emotional trouble. He cited the instance of one young woman who underwent four operations, when her trouble was brought on by the fact that all her sisters were married while she seemed doomed to remain a lonely spinster. Fear, worry, and similar emotions, he said, cause such conditions.

In these discoveries about the dynamics of the mind we have the revelation of the cause of a legion of human ills, but no sovereign remedy is offered. Business men hang " Don't Worry " mottoes on their office walls and resolve to quit worrying, but go right on in the same old anxious thought. Religion, when made a part of our practical everyday life, not only shows how to disperse the mob of anxious thoughts that besets us in the highway of mind but introduces us to a law that will work for us night and day.

The Christian religion as taught by Jesus and interpreted by His followers offers a remedy for every human ill. If it were applied as Jesus applied it, sin, sickness, poverty, ignorance and insanity would soon disappear from the earth. But we must not look for material remedies in the pharmacopoeia of Jesus. He dealt with ideas, the source of everything. He warned against the unbridled anxious thoughts that run amuck when there is no restraining of the mind, and He climaxed His lesson by stabilizing the whole consciousness in God as the unfailing supply and support of man's every need. The 6th and 7th chapters of Matthew are unparalleled in all literature for clarity and simplicity in presenting the way to success in finances. Here you will find most efficient treatments against anxiety and at the same time assurance, under the guise of many comparisons and illustrations, that God does provide for those who trust Him.

The recent revelations of science concerning the real character of the atom and of cosmic space are remarkable in their corroboration of the Bible. Science has completely reversed its former estimate of space as an empty void. It is now regarded as the source of light, heat, mass, power — in fact everything visible and invisible has its origin in the cosmic ether. Jesus evidently knew the ether to be the cause side of existence, which He named "the kingdom of the heavens." He compared it to a net in which every kind of fish in the great sea of existence could be trapped, to a pearl of great price, and to a field in whose soil all things might be produced.

Sir Oliver Lodge once said that there is energy enough in a cubic inch of ether to run a forty-horse-power engine forty million years. Another scientist says that the atomic energy concealed in a single teardrop, if released instantly, would blow up a six-story building. The cells of our body are composed of electrons and protons "whirling in their orbits like cannon balls" and beating like a billion hammers on the corporeal shell in which they are inclosed. Bible stories like that of Joshua stopping the sun and of Jonah and the whale are commonplace compared with the tremendous tales that science tells about the forces that exist in the invisible ether in which we live, move, and have our being. Professor Millikan says: " The atom has revealed that it possesses functions so varied and mysterious that science has concluded that it is mind rather than the old mechanical matter."

Sir James Jeans, the eminent British scientist, says in his book *The Mysterious Universe:* " For aught we know, or for aught that the new science can say to the contrary, the gods which play the part of fate to the atoms of our brains may be our own minds. Through these atoms our minds may perchance affect the motions of our bodies and so the state of the world around us."

Doctor Crile of Cleveland has estimated that the average human body is composed of thirty-nine trillion cells. These cells, so science says, are animated by protons and electrons possessing potentialities beyond human imagination. A philosopher says: " We lie in the lap of immense intelligence, which makes us organs of its activity and receivers of its truth. When we discern justice, when we discern truth, we do nothing of ourselves but allow a passage of its beams."

Jesus did not claim to do the mighty works that were accomplished through Him. In John, chapter 14, He said to those who asked that He show them the Father: "Believest thou not that I am in the Father, and the Father in me? The words that I say unto you I speak not from myself: but the Father abiding in me doeth his works. . . . Verily, verily I say unto you, He that believeth on me, the works that I do shall he do also; and greater *works* than these shall he do." (John 14:10).

Science has revealed that the kingdom of the heavens or cosmic ether is the source of everything except intelligence. We need the illumined mind of Jesus to complete the revelation of science. Doctor Osborne says that if men could be instructed how to release the ether energy hidden in their bodies, we should achieve in a single generation more than we have done in the past six thousand years. Because of the scientific ignorance of men Jesus resorted to parables in teaching the deep truths about life. "Therefore speak I to them in parables; because seeing they see not, and hearing they hear not, neither do they understand." (Matthew 13:13).

Religion, regardless of its many interpreters, has but one goal — the attainment of eternal life by its glorified man. Jesus proclaimed again and again that He came to show us the way to gain eternal life: "What shall a man be profited, if he shall gain the whole world, and forfeit his life?" (Matthew 16:26). Not only Christianity but all religions teach and promise to the faithful the joys of continuous life, but usually in some state of bliss after death.

Eternal life after death is often interpreted as the goal of those who follow Jesus, but a careful study of His words and works reveals that victory over death was one of the evidences that the disciple had attained eternal life. Death came into the world as the wages of sin, and the effacement of sin must automatically restore one to original life. Paul says plainly in Romans, chapter 5, that death reigned until the time of Jesus, who overcame death, and that we should reign through Him in eternal life.

In I Corinthians 15:53, Paul says that the body must be saved from death: "For this corruptible must put on incorruption, and this mortal must put on immortality." " Then shall come to pass the saying that is written, Death is swallowed up in victory. O death, where is thy victory? O death, where is thy sting?" We thus see that the death Jesus conquered — by restoring life to His body after it was killed — was bodily death. We know very little about the death of the soul, but we are made tragically acquainted daily with the death of the body. So, instead of accepting the death of the body as in some way under divine law, let us follow Jesus in redeeming our bodies from this Satanic destruction.

The human family devotes the never-ending efforts of its wisest men, with billions and billions of hard-earned dollars, to the overcoming of disease that the body may be saved from the tomb. To reach this goal it brings to bear every human device, yet meets defeat in the end. Then it submits to what is taught to be the inevitable end of man — and calls it the will of God. But Jesus the Conqueror said: " If a man keep my word, he shall never see death." (John 15:7; 8:51).

The popular religious teachers of Christianity have virtually thrown up their hands in the face of seemingly insurmountable difficulties in the way of following Jesus to the final goal of His doctrine, the attainment of eternal life. Having failed to solve the simpler problem of the cause and cure of the death of the body, they tell us that our great concern should be the salvation of the soul. Although God is omnipresent and all-powerful, the conclusion is that He cannot do much for us until after we are dead. Jesus proclaimed to the Jews who taught a future resurrection: "God is not *the God* of the dead, but of the living." (Matthew 22:32).

The great majority of both the secular and religious world today admit that Jesus has given us the soundest doctrine of morals ever propounded by man. Not only the moralist but the economist and scientist are quoting Jesus as the teacher of the highest principles in their special fields. Professors Eddington and Russell, both eminent scientists, are quoted by the press as saying that when we study Jesus' teaching from the standpoint of science we become convinced that He understood light, energy, motion and space.

Jesus not only understood these finer forces of mind and body as science understands them — mechanically — but He developed His spiritual mind to a point where He could control them. The popular thought about Jesus' teaching is that it is a negative factor in the present world and that the rewards are to follow in a spiritual world. But there is no authority in the Gospels for such a conclusion. Jesus claimed all power in heaven and in earth and authorized His followers to go forth in His name and cast out demons, heal the sick, and raise the dead. The Scriptures say that they did these works and that He was with them, as He had promised — " Lo, I am with you always."

The need of those who claim to represent Jesus Christ is

a greater realization of His presence and power in the world today. We talk too much about the mighty works He did in the first century and too little about what He is doing in the twentieth century. The dynamic power of the Holy Spirit imparted at Pentecost can be had by Christians everywhere if they will only follow the example of those early disciples of the Master. We need more understanding, steadfastness and continuity of faith in our prayers.

The spiritual ethers are vibrant with energies that, properly released, would give abundant life and health to all God's people. The one and only outlet for these all-potential, electronic, life-imparting forces existing in the billions of atoms in the cells of our body, is our mind unified with the Christ mind in prayer. Pray, believing that ye have received, and ye shall receive, is the promise of Jesus. All things for our good are already provided in the heavens, the higher reaches of the mind, awaiting our realization. " Seek ye first his kingdom, and his righteousness; and all these things shall be added unto you." (Matthew 6:33).

The time is at hand when all who believe in the power of God must get closer together on the few simple essentials of His law. The nations of the world have not found the spiritual unity that religion teaches and are looking forward to the havoc of another war. They may reap as they have sown, with the destruction of present civilization, but a righteous remnant will survive upon whom will rest the reconstruction of all the nations into one great federation of the world.

Most persons think of religion in terms of faith. " He that cometh to God must believe that he is, and that he is a rewarder of those that seek him."

The fact is that without faith no one goes very far in

normal life. We do not perform the simplest act without first believing that we can do it. Religion requires the enlargement of faith until it lays hold of God. Those who follow Jesus in the enlargement of the spiritual life find that they must believe further than they can see in order to comprehend even in small degree the tremendous field of action into which His philosophy launches them. Jesus expected those whom He healed to do something themselves, especially to believe that He could heal them. When the two blind men came to Him, He said to them, " Believe ye that I am able to do this? They say unto him, Yea, Lord. Then touched he their eyes, saying, According to your faith be it done unto you. And their eyes were opened " (Matthew 9:28). To the woman who had suffered for twelve years and who was healed by stealthily touching the hem of His garment he reassuringly exclaimed: "Daughter, thy faith hath made thee whole." (Mark 5:34).

Jesus exalted faith to the original creative place in man that it holds in God. Even God must have had faith in the power of His word before the universe was created. In the 11th chapter of Hebrews we read: " By faith we understand that the worlds have been framed by the word of God."

So we see that religion, and especially Christianity, tremendously enlarges the natural ability of man. His faith and trust in the goodness and truth of men must be broadened and deepened until he can look with the eye of faith into invisible nothingness and see it vibrant with mightiness — the faith of God.

But religion does not rest with the development of faith alone, for beyond the scope of the natural man it opens the mind to the understanding of creative principles. Christ opened the understanding of His disciples, and all those who seek Him in faith find that they are spiritually quickened according to their capacity to receive.

Understanding the Christ mind in man and its relation to the universal life energy concealed in every atom, we begin to see what Jesus meant when He said that His body and His blood were meat and drink. When we are spiritually quickened we can say that we have food that the man who functions in flesh and blood alone knows not of. Also the partaking of the Lord's body in a sacramental way becomes a vital process of appropriation of the invisible life and substance sown in our race thought by the superalchemy of the Master.

We all live in the very presence of an all-infolding Spirit, which is life, love, substance and intelligence. Through the development of spiritual faculties, which we all possess in potential ability, we shall come into the understanding and the power of Jesus Christ. " Wherefore if any man is in Christ, *he is* a new creature." (II Corinthians 5:17). But there is work ahead, for " bringing every thought into captivity to the obedience of Christ " (II Corinthians 10:5) is no child's play. Not only the mind but the body as well must be transformed and renewed under the discipline of the Christ: " *So* now also Christ shall be magnified in my body." (Philippians 1:20).

We cannot help seeing that religion is the most vital and important part of our existence. Our religion should give us an understanding of our source, our destiny, and our specific place in the great creative plan.

ALBERT FIELD GILMORE

Albert Field Gilmore was born and educated in New England. He holds the Bachelor of Arts and Master of Arts degrees from Bates College, awarded him in 1892 and 1895 respectively. In 1924 he was honored by his Alma Mater with the degree of Doctor of Letters. For twenty years, 1897–1917, he was associated with the American Book Company. It was in 1910 that his official relation to Christian Science began. For three years he was first reader of the First Church of Christ, Scientist, Brooklyn, New York. For five years, 1917–22, he was the Christian Science Committee on Publication in New York. In 1922–23 he was president of the Mother Church, Boston. In that year also he began his editorial work, serving as editor of the Christian Science weekly and monthly magazines for the next seven years. He was a member of the Board of Lectureship of the Christian Science church, 1930–32, served as a member of the Monitor Editorial Board 1932–5 and since 1932 has been trustee of the Christian Science Publishing Society. He is a C. S. B., an authorized teacher of Christian Science. No one could, therefore, more fittingly represent the Christian Science point of view in this volume. Aside from his official duties he finds time to serve as a member of the Board of Fellows of Bates College, and once long ago, 1901–02, served a term as member of the Maine house of representatives.

His extensive writings on religion have appeared largely in the official periodicals of the church. His books reflect a deep interest in nature and in travel: *Birds Through the Year*, 1909; *Birds of Field, Forest and Park*, 1918; *East and West of Jordan*, 1929; *Fellowship — the Story of a Man and a Business*, 1929; *The Bible, Beacon Light of History*, 1935.

154

X

CHRISTIAN SCIENCE

By ALBERT FIELD GILMORE

THE present is pre-eminently an era of practicability. What is the practical value of any plan, of any proposition or theory? That is the query of the utilitarian, who demands proof as a condition prerequisite to acceptance. Too long, it is urged, has humanity been importuned to accept the theoretical, problematical and uncertain without the practical proof of demonstration. And in no direction is this pragmatism of today more manifest than in the field of religion. The younger generation, in particular, has become a living interrogative regarding the Bible, religion and worship. Emphatically does it raise the question of the practical utility of whatever is presented, no less in religion than in other fields of human interest. It is the purpose of this statement to set forth the teachings of Christian Science, especially as to their demonstrated success in solving the problems of the daily life, in freeing humanity from sickness and sin, from poverty and distress — that is, as the Science of salvation.

Through the centuries of the Christian era, the term " salvation " has taken on a variety of meanings. This statement will be concerned with but one, the significance of the word and its application as used in Christian Science. And in order to understand the subject from this standpoint, it will be necessary to state the fundamentals of Christian Science as taught and demonstrated by its Discoverer and Founder, Mary Baker Eddy.

The foundation of all religion and worship is the assumption that God is: and this fact posited, the questions arise, What is the nature of the Deity? What are the qualities and attributes of the God whom we worship? Is God knowable, and how is an understanding of Him to be gained? Christian Science declares that " God is Mind, Spirit, Soul, Principle, Life, Truth and Love." These seven synonyms describe Deity, and, as presented in the Christian Science textbook, *Science and Health with Key to the Scriptures,* page 465, they are preceded by four descriptive adjectives: " incorporeal, divine, supreme, infinite."

Why these seven words as descriptive of Deity? What is the authority for their use? That God is Spirit, Jesus definitely stated to the Samaritan woman at the well of Sychar. That He is infinite and that He is Love, the Scriptures are equally positive. That God is Life, the source of all existence, is justifiably implied from the Master's teachings. And none can gainsay that the creative power is intelligence or Mind, a conclusion thoroughly corroborated by Paul. The Mind which was in Christ Jesus, which he so effectually expressed, was none other than the divine. That God, as divine Principle, governs His universe with unchanging law is evident from the orderliness of the universe. And that Mind which is infinite Life and Spirit, must also be Soul, the essence of all reality, the essential nature of the Supreme Being. God as the essential of all Being must also be Truth, for only that which is true and perfect can be eternal.

Thus, as the foundation of religion, Christian Science posits God as Spirit, infinite and ever-present; as eternal Life, without material accompaniments; as Love, selfless and all-inclusive; as Mind, that is, as divine intelligence which is conscious of all reality; as Truth, unchanging and eternal; as Principle, the cause and law of the universe; as Soul, the essence, the essential of all existence. While this view of Deity departs entirely from the anthropomorphic sense of God, Christian Science holds that it conforms precisely to the idea of God presented by the Founder of Christianity and his followers, as recorded in the New Testament. And, be it said, since Christian Science accepts Jesus' precepts in their primal simplicity, and proves the logic of its position by fulfilling, in part, at least, the promises of the Master, it is a re-statement of primitive Christianity — without the creeds, rituals and dogmas which have grown up through various interpretations of those teachings.

The next important stone in the foundation of Christian Science is its revelation regarding Jesus, the Christ. Jesus was born of the Virgin Mary, whose concept of God as Father enabled her to become the mother of the Bethlehem babe, later recognized as the Messiah or Saviour. Christ is the divine idea of God, spiritual truth, the truth about all reality, "The divine manifestation of God, which comes to the flesh to destroy incarnate error" (*Science and Health*, page 583). Mrs. Eddy also declares that "Christ expresses God's spiritual, eternal nature" (*Ibid.*, page 333). Jesus was termed the Christ because he expressed spiritual truth, the divine nature, in greater measure than any other who has ever appeared on earth. He was "the way, the truth and the life" because of his consummate knowledge of God and his unparalleled sense of unity with Him. Jesus knew that his divine nature, the Christ, which he so perfectly expressed, was an emanation from God, the Father.

The third essential in the platform of Christian Science is its teaching regarding man. It insists that man in God's image and likeness, as described in the first chapter of Genesis, could not be a material, corporeal creature. The likeness of Spirit must be spiritual. The expression of Mind must be idea. Consequently man is recognized not as made up of blood and bones, of brain and brawn, but as spiritual, the veritable likeness of the infinite God who is Spirit: in the words of the textbook, page 591: Man is " the spiritual image and likeness of God; the full representation of Mind." Manifestly, man is something quite unlike the material mortal included in the general terms humanity and mankind. It was this false concept of God and man, the so-called mortal man and the anthropomorphic God, of which Voltaire cynically remarked, " God made man in His likeness and man returned the compliment! " How plain it is that the anthropomorphic sense of Deity grew out of the belief that a mortal is God's image! Obviously, if this were true, God would assume the proportions of an enlarged human of cosmic magnitude, with the appetites, passions and limitations of mortals. How unlike this sense of Deity is our Master's concept of the loving Father-Mother, who is ever saying, " Son, thou art ever with me, and all that I have is thine."

Logical reasoning upon the subject will leave no doubt in the mind of the inquirer that the mortal, material sense of man could not by any possibility be regarded as God's image and likeness. God is Spirit, eternal and perfect. Must not His likeness express these qualities? Man as God's likeness, expressing all the qualities and attributes of God, is spiritual, intelligent, substantial and eternal, because co-existent with the Father. God without a son would be no Father. Hence man as God's representative is co-eternal with Him. And since this man, this true son of God, expresses God, he possesses no quality unlike God. Consequently he never " fell "; that is, never has departed and never can depart from the primal state of perfection in which God created him. Could

God's handiwork ever become less than perfect, we should have the impossible situation of imperfection from infinite perfection. Furthermore, since the real man has never departed from his original state of perfection, he is not in need of salvation. He is saved now, and reposing in the bosom of the Father; he always has been saved — that is, as God's idea, the expression of Mind, man is forever held in the divine consciousness.

What, then, of the salvation which occupies so important a place in Scriptural teaching and in all theology? Is there no need for it? Yes, most emphatically, and the need is both great and urgent. Who and what is in need of salvation? Not the image of God, the real man, but the mortal, the counterfeit, is in dire need of salvation from the constrictions, false beliefs, and limitations which so generally attach themselves to the material sense of man. Mortals need to be saved from all that constitutes the false, the counterfeit, sense of man. Poor humanity struggles along in its welter of sin, misery, poverty, sickness, because of its lack of comprehension of man's true selfhood as the son of God. It is little wonder that Jesus, conscious as he was of the noble heritage of the real man, the son of God, wept when he beheld the degraded and woeful condition of the inhabitants of Jerusalem. Although much progress has been made in the betterment of mankind's condition during the Christian centuries, there can be but little doubt that he would still shed tears were he on earth today. Poor humanity, for the most part, still stumbles blindly on its purposeless way, unmindful of the blessings that forever attach to the real man, who as " joint heir with Christ " dwells forever in the bosom of the Father, in the household of God.

The problem of salvation, then, is pertinent and impera-

tive and has a practical solution. The term salvation, or freedom, implies restraint or limitation from which release is
desired. Mortals seek release, blindly though it be, from the
vicissitudes of human experience. The sick seek release from
illness, the sinner from the penalties of evildoing, the poor
from poverty, the weary from the need of labor, the worldly-
minded from the cares and burdens of life. Mortals assume
a load of miseries which they carry with them throughout
most of the years of the human span of existence. Why?
Because of lack of knowledge of God, His Christ, and of
the real man. Salvation is indeed their greatest need.

Too often, it seems, salvation is regarded as belonging only
to some future state, as having no possibility of realization on
this plane of existence. What of the words of Paul, " Now is
the accepted time, now is the day of salvation "? Christian
Science emphatically holds that now mortals may be set free
from the burdens of sin and sickness, of poverty and misery,
with which they have become so heavily laden. It accepts
at full value those pregnant words of the Nazarene, " Come
unto me, all ye that labour and are heavy laden, and I will
give you rest." And the coming unto the Christ is a mental
process accomplished by gaining the letter and spirit of the
teachings of Christ Jesus by learning the truth about God,
His Christ, and the real man. Thus salvation is gained not
through pardon, but through reform — not because of any
special divine dispensation, but because of that transformation of consciousness which Paul enjoined upon the Christians in Rome.

When once the realization is gained that the all-loving
Father-Mother, God, has already bestowed upon man as His
offspring infinite blessings, blessings which are continuous,
never withheld, adequate to meet every need, the burdens

of material living are cast off as unreal, even as a false mathematical statement is cast aside when the true computation is presented. Salvation is, indeed, freedom, and is available to all who turn understandingly and with humility and willing obedience to the Father. Jesus' mission was to bring to poor humanity the glad tidings that salvation from all restricting and discordant conditions was and is a present possibility. He was indeed the Way-shower to that perfect salvation which awaits every mortal. For with the laying off of the old man, the false, material sense of man, and laying hold of the real man, God's likeness, the perfect state of man is experienced; and every mortal may assert, as did the Psalmist: " I shall be satisfied, when I awake, with thy likeness."

On page 593 of the Christian Science textbook, " salvation " is defined thus: " Life, Truth, and Love understood and demonstrated as supreme over all; sin, sickness, and death destroyed." Understanding of God who is Life, Truth and Love destroys the belief of man, God's likeness, as mortal and material; and this understanding liberates human consciousness from all restricting claims, even the belief in death itself. Both man's true consciousness and his individuality are reflections of God and his identity is permanent.

The necessity, then, facing every mortal is to gain the realization that man is the son of God, perfect and permanent in his spiritual selfhood, and inseparable from God, the Father. This experience is manifestly individual. Paul was sure of this when he wrote the Christians at Philippi to work out their own salvation, depending upon God and not upon human personality to gain that state of consciousness which is the Kingdom of Heaven. Not vicariously but individually must this way be trod, the way that leads out of the flesh, the mortal sense of man, up to the throne of God, the spiritual state which is conscious only of the things of God. Society will be evangelized as its constituent members individually gain the spiritual concept of man and the universe, that is, become Christianized. The Christ, Truth, the infinite Evangel, is ever knocking at the door of human consciousness, ever ready to enter the mentality open to receive it, to come in, and as a ministering angel bless and heal mortals of all restricting beliefs. Jesus posited as a condition of gaining this salvation, or freedom from material sense, continuance in his word. Then, he told his disciples, " Ye shall know the truth, and the truth shall make you free."

The process of spiritualizing the human consciousness is not, it seems, an instantaneous experience. Mortals grasp the Christ, Truth, slowly, but with the slightest progress in this direction they are blessed with a better sense of life, of its environment and significance. As progress is made spiritward, one by one the shackles imposed by racial and personal beliefs fall off, the way becomes brighter, and the advance less arduous. Through this process, God's presence becomes more apparent, His nature as the loving Father-Mother better understood, the material world seems less substantial, and the things which are not seen, more real. Can one doubt the blessings which accompany this holy experience!

All thoughtful persons today are awake to the great changes which are becoming apparent in the attitude and conclusions of the physical scientists. Some of the most prominent are recognizing the mental nature of the material universe. Each of these, in his own way, has arrived by an intellectual process at the conclusions accepted during the centuries by the idealistic philosophers through a priori reasoning. Bishop Berkeley was no less sure of the mental nature of the universe than was Dr. Johnson of its wholly material constituency. The modern astro-physicist, through resolving matter into its atoms, electrons, etc., has finally resolved it into a mental something not clearly defined.

Christian Science, in a fundamental statement, declares: " All is infinite Mind and its infinite manifestation, for God is All-in-all " (*Science and Health,* page 468). And this Mind is God. Furthermore, since Mind must of necessity express itself in ideas, the universe, the manifestation of Mind, consists of divine ideas having the substance of Spirit. Thus Christian Science posits the universe as spiritually and divinely mental, rather than humanly mental, a distinction of great significance. In this universe is included all that is real, perfect and permanent. True Science, then, is that which deals with reality, with God and His universe of spiritual and perfect ideas. Since this divine Science is exact, practical, and applicable to all human problems, it thus becomes the way of salvation to mankind.

No more poignant question faces humanity than the problem of death and the future state. Of all the clouds which darken the human horizon, this hangs heaviest. The uncertainty regarding the future state (so-called) inculcates grave apprehension. The longing for assurance of continuity of individual existence has been and is uppermost among the desires of mortals. Christian Science furnishes a complete and wholly reassuring answer to this age-old desire. God as infinite Life is the source of all existence. Man who expresses God coexists with Him, with the Father. No son, no Father. Hence the real man as God's likeness, without material accompaniments, has existed forever. When Jesus asserted, " Before Abraham was, I am," he undoubtedly referred to his true selfhood as the son of God, as the Christman. Christ as Truth has always existed and will never cease to exist. Hence the Christ and spiritual man exist in the eternal now, without past or future. Paul declared that the Spirit bears witness that we are God's children, and therefore joint heirs with Christ. Eternity is the spiritual now, in which man co-exists with God. Can we doubt the beneficial results from gaining this understanding? When Jesus declared, " This is life eternal, that they might know thee the only true God, and Jesus Christ, whom thou hast sent," he made perfectly clear the fact that, since Life is God, Life is eternal, and that knowledge of this fact brings into human consciousness that sense of existence which is without beginning and without end, that is, life eternal. Mrs. Eddy has stated the same fact even more briefly: " Not death, but the understanding of Life, makes man immortal " (*Science and Health,* page 485). This declaration opens wide the gate for every mortal to begin immediately to gain eternal life through learning about God. So much of eternal truth, knowledge of God, as is laid hold of now, one will possess forever. So much understanding of God as eternal Life, as unchanging Truth, as is gained now, will continue forever in one's consciousness.

Knowledge of man's present and eternal perfection is now possible of attainment. What could be more inspiring, more heartening, than to know that eternal life may be entered upon here and now through gaining the Mind of Christ. To those who grasp this fact must come a tremendous sense of relief. Fears flee and existence assumes a deeper satisfaction. This is no trivial saying, but a statement of profound significance. No other experience possible on this plane of existence is of comparable importance. And did not Jesus in his inimitable manner utter the same truth? " The kingdom of heaven cometh not with observation," he declared.

" Neither shall they say, Lo here! or, lo there! for, behold, the kingdom of God is within you." And " within you " can have but one meaning, in the individual consciousness. In that Kingdom of Heaven, spiritual consciousness, will be found all that is good and beautiful and true. Thus freedom does not pertain alone to some future state, but is to be experienced here and now in proportion as mortals gain some degree of understanding of God and man.

Sometimes it is mistakenly held that Christian Science is primarily a therapeutic system, the chief purpose of which is to heal disease. This conclusion results from ignorance of its teachings, of their purpose and application. On page 150 of the textbook, Mrs. Eddy, in writing of the main purpose of Christian Science, states: " Now, as then [the time of Jesus], signs and wonders are wrought in the metaphysical healing of physical disease; but these signs are only to demonstrate its divine origin — to attest the reality of the higher mission of the Christ-power to take away the sins of the world." The healing of disease is, as it were, a by-product of gaining the Mind of Christ. It is the proof of Immanuel, God with us. The healing of sin, through its destruction, is similarly wrought. Both sickness and sin are destroyed because they are unreal, that is, not made by God. Manifestly, the infinite Mind, which is also infinite Love, could have no consciousness of evil in any phase or form, of that which has no place in reality. That the beliefs termed sickness and sin are unreal, that they have no place in divine consciousness, is proved by their destruction. The real is permanent, is indestructible. In support of her teaching on this phase of the subject, Mrs. Eddy writes on page 9 of *Unity of Good:* " What is the cardinal point of difference in my metaphysical system? This: that *by knowing the unreality of disease, sin, and death,* you demonstrate the allness of God. This difference wholly separates my system from all others. The reality of these so-called existences I deny, because they are not to be found in God, and this system is built on Him as the sole cause."

In Christian Science, God is the only cause and His creation is good, is harmonious and perfect. Nothing of sin or disease has place in His universe. Sin and disease are figments of the mortal or carnal mind, to be destroyed, healed, by knowing their unreality. And as the truth about man is learned, that he is perfect and permanent, the false beliefs about man disappear as completely as an incorrect mathematical result disappears before the correct computation. It never was any part of reality. Thus sickness is healed by the ever-present Christ, Truth. Sin is destroyed through destroying mental falsities, the belief of pleasure in sinful experience. It is destroyed by knowing its nothingness, its unreality. God's man never sinned, never can sin. Perfection never becomes imperfection.

The understanding of the unreality of sin gives no encouragement to the sinner. Rather, by revealing that sin can bring no lasting pleasure, no permanent good, but instead discord, disease, even death, does it deter him from sinful practice. The third tenet of Christian Science, found on page 497 of the textbook, reads: " We acknowledge God's forgiveness of sin in the destruction of sin and the spiritual understanding that casts out evil as unreal. But the belief in sin is punished so long as the belief lasts." Only as the belief in the reality of sin and pleasure in its indulgence is destroyed is the sinner freed from his self-imposed bondage.

Again, what is the significance of religion in its relation to society? What can it do for humanity in this twentieth century? As society is made up of individuals, its status is that of its constituent members considered collectively. Reformation, regeneration, salvation are gained individually and the group is benefited only as its members are made free. The problem of the reformation of society, then, resolves itself into the necessity for the individual or person to gain the Mind of Christ. As mankind gains this Christ ideal, the purpose and meaning of society is completely changed, the whole outlook improved. In this improved order, selfishness gives place to selflessness, greed gives way to generosity, self-will is supplanted by the desire to know and do the Divine Will, hate is healed by love, false ambitions give way to the desire to serve the divine All-Father, and the joy of the Spirit supplants the fleeting pleasures of human existence. Of necessity, this reformation makes of the individual a better citizen, a vastly improved member of society. Is it not logical to conclude that by this process the grievous ills which now so generally afflict society will be healed? Depression will then give way to normal activity, poverty to plenty, greed and hate to brotherly love; wars will cease, and the brotherhood of man will be established.

HORACE J. BRIDGES

Horace J. Bridges, leader of the Chicago Ethical Society, was born in London, England. He studied at London University and holds the degree of Doctor of Letters from the University of Rochester (1927). Reared in the religious tradition first of the Anglican and later of the Baptist church, early moral revolt against the " sanguinary " Joshua conception of God, and adolescent reading of materialistic science gradually made attendance at church "too insincere to be possible." Happily, however, Thomas Huxley and Matthew Arnold, whom he came to read, brought him to a satisfying religious viewpoint and in one of the London Ethical societies which he presently joined he found an "ideal fellowship" in which he was allowed ample " freedom to 'beat (his) music out' with the growth of time and thought." He soon rose to leadership in the society and from 1905 to 1912 he was associated with Stanton Coit in the direction of the West London Ethical Society. Coming to America, he was chosen leader of the Chicago Ethical Society, where, since 1913, he has made an important place for himself in the religious, moral and cultural life of the city.

Besides lecturing widely outside the limits of his own society, he has been active in writing. Among his books are: *The Ethical Movement, Its Principles and Aims,* 1911, 2nd edition, 1912; *The Religion of Experience,* 1916; *On Becoming an American,* 1919; *As I Was Saying,* 1923; *Taking the Name of Science in Vain,* 1928; and *The Fine Art of Marriage,* 1930. In 1924 he edited *Erasmus, in Praise of Folly.* He is a member of the Unitarian Fellowship, president of Booth House, a social settlement, and one of the founders of the Chicago Urban League (for interracial co-operation) which, as president and board member, he has served for twenty years.

XI

ETHICAL CULTURE

By HORACE J. BRIDGES

The group to which I belong was founded in New York City in 1876 by the late Felix Adler. Its relation to creeds could hardly be better expressed than in the words of Dean Inge (which it acted upon long before he wrote them): " We cannot make a religion for others, and we ought not to let others make a religion for us. Our own religion is what life has taught us."

In accordance with this the Ethical Movement is collectively creedless. No belief, either theological or philosophical — not even any one type of ethical philosophy — is to be imposed upon the members of its Societies, or represented as their official doctrine. Each worker in the Movement is to be understood as thinking for himself, endeavoring to beat out his own music, and offering the results — whether in books, articles, lectures or sermons — as suggestions, and as material for the thought of others to work upon. We are emphatically a society of free thinkers. (Two words, please.)

Our Movement has thus drawn to itself a group of people who were intensely concerned about religion, but so determined to maintain the most complete possible intellectual honesty that they could not make the avowed or implied professions of any of the extant churches. I say implied as well as avowed, because it often happens nowadays that doctrines explicitly repudiated in sermons, or in books written by denominational leaders, underlie and impregnate the liturgies, hymnals, prayers, and modes of worship used by the same leaders and participated in by their congregations. I quoted just now from Dean Inge. His *Outspoken Essays,* and still more his excellent book *Christian Ethics and Modern Problems,* as well as other works, command my high admiration. But how the author of these works manages, without insincerity (of which I emphatically do *not* accuse him), to repeat the Apostles' Creed in daily worship — and, still more, to do what he does on those Sundays when his Church requires him to recite, and declare that he believes, the Athanasian Creed — is an enigma beyond my solving. Although I feel strongly that what Dr. Gresham Machen calls fundamentalism *cannot* now be believed by any moderately educated and intellectually honest man or woman, I still am unable to resist a certain sympathy for him and his colleagues when they resent the presence of ministers who clearly do *not* believe it, in a Church based on it, endowed by dead-and-gone believers in it, and committed to it, in formularies and confessions, as tightly as words can bind men.

So much for the reasons why our Movement is collectively creedless. Each man's religion is what life has taught him. Each — if he agrees with and practices the Socratic dictum that an uncriticized life is not worth living — is engaged, all his intellectual life long, in making a creed for himself, testing its articles as he proceeds, rejecting or revising them; and not until the day of his death can he really say, " This is my final conviction." Regard for truth, as well as personal modesty, should limit us to saying: " This is the truth for me. These are the ' rugged maxims ' that I have ' hewn from life.' Test them in your experience to find whether they are true for you. If not — in so far as they are not — then report your own findings, whence I in turn may hope to profit."

In this spirit, and in strict compliance with the editor's

request that in this book each man should present the distinctive thoughts which constitute the background of his teaching, I offer what the impact of life and experience upon my own mental and spiritual make-up has thus far made true for me. (Space permits only of presenting fundamentals.)

I was born and reared in the Church of England. Ours was a " High " church. Its vicar (for it had started as a mission church a few years before my time) was an uncanonized saint — one of those adorable characters by whose consecrated and devoted lives, through the long centuries, the immense good which Christianity has given to the world has prevailed over the harm done by the incredible creeds, the arrogant authoritarianism, " the pseudo-sin of Heresy and the pseudo-virtue of Orthodoxy," and the worldly ambitions which have built up and maintained the theocratic imperialism of Rome and the pettier dictatorships of some other churches. Later, in my middle 'teens, I came under the influence of the Baptist denomination — to which also, as represented by one or two people with a born genius for goodness, I owe an unpayable debt that it will always be a joy to acknowledge.

Then, toward the end of the eighteen-nineties, the popularized science of the time, and the findings of Biblical criticism, hit me like a thunderbolt and shattered the edifice of my religious beliefs. But I was saved from the materialism and the spitefully anti-Christian secularism which were then even commoner than now, by two influences in particular: Matthew Arnold and Thomas Henry Huxley. Arnold gave me an insight into the minds of Jesus and St. Paul that has proved a lifelong treasure; and Huxley, by his little book on Hume and Berkeley, led me across the *pons asinorum* of philosophy and made me see that mind, or consciousness, is the only reality of which we have first-hand, immediate knowledge.

The attainment of this insight was aided by one or two glimpses of mystical experience, authoritative — as such things always are — for their subject, though not for anybody else. In my case, too, Kant's doctrine of the Categorical Imperative (meaning the inherent and absolute authority of Conscience, so that the difference between right and wrong is as objective as that between true and false) is an experienced certainty. I am convinced that it is really so for every man, and that statements to the contrary, although sincerely made, are due to inadequate introspection and self-analysis. Moral obligation, in the stricter and narrower sense, is but one expression of this irresistible inner law, which is as incontrovertible as the principles of arithmetic. The sacrificial devotion of the scientific researcher to truth and that of the creative artist to beauty are other exemplifications of it. When it came to the point of facing the challenge of the Athanasian Creed — " This is the Catholic Faith, which except a man believe faithfully he cannot be saved " — I had to decide that sincerity was more important to me than salvation. I could not and did not believe it, and the voice that spoke in my conscience sounded more like the voice of God than any other that has ever addressed me.

When therefore, in 1899, I came in contact with the Ethical Movement and found a group of people who cared as I did both for spiritual growth and for intellectual honesty, I realized that I had reached my spiritual home. After thirty-six years this conviction is stronger than ever.

But what sort of creature must man be, in order that he may be capable of the kind of experience I have sketched?

Biologically, of course, he is an animal. Nothing that I know warrants me in rejecting the view that man is first cousin to the apes and descended from a creature in which no trace of the distinctively human nature had appeared. The evidence for this is so compulsive that, unless it is true, it must have been " planted " to deceive us, by a superhuman power with a sardonic sense of humor. Nevertheless man bears a nature, a kind of selfhood, a capacity for experience moral, intellectual and esthetic, which lifts him into a different world from that which any other animal inhabits. His selfhood is not in time, although his body is. Only because he is not in time can he bring together, in a simultaneous act of apprehension, events each of which is over and gone before the next occurs; and only because he does this can he have experience in a sense in which no other animal can have it — the experience of which speech is the medium of exchange, and that can be accumulated and transmitted socially, and constitute education, civilization, science and religion. When a man of science assembles evidence to show that man is a mere complication of the determinate mechanisms of a world of mindless chemical and physical forces, the power by which he reaches his conclusion is the proof that the conclusion is false.

When an eminent mechanist, who happens also to be a humanitarian and a lawyer, demonstrates in a lecture (on Sunday afternoon) that man is an animal, and an animal is a mechanism, and then protests (in court on Monday morning) against a criminal's being treated as though he were only an animal, his protest is the outcry of that most real part of his nature which his theory denies; and it is the trustworthy refutation of his Sunday lecture.

Eternal life is the life of our distinctive humanity. We

experience it when we encounter these "laws which in the highest heaven had their birth, neither did the race of mortal men beget them, nor shall oblivion ever put them to sleep." We experience it when, recoiling in horror from a murder or kidnaping, we yet find that even the murderer or kidnaper, though he has outraged the divine element in himself yet more fatally than that in his victim, must still be treated as a man and not as an animal or a thing. If he is really insane he is not a man, and not a murderer; the killing is then no longer a deed, but a meaningless accident. But if he is sane there will be something in him which will assent to the condemnation we are constrained to pass upon him. Our very condemnation implies a salute to the moral responsibility of which we know him to be still capable.

We experience eternal life when we follow truth to the utmost verge as yet explored by human thought, and then recognize that there is an infinite world beyond our farthermost reaching in which every fact we know would acquire new significance through its relatedness to endless other facts beyond our knowledge. And we experience it, too, when, having struggled along the Socratic trail in quest of beauty and insight into its nature, we come to apprehend its infinite and absolute reality. It is this intuitive and prophetic power of self-transcendence, humbling us by the gulf between what we are and what we ought to be, reducing our achieved goodness, in the prophet's strong language, to "filthy rags" by contrast with the beckoning ideal, showing us our truth as partial error and our beauty as flawed by unexpurgated ugliness, which nevertheless attests our dignity. It shows us that at the core of our being we are identical with the ultimate Reality which is the meaning and life of the universe. We can augur the infinite beyond us only because, in a manner outranging the reach of thought or speech, we are already, and eternally, one with it.

Individual immortality, or any posthumous life short of it, is altogether distinct from the foregoing experience. There is no knowing whether that inmost essence of us, which is eternal because it is a phase of the absolute reality, continues after bodily death to experience an individualized life under the form of duration in time. Any belief — negative as much as affirmative — that we may hold on this question, is purely and simply an expression of faith. Later generations may possibly achieve evidence warranting affirmation concerning it — although a negative demonstration seems logically impossible — but such evidence as psychical research has thus far turned up is inconclusive. There are some who say that survival is " impossible." They say this, however, only for reasons which (as Samuel Butler showed in one of his finest satirical passages) would equally prove to an intelligent embryo that life after birth was impossible. That is, they select arbitrarily a theory of man which preposterously identifies the self with the body, and then conclude, naturally enough, that the end of the body is the end of the self. This negative dogmatism is as unwarranted and objectionable as the affirmative dogmatism it opposes. Like all dogmatism, it is unscientific.

The worth of life depends on its quality, not on its duration. A turtle that lives more than three centuries is not therefore worth fifteen times as much as a John Keats who dies in his twenties, or ten times as much as a Shelley who drowns before thirty. The fifty-two years of Shakespeare and the fifty-eight of Dickens were infinitely more precious than the greater longevity of some selfish centenarian who never had a thought worth uttering or did one truly self-sacrificing deed. To say this is not to forget the difference between moral worth and intellectual capacity. It is in respect to the former that all men are potentially equal, whereas inequality in the latter is universal. The only absolute good is the Good Will, as Kant said — and that is as achievable by any unlettered peasant as by the mightiest deity ever imagined. In any after-life, if there is one, the same law will govern. What we do in and with it, and what we become through what we do, would determine the question of its worth.

The nature of personality — as we experience it in ourselves — and the conditions of moral worth (to be mentioned directly) forbid us to envisage the Ultimate Reality as a person, numerically singular, and separate from us as we are from each other. The infinity of the universe does indeed involve the *possibility* of a limitless range of personalities, some of which may well bear, in mind and power, the proportion to us that we bear to the amoeba. Humanity, as Felix Adler was fond of saying, is but one province of the Spiritual Universe, which is the real universe. But the moral essence of personality depends upon its being underived, an original and not an image, unique, and therefore indispensable. What is gained for the universe if I, " wretched man that I am," am nothing but a degraded *image* of a perfect Author? Why the fantastic superfluity of a creative activity which copies perfection into imperfection — if not utter degradation? Unless I contribute some indispensable atom to the whole — unless my existence adds something to reality without which it would be for ever incomplete — why should I exist? This is the fundamental difficulty of the view that one Person " created " the world and all other persons. Morally speaking, the phrase " created person " is as much a contradiction in terms as the phrase " infinite personality " is in logic and metaphysics.

There is a divine element in the world. We experience it as certainly as we experience evil. We are ourselves its trustees and bearers on earth. Our responsibility is to extend it by subduing the evil within and without us that competes with it and usurps its rightful sovereignty. But it is not to be thought of as a person distinct from other persons — still less as embodying, now and eternally, in existential form, all the ideal values that we must strive to actualize and all the power needed to overcome the intolerable evils against which we must struggle.

Man, as a being developing through time, is wholly and utterly dependent upon a world beyond himself. His bodily life with all that sustains it, and the mental and psychic powers by which he progressively civilizes himself — these to him are gifts, and not achievements. I have always felt very deeply what Dr. Dewey has just finely re-emphasized — the grotesque impiety of any " Humanism " which sunders mankind from nature, and, forgetting its manifest and total dependence upon nature, shouts Promethean defiances at the world for its evil and its recalcitrance to the will of man. A religion that ignores its cosmic roots and linkages seems to me to outrage common sense. But this recognition of our empirical dependence on the Not-Ourselves is wholly consistent with the foregoing assertion of the independence and underivedness of that in us which is not empirical, not the child of time and causation; and this is the essential part of us. In regard to all that is to us gift and not achievement, we are as dependent on nature as an unborn child on its mother. But in respect to what is achievement and not gift — our freedom and moral worth — we are independent, and share the stupendous privilege and responsibility of participating in the creative process of the cosmos.

The realization and acceptance of this boon and task is, to me, what religion should mean. Of course religion aims at salvation — a fine old word, not to be discarded because of some of the " ignoble uses " with which it has been " soiled." But salvation from what, and for what? Hell-fire after death is a wretched mythology, not to say a criminal libel on the character of the God who was supposed to have kindled and fed its flames. And a static heaven of eternal rest and perfect happiness is also a fantasy, pathetically reflecting the weariness of overlabored and frustrated souls. But there is nothing mythological about sin as I shall define it; and it is from this that we look to religion to save us.

Suppose we take the scientists at their word when they tell us that man has evolved by emergence from a simpler animal stage of being. Assume without knowing how (for this we cannot know) that with a certain development in the complexity of the brain and nervous system the bodies of our animal ancestors became organic to the distinctively human element in us. Materialism talks of the brain thinking. This is like describing a telephone as speaking. It is at bottom unthinkable and meaningless. The brain, and whatever else in our bodies mediates thought, exercises not a productive but a transmissive function. We live amphibiously, as it were, between the animal and the spiritual stage — these being not two worlds, but two planes of reality within the one universe. Now evolution, which in the merely sentient realm of life is only a *process* effected through the instincts lodged in animals, becomes upon the appearance of mind a *task*. We are here to conceive ideals and give them actualization. It took a long time for our race to emerge from the somnambulism of animal instinct into the waking life of consciousness, the peculiar characteristic of which is that it is enticed forward by ideals ahead, instead of being driven by blindly felt needs from behind. The instrumentalities of human evolution are will, reason, conscience, and purposes framed and effected through them.

Religious loyalty to man and the universe is the glad acceptance of our responsibility for completing the humanization of our race and the actualization of that increasing good commanded by conscience and foreshadowed by reason. Sin is the refusal of the task. The essence of it is siding with the animal nature which we have in common with other creatures, and foregoing the painful and perpetual effort to make our differential human nature dominant over it.

Speaking with the brevity here compulsory, I would thus state the essential difference between human and animal existence: On the animal plane life is maintained by preying upon other life; on the human level, life is maintained by enhancing other life.

I hope it is apparent that I am not committing the absurdity of forgetting that as animals we must needs do what all creatures do — live by food contributed by other forms of life. I hold that we have a full right, as we have also an invincible need, to use animals as means to our ends. That we should treat them with all possible kindness, and abstain from inflicting upon them any useless or unnecessary pain, is too obvious to need argument. To those of them capable, like dogs and horses, of a quasi-moral relationship to us, we should extend the gratitude and affection which such instinctive fidelity demands. But moral relationship in the full sense is only possible between *persons* — that is, bearers of reason and conscience who can communicate by speech.

The human ideal is to live by enhancing this distinctive life in all its bearers.

This is the commandment of religion (in my understanding of it) to the individual: *So live as to promote and develop the distinctive humanity in thy neighbor.* The foregoing sketch of the essentials of personality emphasizes the uniqueness of each person, and the consequent indispensability of his contribution to the total achievement of our race. I am to look upon each with an eye to the special gift hidden in him, or but partially manifested; and my action upon him must be such as to aid him in the realization of his own highest possibilities — *his own,* as they actually and potentially are, not as I may think they should be.

By cultivating this spiritual artistry and developing the kind of second sight it requires I shall achieve my own salvation in and through the effort to aid my neighbor toward his.

" Salvation," in the sense here intended, is a thoroughly social conception. Individuality is itself a social product, as Aristotle well understood but as later political thinkers have unfortunately forgotten. An ideal society would be one in which the latent possibilities of each member were developed to the utmost, in and through the multifarious modes of activity directed toward enhancing the perfected individualization of all others. This, which we shall never see, is yet what we must work for and follow as the directing beacon of our efforts.

Here, then, we have the bare outline of a religion which relates the ideas of sin and salvation to the manifest fact of evolution. I say manifest fact because, whatever may be the final verdict of science upon the inorganic and the subhuman world, the difference between the men of the Old Stone Age and the men of today is such a fact. We can readily conceive a world-wide human society, all of whose members would compare with us as we compare with paleolithic men. My notion of a religious life is one guided and animated throughout by the purpose of contributing toward the actualization of this prophetic vision.

Does it look impossible? That is precisely why we should labor toward it, age after age, generation after generation, until it no longer looks so. " In our barbarous society, the influence of character is in its infancy." So said Emerson. Well, this defines our task — to advance the influence of character through its childhood and toward its maturity.

The religious life of the past has not been lived in vain. Great parts of it were animated by the very ideal I have sought to express. That our ancestors conceived it in " supernatural " terms, and aimed to achieve it by supernatural means, points (as we must now think) to an error of fact on their part. It does not invalidate the ideal which they expressed by phrases like " the Kingdom of God " and " the Kingdom of Heaven on earth." We are but seeking to translate this language into terms now intelligible when we speak of eliciting and bringing to maturity the best possible self and the distinctive powers of every man and woman, in the only ways practicable — which are through their social relations, interactions and mutual influence.

Our western civilization has for many centuries believed in " salvation through Christ alone." What this century is doing — and will do — is simply to strike from this phrase its last word. Many years ago I ventured to describe Socrates as the intellectual and Christ as the moral savior of the world.[1] By this I meant that each of them, *either* for the first

[1] See my book, *The Religion of Experience.* The Macmillan Company, 1916.

time *or* to a unique degree, manifested a power and disclosed a method indispensable to that enhancement of man's true life which Christ in plain words declared to be his goal. Let me be absolutely clear here: I rate Jesus as a human being, conceived and born as all men are, and living after his bodily death, so far as human society is concerned, only as all good men do — through the influence of their words and deeds upon survivors and later generations. I believe he had no sources of knowledge or inspiration but such as are open to us all. The " mystery " of his personality is unfathomable — like that of all men. The difference between him and others is analogous to the difference between Shakespeare and others: one of degree. Many men have helped to open for us the way of experience which leads to salvation. Jesus and Socrates are pre-eminent princes and pioneers. We owe them a unique gratitude, which yet does not detract in any way from the thankfulness we owe to others.

And Jesus it was who formulated the law of the religious life. " He that loveth his *soul* shall lose it; and he that hateth his *soul* (or life) in this world shall keep it unto life eternal." The repetition, with variations, of this phrase in the Gospels proves it to have been one of his great principles or key-words. Life eternal, as we have said, does not mean temporal duration, before or after bodily death. It means what we have called the distinctively human life — the ascendency of that which, correlated with our animal being, lifts us beyond it into the realm of spiritual reality, that kingdom of Truth, Beauty and Goodness for which man was made; so that, as St. Augustine said, his heart is restless until it rests therein.

JOHN H. DIETRICH

John H. Dietrich is pastor of the First Unitarian Society of Minneapolis, Minnesota. Born at Chambersburg, Pennsylvania, he took his college work at Franklin and Marshall College, from which he received his Bachelor of Arts degree in 1900 and his Master of Arts in 1902. For the next three years he was a student in the Reformed Theological Seminary in Lancaster, Pennsylvania. Ordained to the ministry of the Reformed church, he was pastor of St. Mark's Church, Pittsburgh, until 1911, when he transferred to the pastorate of the First Unitarian Society of Spokane, Washington. In 1916 he was called to the First Unitarian Society in Minneapolis, where he has ministered continuously until the present. The Meadville Theological School honored him with the Doctor of Divinity degree in 1933.

Within the Unitarian Church Dr. Dietrich quickly assumed leadership of that section which has come to be known as Humanist. Indeed, he is frequently called the father of modern Religious Humanism. The titles of his books reveal clearly the emphasis which has characterized his preaching. *The Religion of a Skeptic,* 1911; *Substitutes for the Old Beliefs,* 1914; *The Religion of Humanity,* 1919; *Do We Need a New Moral Outlook?* 1922; *The Present Crisis in Religion,* 1923; *Humanism — a New Faith for a New Age,* 1925; *The Fathers of Evolution,* 1927. Besides these works, he has edited seven volumes of *The Humanist Pulpit* and has published more than two hundred of his individual lectures.

In view of Dr. Dietrich's long record of distinguished leadership in the Humanist movement, it was fitting that he be asked to set forth the Humanist answer to the questions with which this book deals.

XII

HUMANISM

By JOHN H. DIETRICH

As I sit here wondering how to start this chapter, which must contain so much within prescribed limits, my eyes fall upon a book which has stood upon my shelves for twenty-five years. It is *The Function of Religion in Man's Struggle for Existence,* by George Burman Foster. I do not recall much of the contents of this work, but I realize that it is one of the books which years ago played an important role in revolutionizing my attitude toward religion, and the title suggests a clue for the treatment of the goal of religion. I shall approach the subject from the point of view that religion is a function in man's struggle for existence — that in a general way the struggle for existence is the primary thing and religion is one of the tools man has forged whereby he can attain in this struggle a satisfactory, and if possible a delightful, existence. In other words, I place a biological interpretation upon religion and think of it as a phase of the larger process of life.

I have no desire to provoke a controversy concerning the origin and meaning of religion, yet it is futile to discuss the goal of religion until we come to some understanding of its meaning and origin. So let it be understood that I frankly accept the natural origin of religion. There are many who still believe that religion has its source in a supernatural deity, and that its validity is established by virtue of this divine origin; but it is generally believed today by its students that the various forms of religion have grown out of certain phases of human experience, that the gods are the result of religion rather than religion the result of the gods. In any case, I am convinced that religion is of human and not divine origin, existing by virtue of the role it plays in human life and not because of its divine source. I am convinced also that as long as it continues to play an effective part in man's struggle for existence its continuance is assured and that its success will be in proportion to the contribution it makes toward the success of this struggle.

As to the meaning of religion, it is difficult to know what to say, yet the goal of religion is entirely dependent upon what we mean by it. There have been many definitions of religion, but most of them have been made by men to describe their particular attitude toward religion, and therefore they are not available for use in our attempt to define the goal of religion. So instead of taking any particular definition as our point of departure, I will approach the subject in a general way from two different angles — first, from the angle of history, to view it as it manifested itself in the past; and second, from the angle of human experience, to view it as to its bearing upon human life.

Looking at religion historically, we may accept the definition of the dictionary and say that religion is the assumption of a relationship between human beings and superhuman beings, together with the results that follow from such an assumption — doctrines, rites, duties, and personal experiences. Mr. Mencken is thinking of religion historically when he says in his *Treatise on the Gods* that "its single function is to give man access to the powers which seem to control his destiny, and its single purpose is to induce these powers to be friendly to him. That function and that purpose are common to all religions, ancient and modern, savage and civilized, and they are the only common characters all of them show." While these superhuman beings and this relationship have assumed many forms, it is true that they have practically always been present. In this view of religion the goal is to placate the powers which seem to control our destiny. In the later forms of historical religion these powers have been centered in one personal God who sustains and controls the universe and men's religions have taken on the form of seeking and conforming to his will, in which case Cardinal Newman's definition of religion as " the knowledge of God and our duties to Him " clearly defines the goal of religion. If we are to accept this interpretation of religion, there is no use discussing further its goal.

But during the last decade or two, students of religion have been using what might be called the laboratory method; that is, they have been observing religion in its many forms and drawing their conclusions as to its meaning from these observations. The use of this method has led to many unforeseen results. One of these results is that religion is found to be a natural human impulse which may have nothing whatever to do with superhuman beings. Of course, thinking of religion in historic terms, many people insist that once these so-called essential features of religion are dropped, it is no longer religion; but Professor Sellars, recognizing the validity of this criticism, concludes that the term is at present undergoing such a transformation of meaning that the use of it is justified. He tells us that religion really means loyalty to the thing one values, and that this loyalty may be extended to any object or end. We realize the truth of this statement if religion is approached from the angle of human experience, or what might be called the biological point of view. Here we get a large group of new definitions, such as William James's " a man's reaction upon life," Haydon's " co-operative quest for the good life," Ames's " consciousness of the highest social values," Schmidt's " devotion to the highest," and Dewey's " allegiance to an ideal."

Thus, biologically considered, religion is merely a phase of the larger process of life. Biology teaches that life is a constant process of adjustment of the organism to its environment — that the organism seeks always, either through change of self or of environment, to improve this adjustment, to make it as harmonious as possible, to make the best of the circumstances which surround it. In other words, living things seek what they need to enable them to complete their life, to make it as rich and full as possible; and they develop an urge to do those things which give satisfaction. This urge becomes a natural impulse, practically an instinct, as observed in animal life when birds migrate with the seasons. In the lower forms of life this adaptation is mostly physical; but with man, a peculiarly psychical and social being, one of the phases of such adjustment is the development of an emotional attitude toward the universe, including human life, and the relation in which he stands to it. Man is able to contemplate his relation to the whole both in space and in time, and this has filled him with a sense of awe and reverence. He is able to dream dreams, formulate intellectual conceptions of improved conditions, and he has developed an urge to realize these ideals. This is such an important phase of his experience that he has imbued it with sacredness; and in its fundamental sense this is the meaning of religion — the emotional attitude or " sense of sacredness," as Julian Huxley calls it, which man experiences toward the ideal ends of life. So we might define religion biologically as the human effort to realize the ideal; the attempt to ameliorate the conditions of our earthly existence; the yearning for a richer experience, a nobler life, along with the constructive effort to achieve such a life. All the doctrines, all the forms of the various religions have grown out of this phase of human experience; and, different as they may be, the common element in them — and therefore the significant element of religion — is the attitude itself, not the object toward which the attitude is expressed.

Essentially, religion is the human attempt to escape from the evils of maladjustment and incompleteness into the joy of life developed to its highest pitch. It is a human hunger, as real as the hunger for food. People eat what they can get or what they believe to be good for the physical body. Likewise, religion assumes such forms as the creative imaginations of peoples enable them to devise in order to satisfy the hunger and build up their spiritual life. In other words, the purpose of religion is to secure blessings for mankind. Its worship, its sacrifices, its prayers, its duties are all for this end. In the past man's welfare was believed to depend upon the unseen mysterious powers that in personified form peopled the air and the sky. More recently the dependence was upon the one God who dwelt in heaven above, and all the practices of religion were for the purpose of averting his wrath or gaining his favor. But when men see that the blessings they crave, the welfare they desire, the adjustment they need, are based on other conditions — that these things are secured only as the result of a certain type of life among men — what a change comes into the heart of religion! The very ends which religion craves lead it then to pay attention, not to the gods, but to the real conditions of life — to study and observe the laws of the physical world upon which life depends, to study and observe the laws of the mental and emotional realms that life may be enriched, to study and observe the conditions of human relationships that our social life may be improved. Then, instead of praying or sacrificing for health and peace and happiness, they will create the conditions of these desirable states. What value this gives to religion! For if we are really earnest for human life, if we see it as the frail thing it is, dependent for its security, its happiness, even its existence upon knowledge of and obedience to the conditions of life, dependent for its enhancement and enrichment upon the creation and preservation of those values with which we have invested it, how can we be supremely concerned about anything but obedience to those conditions and the conservation of those values?

The goal of religion, therefore, is identical with the goal of human life. And what is the goal of human life? The supreme end of life is to live — or, to put it another way, the great object of living is to attain more life — more in quality as well as in quantity. It is this that men seek even in their wrongdoing. Many people do wrong, that is, they do that which detracts from life, because they are unable to distinguish between immediate and ultimate results or unable to resist the lure of the immediate results in spite of the ultimate effect. But always they are seeking that which to them means fuller and freer life. As Tennyson puts it:

> 'Tis life whereof our nerves are scant;
> Oh, life, not death, for which we pant;
> More life and fuller that we want.

Thus to live and live more abundantly is the purpose of every living thing, from the lowest to the highest. To this end man is ever using his power of thought, ever directing his activities. The only conceivable goal of life is that it should complete itself, that it should fulfill all its enriching possibilities.

Religion is one of the tools which man has devised for the attainment of this goal. In fact, it is the vital urge which drives him on, which prompts him to seek the highest values, that his life may be enhanced. So the goal of religion is to enrich human experience to the utmost capacity of man and the utmost limits of the environing conditions.

It may be asked, then, how religion differs from science or education or philosophy — all of which are directed toward the enhancement of human life. This is true; they are all concerned with improving human life and religion does not differ from them so far as the goal is concerned. It differs only in the kind of thing it is and in the part it plays in the attainment of that goal. These other forces are engaged in finding the way to the goal; religion is the yearning for the goal and the emotional drive toward its attainment. Religion uses all these other forces for the satisfaction of its yearning. For instance, science is engaged in learning how to control cosmic forces for human ends, but science does not urge man to make use of its knowledge. Philosophy is employed in determining what the real human values are, but it does not prompt people to seek those values. Religion takes the results of all these branches of knowledge, and says, "Come, let us seek the highest and the best." Matthew Arnold once defined religion as "morality touched with emotion." In a similar way one might say that religion is philosophy touched with emotion. Philosophy deals with values, discriminating between the true and the false, the beautiful and the ugly, the good and the bad. Religion, accepting the conclusions of philosophy, says to us, "Seek the true, the beautiful, the good." Science gives us the facts; philosophy interprets those facts, pointing out their respective values; religion impels us to seek and grasp the best. In short, religion urges us to seek the higher values, which philosophy points out from the knowledge which science supplies. And in this great trinity of science, philosophy and religion we observe, interpret and seek all that makes for the desired end.

If the goal of religion is identical with the goal of life, then the immediate objectives of religion are determined by the conception we have of life, particularly in regard to its duration. Does man's life end with death or does he continue to live after death? This question no one can answer with certainty, but to me all the arguments in favor of immortality are unconvincing. Even though man lives after death, the character of that life is beyond the range of human experience and understanding, so we cannot make any definite preparation for it, although I cannot imagine a better preparation than the development of the highest and best in human character during this life. So the goal of religion should be the enhancement of human life while it endures on this planet. Until recently the goal of religion was the salvation of man in the world to come. Human life on this planet was considered unimportant as compared to the immortal existence which was believed to await him after death. This earthly life was regarded as a brief training period for that eternity in which man must dwell in either incredible bliss or indescribable horror. The goal of religion was to avoid the latter and attain the former. The methods used were largely supernatural methods; that is, methods whereby men could induce the supernatural power to help them toward the desired end. But now that supernaturalism has been discarded and immortality reduced to a state of uncertainty, the problem is that of understanding and using intelligently all the means at hand for the enrichment of life here and now. The highest and best thing that man can conceive is a human life nobly and beautifully lived — therefore his loyalties and energies should be devoted to the arrangement of conditions which make this possible. The sole issue is how to make this world a place conducive to the living of a noble human life, and then help people in every possible way to live such lives. Stripped of all its incidental embellishments, that is or should be the goal of religion.

This raises the question whether the chief objective of religion should be individual or social. It should be both. I sometimes define religion as ethical enthusiasm directed toward the enrichment of the individual life and the improvement of the social order. These two things are interrelated and complementary. The real objective of course is the individual, because there can be no happiness aside from happy individuals, no enrichment of life except as applied to concrete men and women. Religion, therefore, should always be concerned with the inner life of individuals — the development of all those elements which we rather loosely term ethical and spiritual. But to imagine that these qualities can be built up in disregard of the social environment is to lack entirely any understanding of our complicated modern life, because the spiritual and ethical lives of people are largely conditioned by their social surroundings. We are learning today that human behavior is largely the response of the organism to stimuli in the environment, and that the nature of the responses is determined by the nature of the stimuli. Therefore the most effective method of developing noble lives is through the medium of environment. We must create an environment which will furnish the stimuli that call forth the desired responses, at least an environment that will make the practice of virtue easy and not hard, an environment that will stimulate in each individual the best qualities of his nature. Therefore, while the ultimate goal of religion concerns primarily the individual life, the immediate goal is primarily concerned with the creation of a social situation in which the inherent good in every individual will not only be given opportunity for expression, but will be stimulated to its fullest development.

Another reason why the goal of religion must be largely social lies in the peculiar relation which each individual bears to humanity as a whole. The life of one individual is so tied up and interrelated with all the other individuals that it is practically impossible to do much for one without improving the whole lot. All the things in civilization which we most prize are the product of the co-operative operations of human beings living together, and almost everything that gives satisfaction to life comes through our association with others. To improve ourselves, then, it is necessary to lift the level of the group in which we are merged. Analogies must not be pressed too far, but as the human body is composed of a complex organization of individual cells, so humanity is made up of a complex organization of individual men and women. The health and vitality of the one are dependent upon the health and vitality of the other. Every man and woman is an essential part of the human race, just as every leaf on a tree is an organic part of the tree. There is no more chance of saving oneself in disregard of the rest of humanity than of saving a separate leaf on a tree that has been struck by blight. We must go up or down together, be lost or saved together.

Many will not be satisfied with this identification of the goal of religion with the purpose of life, especially when life's ends are defined in terms of life itself. They will insist that there must be some other meaning to life — some ulterior end, to which life is but a contribution. If this be true, we cannot know what that end is. Human life has gradually risen from crude beginnings through adaptation of form to improve itself. That this human evolution betokens any conscious design or purposed end we cannot discern. So what the objective of human life is to be must be determined by humanity itself. To choose and create such an objective is not only man's privilege but his duty. Even though the force of the universe has pushed forward blindly in the past, all unconscious of what its end might be, it has at last on this planet assumed the characteristics of consciousness and intelligence and may henceforth be consciously and intelligently directed by humanity, at least so far as human affairs are concerned. Since humanity represents the highest product of this process within our knowledge, and since the human race cannot conceive of any higher form of existence than a human life nobly lived in a favorable environment, our objective should be the enhancement and enrichment of human life both individually and socially. It should be the development of all those things which deepen and quicken the individual life, and the creation of a social situation which makes this development possible. So I would suggest an idealized and glorified humanity as the object of our reverence and aspiration, and make religion consist of a devoted attempt to realize through consecrated effort the gradual transformation of human life into its likeness.

How may we proceed to reach this goal? Obviously we must mobilize and master all the knowledge and forces that may help us to achieve this end. This would include all the available information concerning the nature of the earth that we may properly adjust ourselves to it, a full understanding of what man is that we may control his development, a familiarity with the laws of social relationships that these may be improved, a recognition of man's aspirations toward the true and the beautiful that they may be satisfied, and a binding together of all these by the unifying impulse of religion, to supply the emotional incentive which will induce men to make the best possible use of this information in the realization of their ideals. Man may equip himself with knowledge of the natural and social sciences, which may be blended with a proper appreciation of the true and beautiful in a body of wisdom capable of leading him on to his goal of more complete fulfillment. In short, we have knowledge, the accumulated experience of the human race; we have ideals, the result of human imagination of what might be; we have faith, the confidence that our ideals are attainable; and we have religion, the longing to make our ideals actual through this knowledge and faith. Of all these religion is the most important, because without incentive the ideals would be of little use. Religion, purged of its antiquated trappings of theology, ceremonialism and absolutism, may thus be the sovereign quality in human life, integrating the social and emotional urges by gathering them and focusing them in the service of our highest ideals.

So the goal of religion is the development of human life to its highest pitch, and the building of a world which makes this possible, through the use of all available knowledge and of intelligent effort and co-operation. When this goal and method become universally accepted religion will be the mightiest force on earth. Today religion is ineffective, partly because it is encrusted in an outgrown shell, but principally because of the lack of a great objective with sufficient appeal to call forth the deepest personal devotion of men and women. Building new churches, adding to their membership, taking part in the varied activities of church life — how paltry seem these demands of religion as compared with the demands of the age that men everywhere should join hands in building a new world community which will emancipate and stimulate all the better elements of human nature. Religion has been occupied in a will-o'-the-wisp chase to the neglect of man's mundane needs. It has been truly said that " genius has been expended in obscuring the simple truth that there is no responsibility for man's destiny anywhere outside his own responsibility, and that there is no remedy for his ills outside his own efforts." Let men realize this, and we can make this earth a beautiful, healthy, glorious home, with none but the little inevitable tragedies of individual hearts to ripple its smooth surface occasionally, with fullness of life and strength and joy for every man and woman. We can transform the multitude of pale, dull-eyed folk, condemned to stunted minds and coarse tastes, into Ruskin's " full-breathed, bright-eyed, happy-hearted creatures." Burn that one thought — that it can be done — into the mind of the race and the work will begin.

In the field of religion, let men cease employing their efforts in vain endeavors to preserve a crumbling edifice which modern knowledge has long condemned as an obstruction, and unite in the service of their common interests and destiny. Let them make our churches places of meditation on the Great Mystery, places where the natural and healthy emotions of awe and wonder find expression, where the highest human ideals may be consistently held before their eyes, and where people may obtain genuine guidance in the pursuit of those ideals. The salvation of the puzzled peoples of the modern world must come from within, from their own courage and clear-eyed intelligence, from their own moral qualities, from their own spiritual aspirations — the fostering of which should be the main objective of religion.

MARK A. BARWISE

Mr. Mark A. Barwise is a New Englander by birth, education and continuous residence. He was born at Chester, Maine, graduated from the College of Law of the University of Maine, with a Bachelor of Laws degree in 1913 and a Master of Laws in 1914. In addition to his practice of law, Mr. Barwise became interested in politics and served his state as member of the Maine House of Representatives from 1921 to 1925 and of the State Senate from 1925 to 1927. From 1926 to 1934 he was recorder of the Municipal Court of the City of Bangor.

But preoccupation with the practice of law and politics has not prevented him from achieving note in the field of religion. His modest reply, when asked for information concerning himself, that he is "just an ordinary small town lawyer" is belied by the record of his increasingly influential leadership in the Spiritualist movement throughout the United States. Coming into contact with it locally he was attracted strongly by Spiritualism and soon became a leader in the Spiritualist societies, local, state and national. For four years he headed the movement in his own city, for nine years was president of the Maine State Spiritualist Association, and for fourteen years he was a member of the Official Board of the National Spiritualist Association. He is at present chief counsel of the national organization. It was at the suggestion of the president of the National Spiritualist Association that Mr. Barwise was invited to contribute to this volume, as "one of our ablest exponents and well qualified to present the fundamentals of the religion of Spiritualism."

Straightforwardly he has set forth the goal of religion as a Spiritualist sees it. The editor knows of no published statement of the position to compare with this in brevity, cogency, concreteness and yet comprehensiveness.

XIII

SPIRITUALISM

By MARK A. BARWISE

THE National Spiritualist Association at its Pittsburgh Convention in 1919 adopted this official definition:

> Spiritualism is the science, philosophy and religion of continuous life, based on the demonstrated fact of communication, by means of mediumship, with those who live in the Spirit World.

Spiritualism is three-sided. It is a science so far as it deals with the study of mediumistic phenomena, their analysis, classification and generalization; a philosophy so far as it deals with the relationship of its larger scientific truths to the larger truths disclosed by the other sciences, in its endeavor to solve the problem of the real nature of the Universe; a religion so far as it deals with the relationship of these same scientific truths to the nature of the individual, his life here and his life in the Spirit World, the kind of life here and the kind of life there, the contact of the two worlds, and to all the things that affect the growth and development of the individual mind and spirit here and hereafter.

Spiritualists do not make Spiritualism, but Spiritualism makes Spiritualists. Spiritualists do not make Spiritualism any more than astronomers make stars, or botanists make flowers. Astronomers study stars, and botanists study flowers, coming to what conclusions they may. Spiritualists study the natural phenomena of mediumship, and embody their conclusions in books, but the phenomena keep on happening through the laws of nature independently of any book, and probably did happen thousands of years before there were any books.

There are no sacred books in Spiritualism. All truth is sacred, no matter from what book, and no matter if from no book. Spiritualism is unique among all the religions of the world in that it is based wholly on a set of phenomena in nature, on mediumistic phenomena, which includes the teachings of the more advanced spirits through the more highly unfolded mediums. The complete and antithetical difference between Spiritualism and all the other religions may be illustrated by the following hypothetical case: If the Bible and every memory of the Bible should be miraculously blotted out of the world at midnight tonight, there would be no Catholicism, no Methodism, no Episcopalianism, and no Christian religion of any kind tomorrow morning, or ever more in the world; but if every book in which Spiritualism is mentioned, and every memory of Spiritualism, should be miraculously blotted out of the world at midnight tonight, tomorrow, next week, next month and as the months go by, mediumistic phenomena would keep on happening, evidential messages would keep on coming, and inside of five years we should have Spiritualism with all its present-day teachings back again.

Many Spiritualist writers and speakers are in the habit of saying that Spiritualism has always existed. That is not strictly true. Mediumistic phenomena have always existed, or at least have existed since our pithecoid ancestors became distinctively human, as note the countless instances in the Bible, in the classical literature of the Greeks and Romans, in the traditions of the Saints, in oriental myths, in much of the phenomena of witchcraft, in traditions of the American

Indians, and in folklore the world over. But these phenomena did not make Spiritualism until men realized what they meant. Fossils did not make paleontology until men knew what the fossils meant. Through the Hydesville Rappings, on March 31, 1848, and the weeks following, men realized for the first time in the history of the world that their departed friends lived in a realm beyond physical death, in a natural world, and that they could communicate by a law of nature, through mediumship, with those left in the physical form. When men realized that, that was Spiritualism.

Immediately after the rapping experiences of the Fox Sisters, mediums sprang up all over the land, and a great many kinds of mediumistic phenomena took place. These phenomena kept increasing in number and complexity for the next twenty years, with the total volume holding fairly steady down to the present time, and even now new aspects of old phenomena occasionally occur. All mediumistic phenomena are usually divided into two large classes, physical and mental. All are really mental, of course, in the sense that all show intelligence and purpose, but those which take place apart from the medium's body, or in which the medium's mind plays no part, are classed as physical. Among the better known physical phenomena are: raps; the movement of ponderable bodies; apports; independent writing; spirit photography; precipitation of pictures; independent playing of musical instruments; independent typewriting; independent voices; lights; etherealization; and materialization of hands, faces and full forms, which includes paraffin gloves, fingerprints in wax, etc. Among the better known mental phenomena are: clairvoyance; clairaudience; clairsentience; controls; inspirational speaking, singing, writing, painting, etc.; fully entranced speaking, singing, writing, painting, etc.; unknown tongues; and psychometry.

Mediumship is a natural quality or ability or power in one's organism that discarnate spirits are able to make use of to produce the above listed phases of phenomena. It differs in amount and kind in each individual. All these phenomena vary from nothing at all to a slight manifestation, to a little stronger manifestation, to a full force manifestation, and in many cases there may be a combination of two or more phases in one individual.

A study of these phenomena makes Spiritualists, without any choice on their part, by the mere weight of the evidence. All biologists, if they study all the facts that bear on the question, become evolutionists. If they are not evolutionists they are not familiar with the full body of evidence. All psychic researchers, if they study all the evidence, become Spiritualists. Whether they will or no the sheer weight of the facts compels the clean-cut conclusions of Spiritualism. If they remain psychic researchers, or mere " spiritists," they have neglected a large body of the evidence. The Universe has a way of winning out in spite of the most venerable prejudices and hallowed traditions.

Spiritualism, then, is what the spirits teach through mediumistic phenomena. Competent students have studied all this vast array of mediumistic phenomena in circles and seances, in the laboratory, by the fireside in their own homes, on the public platform, have listened to the more advanced controls through the more highly developed mediums, and have come to certain conclusions. Now what is it that the spirits teach? They teach:

That every single human being on the face of the earth, regardless of race or color, is destined to a life beyond death, not as a matter of faith, not on account of a creed, not through the mercy of a god, not through the offices of saint or savior, but by a law of nature.

That every single human being is a spirit now, as much as he ever will be, with mind and soul entity embodied in a spirit body, the exact counterpart of the physical body, which spirit body is what animates and vitalizes the physical body and keeps it alive — the spirit body being formed of atoms of a finer substance which animate the coarser atoms of the physical body.

That the spirit body is formed at the same time and by the same process as the one by which the physical body is formed, by the union of spirit substances from the father and mother, which spirit body is the real body, is that which grows, that which lasts, and that which carries the features, the traits and characteristics derived from and through the father and mother.

That we spirits wear a physical covering over our spirit bodies during the earthly season, just as we wear an overcoat during the winter season, and when the earthly season comes to an end we step out of our physical bodies just as we lay aside our overcoats when spring comes.

That the Spirit World into which we step on leaving the physical body is a natural world in a much higher pitch of vibration, with trees and grass and flowers and brooks, lying right around about this earth, not away beyond the stars.

That the Spirit World is made up of concentric Zones, the first being immediately about the surface of the earth, the reverse side of the physical, so to speak, and the Second Zone about sixty miles out from the earth, the Third a little farther from the Second, and so on.

That we know of Four Zones directly, and three more indirectly, those living in the Fourth Zone reporting that they have contacted three Zones above their own. There may be more, but we Spiritualists are strictly confined to those propositions for which we have evidence. The most highly unfolded spirit with whom I ever came in contact lives in the Fourth Zone, and he has been in the Spirit World a little over five hundred years.

That each Zone exists in a higher pitch of vibration, and is composed of a finer substance, than the Zone next below.

That as each of us steps out into the First Zone we arrive in just the condition mentally and spiritually that we were in here just before physical death, with all our knowledge, our aspirations, our loves, our hates, with everything except the physical body, there being no miraculous changes or supernatural interventions whatsoever.

That there is no Judgment, with crowns for believers and places of torment for unbelievers, but that each person naturally gravitates to that condition and place in the First Zone for which his degree of unfoldment fits him, and associates with those spirits with whom he is in tune.

That the law of evolution obtains in the Spirit World, as here, and each of us in accordance with that law, by aspiration and mental striving, as the years go by, may unfold all of our higher and finer traits and gradually slough off and outgrow our lower and meaner qualities.

That our friends who have been gone long, and consequently are fairly highly developed, may slow down their normal pitch of vibration until it harmonizes with that of us new arrivals, and visit with us, renewing all the old-time delightful friendships, stimulating our interest in all the higher things, and teaching us, so far as we are able to grasp it, all that they have learned of their new world.

That besides those who through love and friendship have been watching over us for years, and who greet our arrival and endeavor to make us feel at home, there are other spirits who will attach themselves to us as guides and teachers, those a little farther advanced, but not so far as not readily to harmonize with our condition. This is done in much the same way as that by which spirits attach themselves to us as guides while we are here, the American Indians through their peculiar magnetic qualities being particularly adapted to this sort of work, especially where they see an opportunity to stimulate the growth of our psychic faculties.

That along with the gradual growth of our mental and spiritual abilities there will go on at equal pace a gradual refinement of the substance of our spirit bodies and a quickening of the pitch of their vibration until we are no longer fitted to the coarser conditions of the First Zone, and we shall be ready to graduate to the Second Zone.

That this graduation does not consist of the death of the spirit body, there being no second death, but much as a rosebud bursts forth after slow and careful preparation the spirit body flowers forth into a finer pitch of vibration exactly adapted to that of the Second Zone, and the transition to that Zone is made — transitions in turn to Zones above being made in a similar manner.

That the Second Zone and each Zone above it are just as substantial and solid to the senses of the spirits living in them as the earth is to us, the trees and grass and flowers and water are just as tangible, and the ground under their feet seems to them just as solid as the earth seems to us, the environment being suited to each grade of inhabitants.

That the goal of life is the unfoldment and development of the individual soul; that the things which enhance that development are good; that the things which retard it are evil.

That there is no evidence from the upper Zones that there is any end to the development of the mind and character of the individual, but that each goes on through the advancing Zones, acquiring as the centuries go by all the great powers and abilities that have been displayed by the greatest geniuses of earth, and in addition thereto acquiring wholly new powers and faculties, as far above our present ken as our present powers and faculties are above those of the lower animals.

These are a few of the things that we Spiritualists have learned as to the definite, tangible, objective reality of the life beyond death, in a natural world, subject to an inescapable natural law. Whether we will or no we keep on living. There is no such thing as Salvation, because there is no such thing as being lost. The Persian story of the Fall, brought back from Babylon by the Jews on their return from the Captivity, is just an oriental myth. It has the same sort of foundation, which is nothing at all, as has the Flood Story. No geologist and no biologist believes the Flood Story. If the Jesus Story is true — that is, if Jesus was a real man and not a myth — it has no saving power, as many of the most cultured and finely attuned spirits with whom I ever came in contact never heard of Jesus while they lived here on earth.

Jesus and Mohammed and Buddha and all the other religious teachers have been of value to the world in so far as they have been able to lift the minds of men from the sordid and material toward the loftier things of life. None of them has had any supernatural power; none of them could turn aside the laws of the Universe; none of them has had access to miraculous power. There is no miraculous power to which access is possible. Nature does not do things that way. We Spiritualists say in our Declaration of Principles:

I. We believe in Infinite Intelligence.
II. We believe that the phenomena of nature, both physical and spiritual, are the expression of Infinite Intelligence.
III. We affirm that a correct understanding of such expression, and living in accordance therewith, constitute true religion.

That is what we believe as to the god-idea. We know of no evidence as to the existence of a god-power or -principle except in " the phenomena of nature, both physical and spiritual." We know of men in the Spirit World who have become almost as gods, but they are men just the same, and were born here on the face of the earth. We know of no higher orders of being, no Angels, Archangels, Powers or Principalities, no Cherubim or Seraphim or Thrones. We know of no demons or devils. There is not the slightest bit of evidence of any being in the Spirit World who was not born here on earth. All souls are formed and are born right here. This seems to be the incubator plane.

Neither do we know of any spirit who was born on any other planet. If other planets in the depths of space, about other suns, are inhabited, they probably have their own spirit worlds about themselves. At any rate we have no evidence one way or the other, and the laws of truth restrain us from indulging in pious vagaries.

The central idea of all religions is the future life. All the elaborate supernatural machinery in the various religious beliefs is of no consequence except as it bears upon and strengthens the belief in individual survival. What the mother wants to know when her boy is shot down in the trenches is, whether he is going to live again in a spiritual world, and whether she is going to see him again in that world. Jesus is of no consequence, the Saints are of no consequence, the Bible is of no interest, all the teachings of all the churches are of no interest, except as they may answer her supreme question as to whether her boy is going personally to survive physical death. The attitude of mind on the part of a bereaved mother is pretty much the attitude of all of us. If the whole world could be definitely assured beyond the shadow of a doubt that there is no possibility of a future life for anyone, we would have no zest for the study of the most exalted of religions. Jesus would be of no more consequence in American and European thought than is Buddha. We should study the history and doctrines of Christianity in a cold, impersonal way, just as we study Buddhism. What gives Christianity its warm, compelling interest to countless millions is the belief that it holds out a hope of a happy future life, at least for the comparative few who can and do believe its doctrines and accept its scheme of salvation from eternal torture. For other countless millions anything like a vivid belief has faded, but about its great cathedrals and little white churches there still lingers a faint perfume of hope that in some way, no longer clearly defined or really believed, but in some inscrutable way, its doctrines may point to a future life. The sad thing about Christianity nowadays is that most Christians are trying to think with their emotions, not with their intellects.

The glory about Spiritualism is that it is knowledge instead of a belief; that it is factual and not textual; that it is based on definite, tangible, present-day phenomena; that these phenomena are experiential and experimental; that the witnesses for these phenomena are present-day witnesses and here to be cross-examined; that Spiritualists have the same attitude of mind toward these phenomena as geologists have for fossils, or astronomers have for nebulae, or physicists have for cosmic rays. Spiritualists have a definite sense of reality as to the future life, not a feeling of pleasant speculation. Spiritualism differs from all other religions in regard to a future life as cash in hand differs from a promissory note.

As we spirits arrive in the Spirit World we have all of our baggage with us — the ingrained effects of all our evil deeds, our low desires, and our selfish purposes, as well as of all the finer attributes of mind and character which we have built up through the years. Slowly as the years go by, with the aid of our old friends and new teachers, we are able to eliminate all these undesirable traits, and to enhance all the lovable qualities. But the climb is by our own efforts. Just as here no one can learn anything for us, each learning all that he knows through his own struggles, so over there no one can be anything for us. Each must be what his own efforts attain. We may have teachers, we may have guides, but each of us must do his own work in building mind and character. There is no vicarious atonement.

As we progress on the Other Side and our spirit bodies become more refined, they become more finely attuned and vibrate on a higher key. Our spirit brains catch pitches of vibration unknown to us before. A control of an old friend of mine said to me a few years ago: " You will never know color in all its beauty, nor music in all its richness, until you come over to my world." All our sense impressions will be more vivid. Our minds will be keener, our thoughts clearer, with no blind spots in our memories. Our feelings will be much more acute. We shall be keyed to a greater intensity. Life will be fuller and richer than we have ever imagined.

When we arrive in the Spirit World, as I have said above, we shall be welcomed by our nearest and dearest. Things will be prepared for us, just as they were prepared for our arrival here. We shall have clothes and homes, and, so long as we think we need them, things to eat. We shall soon learn, however, that it is not necessary to eat, that we shall receive all the sustenance we need from the atmosphere we breathe. We shall learn after a little that we can travel by the power of thought, and almost with the swiftness of thought. We shall learn too that the scope of our wanderings will be confined to that pitch of vibration to which our spirit bodies are keyed, and to lower pitches; that we may lower the pitch of our vibration and visit earth scenes, but that we cannot raise the vibration and visit the Second Zone until we have grown up to that condition which harmonizes therewith.

One of the new and wonderful feelings which will dominate us for a time will be the feeling of an immense freedom. The realization that all these heightened powers are within reach; the ability to visit to the ends of the First Zone away around the earth at a moment's notice; the knowledge that all the fetters of matter, the burden of growing old, and the irrepressible anxiety of physical death are gone for good, will make us feel like newly emancipated slaves. The knowledge also that all our abilities may be tremendously increased — if a man was a good musician, he can be a better one; if a good painter, a greater one; if a good mathematician, a profounder one; that whatever our ambition, if for the higher and finer, it may be attained — will open up a new world of vistas down which we shall gaze with ever increasing wonder and delight. No more anxiety about making a worth-while living, but all our thought and effort will be toward making a worth-while life. We shall learn also that just as a teacher learns by teaching, we shall all grow by helping those a little below us. Part of our time will be devoted to self-improvement, and part of it to assisting others less advanced than we. We shall all be students and we shall all be teachers in the great school of life in the Spirit World.

Children who pass to the Spirit World grow up in that world, and they grow up to have the same general features and family characteristics that they would have had had they matured here. Old people who are bent and decrepit gradually return to that condition of spirit body in which they attained their greatest development while here, to a hale and robust sixty, or so. There is no sickness or weakness or decrepitude in the Spirit World after we have been there some little time and become thoroughly acclimated. The Spirit World is a place of health, vigor and good cheer. About the only hindrance to our general happiness will be an unavoidable grieving over the wicked and foolish things that our friends and relatives will be doing back in earth life.

Mediumship is not of the physical body, but of the spirit body. If one is a medium here he takes all the mediumship that he has unfolded with him into the Spirit World, where it will unfold still more. Through that mediumship he will be able to get in touch with those in the Zones above him, and give messages to those about him, just as he used to get in touch with those in the First Zone and give messages to his earthly friends.

To attempt to make clear the nature of Spiritualism within the limits of a brief chapter, and so set forth its goal, is like trying to write on a postcard an article on organic evolution. But in a word I may say that the goal of Spiritualism is to teach all those amenable to evidence in religious matters these tremendously emancipating facts: that life for all is continuous in a Spirit World; that there is no death for anything but the physical body; that the Spirit World is a world of natural law; that there are no supernatural beings, schemes, plans or machinery; that life Over There is a continuous and progressive unfoldment of mind and character from lower to higher planes of being; that the Spirit World is a world of boundless opportunities, but one of exact justice, in which each of us will attain exactly what he earns; and that as the centuries go by, if we work hard enough, we shall enjoy a breadth and a depth of mind, and a fullness of soul, undreamed of in any other system of thought, Christian or Pagan.

ALBERT POWELL WARRINGTON

Albert Powell Warrington was born in Berlin, Maryland. After leaving high school he entered the railway service, rising in a few years to the position of traffic manager. The law, however, proved more attractive to him than railroading, and he set himself to prepare for its practice, training under Professor John B. Minor of the University of Virginia. Strongly attracted by Theosophy, in 1896 he joined the Theosophical Society of Adyar, India, an international association of students of comparative religion and the hidden laws of life, bound together by the spirit of universal brotherhood. He retired from active practice in 1911 in order to give himself wholly to theosophical work, in which he soon rose to a position of leadership.

He has served as Fellow, as Lodge President, and as the American National President of the Theosophical Society; as editor of *The Theosophic Messenger* and of *The American Theosophist;* as vice-president and, on the death of President Dr. Annie Besant, as the Society's International President *pro tempore;* and as editor of *The Theosophist* during the many months of interregnum while the world-wide election of a new president took place. For twenty-one years he was Dr. Besant's active agent for the Western Hemisphere in the Esoteric School of the Society. At present he is vice-president of the Krotona Institute of Theosophy of Ojai Valley, California, which he founded in 1912. He has but recently returned from an extended visit to the Far East in the interests of Theosophy. His writings include chiefly magazine articles and editorials, and the article on Theosophy and Occultism in the *Encyclopedia Americana.* His long career as a prominent figure in Theosophy fits him admirably to write as a Theosophist in this symposium. He is a thirty-second degree Co-Mason.

XIV

THEOSOPHY

By ALBERT POWELL WARRINGTON

RELIGION offers to the individual man safe and happy guidance throughout the journey of life and the promise of ample blessings in the after-death state; to socialized groups of men, whether large or small, national or otherwise, it offers the truth of right living whereby peace and concord may be made to reign in the world-wide human family. When the true spirit of religion finds its normal place in the hearts and minds of a people, no greater blessing can come to them from any source. True religion begins its ministrations at the cradle and continues them to the grave. There is even a period before birth and one after death to which its beneficent influence is meant to extend. Life's road is dark and stony, and we come into it, over and over again, ignorant and impressionable. Along the way there are endless pitfalls and dangers, and one ordinarily learns how to pass wisely and safely through them by experience, by trial and error. But one may learn much, if he will, by guidance, which is but the essence of the experience (and hence the wisdom) of those who have gone before; and the way of this guidance has been set down by the wisest, or by their pupils or disciples after them, as wayside signs for the travelers coming on behind. It is thus that some of the records of religion have been made, thus that its guidance has ever been provided.

It is likewise true that some of the records have arisen from revelation, or higher knowledge imparted by a higher being to or through one who has qualified himself by exemplary living, self-discipline and service to be the instrument of such revelation and to some extent to understand it. Again, some of them have arisen from inspiration wherein the inspired one, being harmoniously attuned to his own higher self — that storehouse of his experience in past lives — derives knowledge therefrom beyond that which he has gained in this life; and this he sets down for the helping of others. And again other records have been based upon the life events and teachings of a divine incarnation, such as the Second Person of God the Cosmic Trinity, Who has always come when the world has had need of Him. For the sake of firmly establishing righteousness, he is born from age to age.

As has been said by one of the leading minds of this age: " The religions of the world are the partial unveiling of Truth — that is, the unveiling of such portions of Truth as are needed to help the stages of evolution present at any given time." Thus, fundamentally, religion is intended to disclose the unknown facts of the world we live in and its obscure laws, and to direct mankind in the knowledge of how all may live in harmony with those laws, operating, as they do, in the material, psychological and spiritual realms. Deliberate and continuous transgression of these laws whether by the individual or associations inevitably brings dire results through the laws themselves in the natural course of their operation, and the ethical teachings found in religion are intended to indicate which course of life lies in closest harmony with Law. Those living accordingly may be said to be safe, or saved from sorrow — one meaning of the plan of salvation, so widely dealt with in religion.

In considering the general theme of salvation, as called for in the editor's plan for this book, one is conscious that in

tradition it has been mistakenly said that religion exists to
show the way of man's salvation from damnation in the fires
of an eternal hell provided by the wrath of an all-wise, all-
powerful and loving God; but does this really seem to be
a consistent outcome of the Great Heart of Love? Is it not
rather one of those unfortunate misunderstandings of fallible
man? Salvation or liberation there surely is, but not from a
diabolical fire that eternally tortures and never consumes.
Rather is it from the fires of one's own passions unwisely developed and indulged in for one's separate, selfish gratifi-
cation. Religion has ever pointed out that such energies
are not to be prostituted to man's baser uses but must be
transmuted into spiritual graces and power. Nor can there
be salvation from anything that could be called the wrath of
God. Law — the law of God — there surely is. We can
understand how, when primitive man transgressed the Law
and suffered, he believed that he must be suffering from the
wrath of an all-powerful and angry being; but no such
savage vice could be attributed to the divine Father of love
by the enlightened, civilized mind which perceives the operation of Law throughout all human as well as cosmic nature
and strives to understand that Law as it operates in all
phases of man's being.

There is, however, a post-mortem method of self-discipline,
which may be painful or otherwise, according as one has
lived here, and which inescapably comes to one in the first
after-death state before he is ready to pass on to the blissful,
inter-birth heaven state. But this is essentially instructive
rather than punitive, though in extreme cases there may be
elements of considerable psychological suffering in it of a
purificatory nature. But it must not be forgotten that such
suffering is self-inflicted in the sense of being caused by

one's own thoughts and acts indulged in during the life here which have run counter to divine Law.

To be liberated from one's ignorance and enthralling limitations is to acquire wisdom and essentially all the power, love, beauty and goodness that are the handmaidens of wisdom; and this is the greatest salvation for man. The religion that teaches the way of this the only true salvation is the religion that truly binds men back to the One Source of all Life, as the word implies, for there is but the One Life and in That we live and move and have our being — all as sons of that Life or God, in various stages of cosmic growth.

Practically all of the world's scriptures are of Oriental origin, and any one familiar with the Oriental mind knows that its mode of expression is through imagery and symbol. The parables of the Christ were not unique in this, but followed a hallowed practice among Asiatics which continues to this day. As the culture of the older races becomes more generally known, it is not difficult for the advocate of intelligent criticism to indicate how inept it would be to approach the indirect methods of the East with an understanding that can only be properly applied to the methods of the more direct and forthright West. It is through such misunderstanding that the literalism of the Occidental mind has proved to be a stumbling block to the intelligent comprehension of Oriental thought. Hence the misinterpretation shown in many traditional doctrines, and, one may add, notably in that of salvation.

As salvation plays so prominent a part in the theology of the West, it may not be out of place to take a view of it from an angle not commonly seen by the student. So I will venture broadly to sketch in what to the spiritual oc-

cultist is a more obscure or mystical meaning than that suggested in the foregoing. In the beginning of a world manifestation, after God as the Great Architect of the Universe
had vivified and formed the primordial substance of sleeping Cosmos into the state which qualified it to respond ultimately to its every potential rate of vibratory activity, He
put forth from His Being a group of spiritual entities or
spirits of His spirit having but the consciousness of a group,
which, after eventual earthly manifestation and individualization, became what we know as mankind. These beings
only reached the density of manifestation which is physical,
and individualization from the group consciousness, after
aeons upon aeons of involvement or descent into matter,
by pressing ever farther and farther downwards into ever
increasing densities of matter. This vast group embodied in
latency each of the three aspects of the Primal Trinity, although, when they first appeared on earth as individuals,
they occupied crude, primitive, human forms. To these
forms were brought all the fruits of the anterior forms
such as are afforded by the elemental, the mineral, vegetable
and animal kingdoms, which kingdoms, embodying as they
did and do two of the aspects of the Cosmic Trinity, had
provided for humanity the organic substances wherewith
the bodies of its individuals should be formed.

But the assumption of the human form by the members
of this group was the result of a special downpouring, into
the somatic substance made ready, of the third aspect of
God's consciousness, which gave to the forms the addition
of the human ego, or soul. This was the greatest event that
had thus far occurred in the long cosmic process. It meant
the individualization of the whole group as separate entities,
countless in number, possessing potential minds and a frag-

ment of His free-will. This significant event may be called a stage of salvation, for it saved that phase of involving divine consciousness, which had gone before, from deeper material involution, and marked a significant stage of its ascent out of matter to be taken by gradual, evolutionary steps onwards into its eventual immergence again into its Source, enriched by its material experience for purposes best known to that universal Source.

The higher embodiment thus attained thenceforward began a new stage in the cosmic process — that of consciously reversing the impulse that had insured an orderly and effective involution, by making the effort to rise out of the bonds of matter through compliance with the ethics of evolution to be learned from right guidance and first-hand experience. Hence the presence in man of the war of the members — one force conventionally called evil (the remains of the involutionary process) and the other known as good (the beginnings of the evolutionary process).

When, in the course of very many incarnations (during many millions of years, at least on the earth planet) man shall become capable of accomplishing the very great task of making himself so strong, pure and wise, in universal, all-embracing love, wisdom and power, that he will be forever proof against permitting the forces of so-called evil within him ever to influence or entrap him further into their self-seeking ways, he will then be said to reach the next significant stage of salvation, sometimes called in mystical symbology the second birth. This stage represents the first step toward the gradual and final evolvement (still by repeated earth experiences) out of the stage called human and into that known as divine, or the stage succeeding the human in orderly cosmic growth. From this point onward the candidate for divinity, who as son seeks a closer walk with the universal Father, has but one purpose in life — which is to give every power he possesses toward the enlightenment of humanity, that all may be enabled sooner to see the truth which has set his feet on the path of Holiness.

Until salvation is thus made secure, or until a stable condition of safety is attained from the domination of the involutionary or separative, materializing forces, one may greatly prolong his period of successive incarnations on earth, and so reach human perfection at a later period than those will do who have succeeded in becoming dominated by the evolutionary or unitive, spiritualizing forces. As planets travel in orbits like great cosmic wheels, so does man travel in orbits of consciousness through life and death and life again unto a high and far-off goal which ever recedes as he expands in his endless cosmic growth.

Technically this stage of safety, thus entered upon at what is known (in Theosophical writings) as the first great initiation, must be followed by three other stages or initiations before, in a human sense, perfection is attained. At that stage the initiate may pass out of the human evolution altogether into the divine, where he may either work with the angelic hosts or voluntarily sacrifice this joy by returning to share his power and wisdom with humanity. But these initiations are stages of growth which can be consummated only in states of consciousness experienced during profound sleep of the body, but available nevertheless here and now as in the past to the eager aspirant who has determined to find the way. In modern days this way has been pointed out more in detail by such writers as the Rt. Rev. C. W. Leadbeater (*The Masters and the Path*), Dr. Annie Besant (*In the Outer Court, The Ancient Wisdom,* etc.), J. Krishnamurti (*At the Feet of the Master*), Mabel Collins (*Light on the Path*), and H. P. Blavatsky (*First Steps in Occultism, The Secret Doctrine, The Voice of the Silence,* etc.).

By one of these writers a correspondence is found between these four stages on the Path of Holiness with the stages of Birth, Baptism, Transfiguration and Crucifixion of the Christ-man on earth, and by another with the stages of Conversion, Purification, Illumination and Perfection.

In passing, it may be stated that one might, if one so chose, deliberately set out to live a diabolical life of opposition to the good law, and if this be persisted in, one's subsequent incarnations would gradually fade out, and that which survived as a unit of the One Consciousness would, after aeons of sleep, emerge again to re-enter the stream of life at a later world-period, for another and perhaps a more successful effort; for every fragment of His consciousness is eternal, though the forms it successively inhabits be finite. If this situation spells "lost," the meaning can be taken only in the sense of aeonian delay. For after all there can be but the One Consciousness in all the universe, though a phase of it be fragmentized from age to age for ends we have no means of fully comprehending. But to speak of any part of His consciousness, His life, or His substance as lost or damned is unthinkable, for at the end of a periodic cosmic manifestation, whatsoever He put forth into it is recovered again, redeemed, or saved, whether its ends have been achieved wholly or only in part. In the latter case, there will be future days of manifestation for its ultimate perfection, so perfect is His plan.

In a human sense salvation is an individual matter. One could see no meaning in a "saved society," as such, under conditions as they will be for a very long time to come. But in a future world-period, many millions of years off, progressive conditions will necessarily be such that only those who have attained to human perfection will go on into the still higher reaches of evolution, and these very distinctly will be the saved ones, as a group, in the sense of being the garnered fruitage of the present evolution. The rest of the human family, not having reached this stage, will have their next opportunity to pass this same critical point in evolution (a kind of "judgment day") at the same evolutionary juncture (or sooner) in another world-period, after enjoying an interim of rest of long duration, when not only mankind but all nature will sleep until the dawn of the new cosmic day. Perhaps one may see in this statement a division of "the sheep from the goats," conventionally supposed to take place on a judgment day. But in this there still remains hope, for in a good universe created by a good God no one of His beloved sons can ever be doomed to eternal misery.

Traditional Christian doctrine can be seen as adumbrating this universal cosmic process when, from its inner interpretation, it is understood that man, in his constituent elements, is a threefold reflection of the triple Logos — the Father, the Son and the Holy Ghost — as shown in his spirit, soul and body, to use St. Paul's designations. Thus the spirit is the Father in man; the soul, the vehicle of the spirit, is the Christ in man; and the body is the Holy Ghost in man, the temple of the living God on earth.

It was the Holy Ghost aspect of God's Consciousness that first descended and fertilized, or vitalized, the virgin cosmic field. Then vast ages later, there followed the descent of the second or Son aspect into the virgin field thus energized, to mold this vivified substance into forms or organisms as vehicles for a state of consciousness to be graduated from the rudimentary simplicity of the mineral into ever increasing complexities extending to the highest animal, thus establishing evolving, pre-human states of consciousness, not yet become self-consciousness. Self-consciousness came after the later descent — that of the third outpouring, or the Father aspect of Divine consciousness. In this outpouring He breathed into the foremost of the organisms thus developed the germinal souls of men, which in this way became the subtle vehicles of those divine spirits of men, who thereafter manifested in human forms as the sons of the One Spirit, whose task it is to master the realms of matter for That One Spirit of all, unto the perfection of man and the glory of God.

This means, as said in one of the great scriptures of the world, that with a fragment of Himself God created this world *and He remained*. That is, the Creator put but a fragment of Himself into the creation of His Universe, and beyond that He remained unchanged. That " fragment " consisted of three separate outpourings or acts of descent: (1) the vivifying of sleeping primordial substance; (2) the formation of worlds, kingdoms of nature and organisms out of this substance as vehicles of a growing, expanding consciousness; and (3) the pouring down into the highest of these organisms of that aspect of His life which became the subtle vehicles of the Sons of God called the souls of men. And this was the culminating act of His Creation, the purpose of all that had gone before. This act constituted a redemption, an act of salvation, or that process of drawing back into the One Source the fruits of the two prior outpourings from His Being. And all this is, to this very day, a continuing process in the life of the worlds and will remain such until all things shall pass once again into the periodic sleep of Cosmos, only to awaken again and again for further manifestation and so on infinitely, each manifestation producing, as the fruit of a universe or system, countless groups of perfected men become deities, who in their turn enter the stupendous fields of Creation as creative servants of the Most High and so on and on — who can say whether on to anything that could be thought of as a limit?

Such may be said to be the general trend of information which the student of occultism gains concerning what may be called the plan of salvation. It has been sketched here that it may be compared with other teachings on the subject which may be more familiar to the majority of readers.

From this point of view, salvation takes on a certain cosmic orderliness and grandeur that is indeed impressive. For its realization there is ever the need of right religious instruction showing how man must struggle to make the True, the Good and the Beautiful permanently triumphant in his life; how in thought and deed he may strive to develop a Christlike character here and now on earth; and how this destiny, in the goodness of the All-Father, is insured sooner or later to all — to some who cling to selfishness and separateness, by a slower process, to others who prefer the way of unselfishness and unity, by a more rapid achievement. With this knowledge, how magnificent and wise would seem the scheme of life! No effort is too great to help accomplish its purpose.

Thus all true religions have the sacred duty of devoting their every energy to the wise training of man gradually away from his necessarily inborn involutionary instincts into his task of acquiring those of the evolutionary upward way, which insures the achievement for which the great journey was planned.

In all times, however, corruptions have crept into religions through the inevitable defects and limitations of human nature. These have hindered instead of helped the individual to free himself from selfish egotism, ignorance, superstition and material entanglements, which ultimately must be exchanged for the unselfish principles of that brotherhood of man which is the true birthright of the sons of God. But such corruptions ought not to blind the earnest student of religion, for the fault is man's and man's only. Wherever religion has failed of its purpose it has been because of the prostitution by man of its pure gift, which he has confined to his own darkened limitations.

In trying to understand religion, as in all subjects involving essential human values, one has to apply a cultivated discrimination; for spiritual understanding without true discrimination must indeed always be limited. Through this indispensable quality one accepts what seems reasonable and ennobling, and rejects, or holds in suspense, all else for the time being. Any other attitude does violence to all that one holds as true in regard to the hidden god in man, who in the end must tread his own path out of the bewildering, blind darkness of matter into the Light whence he came forth when time was not. For after all every man has his own way of return appointed throughout eternity. What religion can do for him (and surely that is of vast importance) is to

> Point out the " Way " — however dimly, and
> lost among the host — as does the evening
> star to those who tread their path in darkness.

LEO JUNG

Rabbi Leo Jung was born in Moravia. He was educated in Hebrew high schools and Rabbinic academies of Hungary and Germany and in the universities of Vienna, Berlin, Giessen, London and Cambridge. He earned the Rabbi's diploma (Semikhah) and the degrees of A.B. Hon. from London and Cambridge, M.A. (Cantab.), and Ph.D. at the University of London. His first rabbinate was at Knesset Israel Congregation, Cleveland, Ohio, in 1920. In 1922 he was called to the Jewish Center in New York City, where he has since carried on a very active and influential ministry. He has been vice-president of the Union of Orthodox Jewish Congregations of America since 1924; was president of the Rabbinical Council, 1928–34; member of the Presidium since 1934; Council of the Agudat Israel, the World Organization of Torah-true Jews, since 1923; member of the cultural committee, Joint Distribution Committee, since 1926; Council of the Jewish Agency since 1929; on the executive committee of the Goodwill Union since 1928; and vice-president of the Family Institute of New York City since 1929. Since 1931 he has served as professor of ethics at Yeshivah College.

His list of books includes the following: *Foundations of Judaism,* 1923; *Essentials of Judaism,* 1924 (sixth edition, 1935); *The Story of Fallen Angels in Jewish, Christian and Mohammedan Literature,* 1926; *Living Judaism,* 1927; *Aspects of Judaism,* 1933; and *Mistranslation as Source of Folk-lore* I, 1935. He is editor of *The Jewish Library,* volumes of which appeared in 1928, 1930 and 1934.

Within the Jewish group, Rabbi Jung represents orthodoxy, or, as he prefers calling it, Torah-true Judaism. It is safe to say that no exponent of that point of view is read more widely or with greater respect by Jewish or Christian readers than he.

ORTHODOX JUDAISM

By LEO JUNG

HUMAN history has been marked by a multitude of religious experiences, by a number of religions, and by necessarily inadequate attempts to articulate the significance of these for human beings. At best, expression about religion is one's personal expression of religion. It is in this light that these few paragraphs are offered.

The diversity of religions and religious experiences has not excluded an essence, a religious essence, common to all. This common experience has joined men in a consciousness of their connection with an extra-personal being, God, and through him with all human beings. Religion designates a loyalty by human beings to human beings as a direct result of the larger loyalty that embraces all. Religion defines the relations between God and his creatures. In so far as different ones among us have viewed differently this relation, our religious experiences have varied, our religions have differed.

The ultimate goal for my religion, as it must be for all religion, is the penetration of every nation with the living ideal that issues from this relation of God and his creatures. The ultimate goal should unite mankind in good and beautiful life, in a life in which sin or evil or wickedness no longer exists. The ultimate goal can be achieved when life is viewed as an opportunity for doing good in conformity with the will of God. That this opportunity is often blocked or canceled by temptation, that it is delayed through the loneliness and despair existing in the hearts of men is true. It is this latter fact which begets the strife between good and evil, between spirit and matter, between beauty and ugliness, between truth and falseness. Defeat will destroy not only religions but religious experience; victory will hasten the realization of the ultimate goal. We believe that the tendency of human history toward this ultimate goal is advanced by the Father of human life.

If the foregoing is correct, then it was inevitable that there should be different religions or at least that there should be different religious experiences. The experience of Jews has contributed one religion revealed in the Torah. This we call Judaism. However, it is not to be denied that even within the framework of one religious group or one religion diversity inevitably obtains. Each man's conception of Judaism is the distillation of his individual experience. In no other way can it be evaluated.

Judaism defines the relation of God and his creatures so as to make of it an all-embracing relation. Since the ultimate goal of life can be won only through God, Judaism holds that all things in life, in our daily living, must have direct contact with God. No aspect of life is excluded from his concern. Judaism holds that in so far as the purpose of life is ethical perfection for all individuals, then this ethical perfection is in no manner more encouraged and made more possible than in the avenues of a religion which not only affirms life's values but looks upon all experiences of life as related to God and therefore comprised in his laws and will.

This central point in Judaism can perhaps be illuminated by a brief reference to the Torah, the law of God. (Torah — literally " direction " — designates not only the Pentateuch, but also the whole of Jewish religious literature and the living tradition of Israel, to whom this divine guidance or direction was vouchsafed.) No detail of life is omitted from its consideration. Each detail of life is considered so as more and more to spiritualize life. As a law of life, of the whole of life, the Torah would neither neglect the urges of the body nor make of them ends in themselves. Body and soul — their needs and their possibilities — are the concern of the Torah. Hence the infinite number of rites, hence the minutiae of dietary laws, hence the pervasive character of ceremony — all symbolizing the religious significance of each action of life.

The goal of Judaism does not depend for its realization upon a set of theological beliefs. Judaism does not depend upon the punishment of damnation or the reward of salvation to spiritualize the whole of life. Rather, the whole of life is an adventure each aspect of which may be made holy if it is related to all other aspects, and these to God and his will. Thus the Jewish religion offers an organic conception of life, organically related to the will of God, making for holiness and happiness. The Jewish religion insists that the whole of life be permeated by this concept, this way of life, the guide to which comes from the Torah.

Man can be good and happy only at the same time. In Judaism the term " holiness " plays an important role. Israel is commanded, " Be holy, for I the Lord your God am holy." In God, holiness means freedom from all the limitations of natural phenomena — hence, omnipotence, omniscience, inward harmony, the blending of all wisdom, all goodness, all power.

Holiness as a categorical imperative for man means the endeavor to reach, within human limitations, a similar power, a similar harmony, a similar freedom. Jewish tradition defines holiness in man as freedom from every wickedness, every ugliness. This freedom is impossible without man's reverence and love of God, the numen. Without this anchor, moral standards will be lowered or adjusted to appetite. But holiness is more than righteousness. It is righteousness based on, conscious of, and directed by a sense of awe before the ultimate perfection and harmony of God. Holiness in man is his *imitatio dei*. Holy are all such men and women as deliberately, selflessly, and abidingly strive to imitate God. The entire Law has for its aim the hallowing of life, to be reached through good deeds, through observance of Sabbath and holyday, through the sanctification of God's name. God, by reason of being God, is free — a free spirit, a free untrammeled Creator, the first and only cause of everything, in constant contact with his creatures and concerned about their welfare. Hence his revelation to them of his will is the only complete guidance toward happiness and perfection.

A philosopher whose profundity has been recognized by the modern world closes his most important contribution with these last and significant words: " But all noble things are as difficult as they are rare."

This quotation is particularly Jewish, for although many may subscribe to the generality and fullness of the religious life as indicated above, few will be courageous enough to fulfill the practical requirements for its realization.

Judaism has provided a method to concretize in all of life's situations this spiritual significance of life. Judaism has insisted that unless our actions are consciously invested with conscience, they fail to bring us closer to God. Judaism has maintained, moreover, that as God-consciousness is the first requisite of any religion, so we Jews must symbolize in each experience our awareness of God. In several religions and particularly in Christianity these experiences have gone to make up what are known as the sacraments, limited in number. In Judaism there are no sacraments as such, or, to put it another way, all acts can be made sacred.

Briefly let me remind my reader that when he finds " Love thy neighbor as thyself " twice enjoined in Leviticus, the third book of the Torah of Moses, the very same chapter in each case insists on the practical realization of its implication. It demands part of our annual harvest as our minimum contribution to our poor neighbor. The ceremonial of Jewish holydays produces a veritable symphony of goodness, from the gift to the poor on the eve of the holyday " so that the stranger at our gate too, may rejoice on the day of our feast," to the many religious acts and symbols expressive of cosmopolitan human sympathy.

The ceremony, indeed, is the method of Judaism. It connects practical life in all its richness and activities with the spiritual truths of religion; it gives tangible expression to these ideas and ideals. Judaism not only states the ideal, but consistently, in every instance, provides the method, and outlines the path toward its realization. This is another aspect of the mistrust the Torah has for mere theoretical speculation unrelated to conduct.

The *Mitzvah* or ceremony speaks both to the Jew and for him. By insisting on certain actions and prayers in moments of great emotional disturbance, the ceremony reduces the expenditure of emotional energy and steadies our heartbeat, preventing us from losing balance in hours of extreme happiness or unhappiness.

The ceremony speaks *to* us, pointing out spiritual vistas to encourage our moral effort; the ceremony speaks *for* us, articulating our sorrows and joys, when expression, though vital, is impossible because of pent-up feeling. The ceremony thus trains us in self-restraint and in constant vision of that good and beauty which we are to achieve by our own effort. Recognizing the need for uplifting above the humdrum drabness of life, the Torah through ceremony diverts our gaze beyond the sphere of cut-throat competition, social annoyances and personal disabilities toward the contemplation of a better world, of which we should not merely dream but for the consummation of which the ideal calls and the ceremony guides our steps.

A single instance should suffice. Most people suffer from a lack of social imagination. That is why there is such widespread and profound lack of genuine human sympathy. The Jew receives this message through a ceremony at a moment when, without this reminder, he might be exclusively and narrowly nationalistic.

The Passover eve service is dedicated to recalling the sufferings of Israel in Egypt and his deliverance from under the heel of the Pharaohs. At the beginning of the night, the Jew performs the ceremony of Kiddush. Kiddush means sanctification. The Jew takes upon his soul the sanctity of the holyday by pronouncing a blessing over a full cup of wine. A full cup of wine is the symbol of happiness, a symbol based on the biblical expression, " the cup of my salvation is full." This ceremony introduces every Sabbath and festival day.

In the course of that Passover eve service, reference is made to the ten plagues with which the Egyptians were afflicted. When this account is about to be read, another ceremony is performed. A full cup of wine is taken, and with the mention of every plague some wine is poured away. The children, for whose benefit this service is arranged, are encouraged to ask the meaning of this ceremony and they receive the answer: " The Egyptians were our cruel oppressors. Tonight we recall God's redemption of his people and our hearts are full of gratitude and joy. That is why we make the blessing over the full cup. But the Egyptians were human beings, and, although they were our enemies, we are sorry when we recall their sufferings. They, too, were God's children and we must feel with them. Our cup of happiness cannot be full as we read the tale of the ten plagues. That is why we pour away some of the wine whenever one of the plagues is mentioned." The humanizing influence of this ceremony at this moment can hardly be exaggerated. It is an unforgettable lesson in good will.

The Torah sets forth the command, "Love thy neighbor as thyself." As a means toward the realization of this precept, the Torah enunciates the principle of equality of the foreigner before the law; of the civic duty to help the poor, and to take care of the stranger. Such activity, not dependent upon a man's temper or mood, but representing the legal minimum of his contribution to social welfare, is the first step toward the realization of that ideal. The obligation to take care of the non-Jewish as well as of the Jewish destitute helps to make these steps more valuable, to train the Jew in a general humanitarian tendency. Our ceremonies are the sources of humanitarian vision, the springs of kindliness which feed interdenominational friendship and influence action.

But behind them all is the conviction that all these deeds, productive as they are of social welfare and individual nobility and happiness, derive their ultimate sanction from the fact that their performance is the revealed will of God. To the Jew, the one good in life is conformity with the will of God. Sin is refusal to accept the law of God or action against it.

These principles are based on God, the immutable standard of goodness, righteousness, wisdom and beauty. God is the source of every goodness, and God-consciousness is the breath by which the righteous live. All the ceremonies are designed to create and support God-consciousness. In detail they help the Jew to progress on his way toward the realization of his ethico-religious ideals. In totality they surround him with an atmosphere of Godliness, in which the opportunity for evil is necessarily limited and every will for good normally encouraged.

Devotion to God in Judaism must not be confined to certain periods of prayerful attention. It must be as rich, as broad, as continuous as life itself. The system of symbols and ceremonies of thoughts, words and deeds, interdependent and mutually fruitful, attunes the Jew every hour of the day, every day of the year, to the great ideals of man by keeping awake in him the love of God. The forms of Judaism are its contribution, too little known, to the esthetics of man. They are the humanistic Jewish art that works not on marble, but on human beings, shaping their character, encouraging their moral and esthetic sense, bringing home to them the beauty of truth, peace and kindness. They are a system of life and thought devised to express a living monotheism.

The Jew, according to the Bible, is not the only child of God, but his spiritual first-born, carrier of the Father's message. He is charged with the message and to safeguard it he must go his own way, live his own life, protect the separateness of his march through history, protect the very uniqueness of his destiny, resist every influence that would change his message, develop through centuries his mode of expression, the force of his example, the influence of his heirloom, the Torah, so that his labor for the ideal may be successful.

The ultimate goal is the penetration of every nation with the living ideal of ethical monotheism to a degree which will beautify life, unite mankind, and banish wickedness from the world.

But this must not be thought of wholly in this-worldly terms. This world is like an ante-chamber to the world to come. We are unable to approach the Deity and to understand the ultimate verities of life because we are psycho-physical beings, and the body cribs our mind. In the world to come (meaning the life after death of each individual) we are freed from the limitations, spiritual and mental, of the body. There is neither eating nor drinking; the righteous enjoying spiritual bliss and the gift of full understanding, full communion with the Lord.

The more we refine our personality here, the more spiritual our life, the more profound and complete our participation in the world to come. Though there are no details about this fundamental creed, the pious Jew is convinced that life continues beyond the grave.

Clearly to be distinguished from *olam haba* (the " world to come ") is the Messianic Age which is to be achieved by man's effort under God's guidance on this globe.

The task is dependent on the capacity of Israel to pursue his way through the ages, trained in God-consciousness, isolated during the centuries of struggle, in the world but not of it. The discipline of suffering for the ideal, the discipline of struggle for freedom of conscience, the hard battle against passion, desire, and every vanity are to help the Jew retain his identity, and through his identity the undiluted strength of his message, his God-consciousness as the single propelling force in his individual and collective life. Hence every Jewish ceremony is part of the God-given way of life, every commandment based on the will of God, every step the Jew takes is either prescribed by God or nullified by its nonconformity with His will.

When the message underlying the Jewish ceremonies is appreciated these become the wings by which the Jew lifts himself into the sphere of his historical ideal, defeating the downward pull of gravitation. If, however, they are not related to the totality of Jewish life, they may become a leaden weight.

The Jewish ceremonies are the wheels of the Jew's progress toward social righteousness, but if through ignorance, lassitude or indifference their meaning is not known, they become clogs. Some Jews, impatient with the slow progress of humanitarian effort, unaware of the fact that wheels need a driving spirit, discard the wheels, deny the value of ceremonies and censure the vehicle for its inability to move forward.

The ceremonies also create the most potent Jewish survival value — a congenial, healthy Jewish environment. We are a minority. A minority comes into being out of a consciousness of some immanent difference which distinguishes it from the majority. A minority can survive only as long as a consciousness of this difference and a recognition of its worth prevail in the minds of its members. It may be astonishing to friend and foe that we Jews are but one per cent of humanity. It is a surprisingly hard task for a scattered minority of one per cent to reach longevity. The struggle for national survival is accentuated by the leveling tendencies of the industrial age and by international, interracial, interdenominational class struggle. All these tendencies represent so many unceasing assaults on our personal Jewishness, on our national existence.

We Jews want to live. We consider our historical record to be more than justification of our desire for continued separate existence. We have earned such triumphs as well as scars in our historical migrations that we stiff-neckedly refuse to die. Moreover we know that we cannot make any further Jewish contributions to the common treasury of mankind except out of a virile environment, in which our assets can be developed, reinterpreted, reinforced. From the colorless abode of assimilation we have no message for the world.

We want to continue because of our uncompleted task — to bring, through the example of Jewish life and lore, all nations nearer to the One God. We have no refuge, no unassailable fortress other than Jewish life, the atmosphere in which the Lord is set continually before us. The laws of the Torah in their totality create the Jewish environment, in which the Jew works out his salvation for the salvation of mankind. Through a number of customs, laws, regulations, admonitions, encouragements, cognitions, the Jew is to be kept in contact with the divine spirit. No secular pursuits need interfere for one moment with this essential relation, which is the true object of religion. On the contrary, by means of customs and laws every action becomes sublimated into a channel of communion, into an act of worship. The Jew can thus achieve spiritual victory without doing violence to human nature, without fleeing hermit-like from the world, without sealing his senses to the beauties and blessings of life.

Everywhere a persecuted minority, bereft of social control, the Jewish people have been dreaming, praying and, through deeds of charity, contributing to the emancipation of humanity from inhumanity. To the modern world the Jew would bring this solution of its most pressing problems. He would join every group which bases itself on the ethical monotheism of the Bible, would endeavor to abolish war, promote social welfare and civilize mankind to an understanding of the blessings of peace.

According to Jewish law and sentiment (codified especially by Moses Maimonides at the end of his "Laws Concerning Government"), the Jew would seek the welfare of mankind through co-operation with other bodies tending in the same direction.

The prophet's admonition, "Seek the welfare of the country wherein you reside"; the rabbis' decision, "The law of the country is binding upon every Jew (where it does not interfere with Jewish observance or religious principles)"; and the Code's teaching that Christianity and Mohammedanism are to co-operate with Israel in bringing about the Messianic Age, would be the guiding principles of all activity.

How Judaism might contribute to the solution of some of the grave problems of society may be indicated briefly by two or three illustrations:

(a) Most important is the Jewish solution of the marriage problem. The laws of nature call for early marriage, as soon as possible after mental and sexual puberty; but economic conditions have tended increasingly to retard the age at which young men contract marriage. Hence youth has been driven to dangerous sex experience, to sex excess, or to unhealthful prolonged self-repression. Another difficulty has been that of adjustment in marriage, the balance between sex urge and consideration of the partner's constitutional and congenital complexion.

Jewish law insists on early marriage. In Jewish life early

marriage has been a fact of great importance. The parents —
to enable their children to marry as early as possible — provided partly or wholly the means of sustenance for the first
few years of their married life. Endowment insurance by
parents for the first few years of their children's married life
might be the modern application of this Jewish principle.
The dowering of poor brides has been a communal responsibility in Israel and a self-evident task of Jewish congregations
in all ages and countries. Thus the bane of "bachelor-
morality" as well as the disillusion of poverty in marriage is
avoided. Parental responsibility is made to extend to their
children's married happiness. The laws of nature, the laws
of God, are so considered.

Jewish marriage law provides for woman's essential freedom by special enactment which takes into account her
physiological and psychological peculiarities, protects her
against becoming merely a means to the husband's end,
guards her moral and physical welfare also in marriage.
Consent in marriage is a postulate of Jewish law; enslavement
of his wife renders the husband an outcast. Jewish marriage
law is responsible for the high level of Jewish married life, for
the excellent health of the Jewish wife and child, for the
close bond of family love prevalent in the Jewish community.

(b) Judaism effects the abolition of hereditary pauperism
by assuring "von Staatswegen," as from the State, a minimum of sustenance to every man and family. According to
the Jewish law the State furnished the use of a tract of land
to the family.

In times of poverty, sickness, or other misfortune, the owner
could sell its leasehold for a period not beyond the year of
jubilee, for no longer than fifty years. His field would return to him, at the latest after a generation, and his children

could again enjoy its possession. With the increase in population, the form of principle changed, its essence persisted: it is the obligation of the State to provide opportunity for work. Every man has the legal right to work, and it is the obligation of the State to provide it. Modern society has not yet grasped these elemental facts. A movement toward such consummation would ultimately free humanity from slums and their evils, and all the horrors of class war.

(c) Arbitration in disputes between merchants, between capital and labor, has been for centuries the practice in Jewish life, set forth in the details of the Jewish code. Arbitration gives promise of being the solution of the very dangerous labor problem all over the world.

These are the solutions offered by Judaism to a few of a large number of modern problems: whenever applied, they have been productive of excellent results.

Judaism has this fundamental message for modern man: religion must be the upward moving force in every aspect of life. Hence the religion of the Jew is all-embracing in its ideals, summoning us to effort — individual, national, international. Judaism demands from every Jew that he dedicate a certain amount of time and energy toward the general betterment of man. This requirement is negative as well as positive. It includes prohibition of social wrong; it enjoins co-operation and help. Beyond this minimum, the Torah leaves a wide margin to individual enterprise, its purpose being to enrich and encourage man's striving after happiness. But throughout all human activities Judaism stresses its demands for righteousness and helpfulness.

To make himself at home in this world is the primary need of man. He must have a point of vantage from which to survey the field of his work. Belief in God extra-personalizes, or, to use a scientific term, gives objectivity to, Man. For the Jew who believes in his religion this belief is made real through the Torah. From it is derived the ultimate purpose, the Messianic Age, achieved not only by the grace of God but through Man's own labors toward perfection.

The beginning of history, according to the Torah, saw One God and one man created by God. The fullness of time, the latter days of prophetic messages will see the One God acknowledged by all men, and the human race united and living in harmonious co-operation as the consummation of man's ideal.

The faith in God gives us not only the interpretation of the universe but also provides standards and guidance. *Yirat het,* literally " the fear of failure," is the flowering of that thought. " I'd rather be considered a fool by man all my life than a failure before God for even one hour." Sin is failure before God.

The basis of Jewish serenity is the faith in the fundamental goodness of man. Judaism brooks no despair in human nature, but would sponsor a keen consciousness of its potentialities. For " Thou hast made him a little bit less than the gods and Thou hast crowned him with honor and glory."

By reaching moral perfection the Jew is to find his peace, himself at home in the world, himself part of the cosmic rhythm. His way toward the height of Judaism is to bring him meaning, goodness, peace and happiness. Stagnation would not spell damnation, but worthlessness, colorlessness, meaninglessness, peacelessness, unhappiness.

These, then, are the elements of the Jewish religion: consciousness of God; belief in his word so that it becomes practical in the activity of every day; confidence that under the common fatherhood of God this will lead to the unity and happiness of mankind. With these the Jew goes forth inwardly serene. He knows that as he performs the ceremonies of the *Tefillin* each morning he places on his head, the seat of thought, on his arm, the instrument of action, opposite to the heart, the seat of feeling, the text of the commandment, " Thou shalt love the Lord thy God with all thy heart, and with all thy soul, and with all thy might." Thus he begins his day teaching and each day until his death he learns that all our thoughts, feelings and actions must conform to the will of God.

SOLOMON GOLDMAN

Rabbi Solomon Goldman ministers to the large and enthusiastic congregation Anshe Emet, Chicago, Illinois. Born in Kozin, Volhynia, Russia, his early training was received in the Isaac Elchanan Seminary, New York. He graduated with the A.B. degree from New York University and has since done graduate work both at Columbia University and at the University of Chicago. In 1918 he was ordained rabbi by the Jewish Theological Seminary of New York. His first synagogue was the B'nai Israel Congregation, Brooklyn, 1917–18. Following this he went to the B'nai Jeshurun Congregation, Cleveland, 1919–22, and thence for seven years' service at the Jewish Center, Cleveland. Since 1929 he has been at Anshe Emet, Chicago.

Aside from his busy pastorates, Rabbi Goldman has been active in many of the general Jewish organizations as well as in civic affairs. He has served variously as vice-president of the American Zionist Organization, president of the National Hebrew Association, delegate to the World's Zionist Congress in 1933, on the board of governors of the Intercollegiate Menorah Society, and on the Hillel Foundation Commission.

He has been a frequent contributor to various magazines, was joint editor of the *Brooklyn Jewish Forum,* 1909–10, and is associate editor of the *Journal of Religious Education.* In 1931 he published *A Rabbi Takes Stock,* and was co-author of *Hashebil.* He was editor of the *Schechter Memorial Volume; Frischman's Stories;* and *Feierberg's L'on.* He wrote the script for the remarkable pageant *The Romance of a People* given during the Century of Progress in Chicago in 1933. In his interpretation of Judaism, he has differed somewhat from the three main official positions, Orthodoxy, Conservatism and Reform. He begins with the nationality, or peoplehood of Israel, as against its theological heritage.

XVI

NATIONAL JUDAISM

By SOLOMON GOLDMAN

WHAT does religion offer man? Before we attempt an answer to this question, we should perhaps ask whether religion offers the same thing to all men. Is there anything in life which can have the same significance or appeal to all? Is that true of poetry, music, sport, food, sex, politics? What does poetry offer the callous, music the deaf, sport the cripple, food the sated, sex the eunuch, or politics the hermit?

What does religion offer? To whom? That man running by the church contemptuously, whither is he running? What does he want? Does he himself know? What is he seeking, liberty or libertinism, happiness or pleasure, salvation or security? Is he a poet, philosopher, physicist, cynic, theologian, or psychopath? Is he healthy, kindly, affectionate and altruistic? Or is he bilious, irascible, sullen and selfish? How about his diet? Is he a glutton? Is his head always in the fog of dulling vapors?

What is he, this man, and what does he want? What can, or what should religion offer him? What do we mean by religion? Do we have in mind loyalty to life's values, an attitude toward the cosmos, or institutionalized religion? If we think of the last, it were feasible to eliminate from our discussion, for the moment at least, the sensitive artist, the ruminating philosopher, and the eager scientist, or all men whose surplus energies do not go to waste but are absorbed in their creative faculties. Men whose impulses, passions or drives are subject to the discipline necessitated by the search for truth or beauty do not, as a rule, wreck their lives on the wheel of fortune or scuttle their personalities in the bogs of environment. Neither preacher nor psychiatrist can claim them. What makes them sacrifice the delights of the flesh, the idle gallantries of society, the graceful flatteries of caste, to a syllogism, formula or sketch? Nobody knows. Perhaps they themselves least of all. Such men often find their salvation in their own inner strength. There is little that they can be offered. They certainly cannot be preached at. One often wonders whether an Isaiah would have been a regular attendant at a synagogue where a Jeremiah was the preacher. The answer undoubtedly is that Jeremiah never could or would have preached to order.

Let us then, for the moment, leave humanity's chosen few to quest their happiness in their own way, and turn our attention to the average man. What does religion offer him? Well, what does he need? What bothers him? Is he disturbed by the misery of humanity? Does he want a formula for cosmic origin or ontological proofs of metaphysical Being? Is he concerned with the exact meaning of Revelation? Is he seeking eternal bliss, grace and salvation? What do these concepts mean to him? If we reduce them to the simplest terms and expunge from them all theology, will that help the plain man much? Will he grasp their meaning? What does he essentially desire? There are certain drives and hungerings he wants fulfilled. There are certain values he seeks to wrest from life. He needs food, love, sympathy, health, recognition, rest, amusement. Frightened, or at least made lonely, by death, he craves the assurance that the grave is only a temporary abode, and that somewhere in the beyond he will meet his loved ones again. His unhappiness is in the main due to the conflict generated by his impulses.

Judaism seems to have understood this plain man well. It has encouraged him to love life, and to seek here on earth health, longevity, comfort, peace, joy, blessedness. To achieve that it offered him what he most needs, namely, discipline or the Law. It rarely overburdened him with philosophic speculation or theological discussion. Not that Judaism was free from positive affirmations in matters of faith. Assent to dogma was not optional. The besetting sin of Adam and the generations of the deluge, later Judaism concluded, was heresy. The most hateful man in the world, a famous Rabbi had declared, was the infidel. Official dogmatism, however, and its twin-sister, heresy-hunting, never did thrive in Israel. With but few exceptions, the mighty men of Israel spoke to the plain man in the plain man's language. Their images, figures of speech and parables were of everyday experience. Their teachings were not above the mentality of the plain man. He grasped them intuitively.

What do the Bible, the Talmud and the Codes emphasize if not simple human relations, the standards and criteria of associative living? Rest on the Sabbath; respect for parents; kindliness to servant, stranger, orphan, widow and beast; certain sex restraints; honesty in business; sacrifices as thanksgiving, petition or atonement; joy and festivity on Sabbaths and festivals; safeguarding of women's rights in marriage and divorce; restraining of the thief, adulterer and murderer — all these the plain man easily understood. The Torah, to use the all-embracing term, sought to condition him for love, justice, mercy, humility, brotherhood and friendship. The goal of religion was stated with grand simplicity: "It hath been told thee, O Man, what is good, And what the Lord doth require of thee: Only to do justly, and to love mercy, and to walk humbly with thy God." Lest the plain man be still puzzled despite such a divinely simple statement, Hillel offered him a measuring rod: "What is hateful unto thee, do not do unto others." That he declared to be the hub of Judaism.

There are, indeed, verses in Isaiah and Ezekiel which describe the majesty of the divine in words that tax the imagination. Hillel, too, Jochanan ben Zakkai, and Akiba were wont to indulge in speculation, but this they did privately and reserved their vague conjectures only for the most brilliant and worthy of their disciples.

On the mind of the plain man Isaiah's visions of the glory of God had but little effect. He did grasp and could readily remember the parable of the vineyard. He knew from personal experience the difference between sweet grapes and wild grapes. The silver which had become dross and the wine which had been mixed with water were not unknown to him. The winebibbing heroes, wise in their own eyes, calling evil good and good evil, justifying the wicked for a reward, and taking righteousness away from the righteous, were easily comprehended by the plain man. He was more than once victimized by the plutocrat, who joined house to house and laid field to field, driving him from his heritage and reducing him to a lowly proletarianism. The Prophet's immortal visions of peace spoke to the very depths of his heart. How he did fear the wolf, the leopard, the young lion, or bear! How often had his child been the victim of the asp or basilisk, and who was there who wanted to leave the family hearth to go forth to war? There was such a shortage of iron in the land that it were a blessing to be able to beat swords into plowshares and spears into pruninghooks. How soothing were these words of Isaiah! It is true that any king or any false prophet could easily throw an Isaiah to a duped, infuriated mob and have him martyred. But after one or two generations he came to be revered by the people as the noblest spokesman of their innermost desires.

What did the plain man know about Hillel, ben Zakkai or Akiba? Nothing, except that they were humble, kindly teachers of the Law, explaining the will of God as revealed to Moses and the Prophets. These men were offering discipline as the only way to salvation, to inner harmony and peace, as well as to joyous, blessed, peaceful, associative living. They taught the Law in all its weary, petty details. "Pure," "impure," "innocent," "guilty," "thou shalt," "thou shalt not," were the everlasting burdens of their message.

They were denounced as Pharisees or legalists. A whole world was crumbling about their heads. Their own country lay in embers and ruins. A new world was born, a world which often turned upon them with implacable fury. But these Pharisees went their way unperturbed, with a calmness which Olympus never achieved, offering a way of life, a social pattern, a discipline, a Law — aye, laws in their minutest detail. They were born teachers and psychologists and understood the plain man and his needs. They knew that man must be restrained and instructed by habits, customs and practices. It is not sufficient to preach ideals, emphasize faith, and leave the molding of character to chance. The human organism tends to act. It is impelled by desire. The "evil tempter," lodged in the heart, knows no rest. He keeps himself busily engaged, working twenty-four hours a day, three hundred and sixty-five days a year. No mean fellow is this foe. To combat him there are only the weapons of self-control, restraint — that is, the group pattern of conduct. But how shall these weapons be forged? By the Law, said the Pharisee, by the established standards of piety, through the daily exercise of self-restraint in every walk of life.

The reader of Moore, Herford, or even Lake and Jackson will easily convince himself that the plain man was never reduced to a robot performing *mitzvot*. He was never, never sacrificed to the Sabbath. Spirituality, faith, grace, salvation were ever given pointed and challenging emphasis. With simple aphorisms, concise *logia,* charming parables, the Pharisees stimulated and led men to the practice of duty, to noble living and pure feeling. In no literature is man given loftier position than in the writings of the Pharisees. To them, the frail descendants of Adam, obeying the Torah, that is, living the good life, are superior to the angels ministering before the Divine Presence. Indeed, " Wherever thou findest the footprints of a man," they taught, "there stands God."

The student of Greek literature turning to the Pharisees cannot but be struck by their wholesome respect for the worthiness of man. One seldom encounters in their writings the depreciation and disparagement of the human in which the Hellenes frequently indulged. The Rabbis were not unaware of the frailty of *homo sapiens.* To this day the Jew recites in the synagogue a pharisaic prayer which contains the following unforgettable utterance: " What are we? What is our life? What is our piety? What is our righteousness? What help is there in us, what strength, what valor? What can we say before thee, O Lord, our God and God of our fathers? " What then emboldened them to esteem man so highly? The answer is to be found in their unique understanding of the essence of religion.

Religion, to them, is practically synonymous with the Law, even as in Paganism it was with art. Both attempted to deal with the evil tempter, with the drives of men. Judaism employed the technique of law — control; Paganism that of art — sublimation. Sublimation assumes for the body autonomous, independent existence. Matter thus becomes its own end. There was, therefore, in Paganism the dichotomy of man into body and soul. Gradually this resulted in the deprecation of the body. As an end in itself, the physical frame was found wanting, and was condemned by the pagan Plato as vehemently as by the Christian St. Jerome. It was the price of sublimation, of primitive materialism. The plain man found in art no sublimation. Aphrodite or Dionysius fanned his desires to mad fury. In fear of his own body, he fled to the Mysteries with all their superstition, self-torture and asceticism.

Judaism never countenanced sublimation. It did not recognize matter or body as an end in itself. The body, indeed, was important, but always as a means, never as an end. It existed solely for the sake of helping man perform the *mitzvot*. It was never considered an autonomous entity, and therefore never came to be stigmatized as the cesspool of evil. The Law was always there to train the body and help it become an effective means to a noble end.

The Jewish attack on Syrian and Roman sport, theaters and circuses was evoked by the fact that they tended to make the physical an end in itself. To make of it an end in itself ultimately means to strengthen the Tempter and to perish in his service. When a Rabbi today waxes eloquent over prize fighting and brings a Jack Dempsey to address his congregation, he may, indeed, be the spiritual heir of a Menelaus or a Herod. With Judas Maccabeus or Hillel, with the Pharisees he has little in common. What does Mr. Dempsey represent? He symbolizes the eminence of matter, or, at best, dexterity. But dexterity to what end? Solely to mar and bleed the face and body of a fellow man. To strike a man, the Pharisees declared, was not only to desecrate the image of God, but an injury might constitute a hindrance to the performance of *mitzvot*. Without the *mitzvot* life was meaningless, and without the body the *mitzvot* could not be performed. Therefore the Pharisees piled up precept upon precept, practice upon practice, to restrain and sanctify the body and keep it fit for normal, wholesome, associative living.

But why keep fit? To what end was the body to be cherished and trained? What was the purpose of life, or goal of religion? The answer to these questions might have been expanded into weary volumes of logic, metaphysics or ethics. The Rabbis preferred to remain blessedly simple. There isn't a philosophic tyro who could not shoot holes through the armor of rabbinic reasoning. Even if one grants their premises, one still finds in Talmudic and Midrashic literature numerous contradictions in the discussion of the problems of Evil, Freedom of the Will, Creation, Revelation, Grace, Immortality. The Rabbis drive no philosophic thought to its logical conclusion. Their formulations are not precise. They are in the main easygoing, *gemuetliche* comments on life which may sound childish to our sophisticated ears, but in the final analysis are no less conclusive than the more exact statements of an Aristotle or a Kant. The Rabbis have this advantage; their language is vivid, living, and speaks more intimately to the heart of man.

Every religious conundrum the Rabbis unraveled with the simple commandment, "And thou shalt love the Lord thy God." How does one show one's love for God? By performing the *mitzvot*. Why love God or perform the *mitzvot*? Because that is the will of God. Why has God willed it? Because the *mitzvot* make for the well-being of society and assure the individual health, longevity, comfort, peace. The *mitzvot* achieve these ends by restraining the evil tempter, purifying the heart, and curbing selfishness, thus making man fit to live with his fellow men as a desirable member of society. But why should the individual want to restrain his personal liberties and adjust himself into a restraining social order? Neither the Bible nor the Talmud consumes much space in the consideration of such a challenging proposition. They had many ready answers. It was, for one thing, the inscrutable will of God. All men were the children of one father and therefore ought to be happy to dwell together. All men were created in the image of God, therefore their society was desirable. The individual could not with his own limited capacities achieve personal security or happiness. He would be foolhardy to hope for joy, blessedness, peace in the midst of a world of universal misery and strife. He is therefore inescapably dependent on society. Society without justice is a jungle. In the jungle there is no health, longevity, piety or peace. Then let man perform the *mitzvot* and submit to the restraints inherent in co-operative living.

In the Old Testament the outlook upon life was essentially this-worldly. The purpose of life or the goal of religion was to create an ideal society so that man might find personal happiness in the midst of the common good. It is true that there are some phrases in the Jewish Scriptures which have an other-worldly ring, but they are too few and vague to bespeak a deeply rooted universal conviction. The story of Job, if not the doubts and speculations of Ecclesiastes, will forever persuade the unbiased that to the Jew of biblical times this earth was not a mere vestibule, cold and dismal, to be rejected and despised as meaningless and unworthy. Not one of the *dramatis personae* suggests to Job the solace of immortality, the comfort of perpetual bliss in a glorious paradise. The narrator was decidedly a lover of earth. (Job 42:12).

In the Talmud, to be sure, a more impressive case can be made for other-worldly salvation, paradise, and hell. But at no time was the biblical *Anschauung* completely forgotten. Talmudic and medieval writers, though considerably interested in immortality, and in reward and punishment beyond the grave, nevertheless clung to a this-worldly outlook. The Kingdom of God or the Messianic era was never conceived as something vaporous and spiritual. It was envisaged as concretely human, perhaps *alzumenschlich*. Maimonides, who more than any other Jew spiritualized every element in Judaism, nevertheless conceded that with the coming of the Messiah a human being will live longer, be healthier and more comfortable. Paradise or *Gan Eden,* he suggested, was a fertile, choice spot located somewhere on this earth with many brooks and fruit trees, growing plants marvelously sweet and medicinal. In brief, it should never be forgotten by those who press other-worldliness on Judaism that it was the belief in the resurrection of the body, not in the immortality of the soul, which found its way into the prayer book.

But let no one form a hasty conclusion and thus brand the Torah and Talmud as earthly and materialistic. The Jew never made " the material an end in itself." " Were man's happiness to consist in pleasure," is the striking utterance of a medieval Rabbi, " he would forever remain envious of pigs. Were he to mistake wealth and honor for happiness, he would forever live at the mercy of others. The greatest human good is much nearer at hand. It rests within man, in spiritual living." Rabbi Adret tolerated food in the world to come not for itself, but only because it invigorated the mental faculties. Only fools, says Maimonides, look forward to the coming of the Messiah in order to enjoy the abundant food, drink and merriment that it will bring. The sages and the prophets, he continues, longed for the cessation of wars, the freedom from economic struggles, only as a means to an end, the end being the contemplation of God and the universe. Isaiah's triumphant vision of a world in peace, he notes, concludes with the lofty envisagement of a world full of the knowledge of God.

Very few Jewish teachers stressed intellectual excellence to the same degree as Maimonides, but no one of them was ready to tolerate ignorance. Ignorance, brutishness, egotism and impiety were to them synonymous. The learned bastard was superior to the noble-born illiterate high priest. Study was life eternal: compared with it prayer was only the life of the fleeting moment. Even though the glory of God was present everywhere, the sages preferred to pray in the schoolhouse. The end of life or the goal of religion, the Rabbis would have said, was wisdom. But wisdom was not, as in the case of Maimonides, metaphysics. It was rather the funded experience of the nation, rooted in the revealed word of God. It was the intelligent fulfillment of life in society. Wisdom, even as Torah, comprehended the national pattern of life as much as knowledge. The reward of wisdom was health, longevity, joy and peace; the way to wisdom was the performance of the *mitzvot*.

On the whole, the average man everywhere recognized these simple ideals as indispensable. While he was driven by an ineluctable force to satisfy his hungerings, he was nevertheless abashed by his excessive appetites, selfishness and greed. He really aimed only at satisfaction, not stupefaction; fellowship, not strife. In the Occidental world, with which the Jew came to be identified, the plain man has gone through the ages rather complacent and satisfied. When agitators, prophets or demagogues made him aware of his misery, he smashed images, burned heretics, stormed bastilles, ground monarchs to pulp, exhausted his anger, and retired once more to bear his burden docilely. By the philosophers he remained untouched. He read neither Kant nor Spinoza, and he had not heard of either Maimonides or Aquinas.

The plain man was not a serious problem to organized religion. He accepted its simple statements and remained unaware of its syllogistic dogmas. He surmised that some kind of a God created, in some sort of way, the world; that God had told the clergy what was good. It was his business to obey. Most of the time he did. Sometimes he faltered and expected punishment, but then God was forgiving. Man preferred to think of reward rather than of Hell. The clergy, too, generously offered intercession in his behalf. Among the learned men there were profound controversies over canons and creeds, but of these he could make nothing. Sometimes the man of God in whom he trusted told him that such and such a man or such and such a group of men were heretics and therefore a menace to his well-being. He then went out, annihilated them, and received the blessing of the men of God. He felt relieved. He could now sin a bit more recklessly — the zeal he had shown for his faith assured him salvation. The men of God had said so.

Occasionally he received a terrific jolt. There wasn't in the world all the kindliness, mercy, justice, or even fair play that he was led to expect. The lord of his manor was a dissolute rascal, but throve. The king violated every law of decency and yet remained king. No thunderbolts from heaven destroyed them. He himself, on the other hand, barely had enough to eat. His wife's strength was sapped by stillborn children. His eldest son, who was to be the support of the family, was ruthlessly shot down by some drunken dukeling on a wild chase. He conceded that he was a sinner, but with all his humility he vaguely sensed that he was no worse than the princes and lords upon whom heaven was showering its benefits. What was happening to him was neither merciful, nor just, nor fair. But the world was too big for him. It was all in the hand of God. There was no use being skeptical. It only would mean damnation in the world to come. Occasionally a philosopher challenged the whole scheme of things. But the philosopher himself was a skeleton in rags eating the crumbs of some Maecenas. He could effect no change in the scheme of things, neither for others nor for himself. His prattling brought no results. The men of God said that he was anathema, the Devil's disciple. The men of God were probably right. The philosopher died a martyr, or a prisoner, or in exile.

The church fared well. Its devotees were legion. If the man of God, like the philosopher, could not affect this world, he was yet master of heaven. He offered perpetual bliss in the world to come. But then something startling happened. There appeared men who could actually effect changes. They built better houses, softer chairs, invented eyeglasses and eardrums, stamped out plagues, removed mud, constructed bridges, built automobiles, healed the sick, and filled the earth with light. These fellows were not theorizing. They were doing things. There were perhaps some theorists among them too. But that was a matter of no concern to the plain man. He had no more read Galileo or Newton than he had read Abelard or Descartes. The plain man is incapable of philosophizing. He wants his drives fulfilled. That's what the inventors — or was it scientists? — were doing for him. He discovered that things might be better on this earth. Men were now doing things which the men of God had for ages declared were beyond human capability. The plain man became somewhat skeptical of the man of God, but not because of some theory of evolution, not because of biblical criticism and archeology, or idealism and mechanism. Nothing is quite as ludicrous as the attempt to salvage religion with the Second Theory of Thermodynamics or with the Principle of Concretion, as though either the pulpit or pew can grasp with any degree of intelligent enthusiasm these involved nebulous hypotheses.

The fundamentalists and modernists are chopping logic while the rotarians, bankers, unions, moving picture magnates, baseball managers cater to brute appetites and offer the material values for which man has always searched. So many advertisements beckon him, offering him his heart's desire, health, longevity, comfort, amusement. The mad rush for fulfillment is overwhelming. The interest in this world is all-absorbing. What chance, then, has the church, with its other-worldly outlook and its learned discussions on how to square atomic fortuitousness with Divine Purpose?

Had science achieved social organization as it has built material values, the doom of organized religion would now have been sealed. But that is precisely where science has failed and religion blundered. Science failed because it was self-centered, indifferent to the effects of its inventions on the individual and society. Religion blundered because it attacked science in the name of truth and not in the name of goodness. It demanded belief where there was a crying need for character. Religion has not yet lost the battle. Just now the crowd is exceedingly restless. Invention and advertising have not fulfilled their promises. Man has found no satisfaction, no peace, not even rest or health or longevity. His appetites have rather been sharpened. He does not cease desiring. Surfeited for a day, he craves only more passionately on the morrow. Then again, in the midst of shrieking advertisements about plenty he is frequently starving. Kings and dukes are dead, but grafters, plutocrats and dictators multiply. There is enough to waste, but he and his are naked and hungry. Again he is hungering for security, joy, peace, for the better world order that the religion of old had promised. Discussions about the eternity of the universe, *creatio ex nihilo,* revelation, will neither check nor quench his thirst. He wants a simple pattern of life that will make for fulfillment. He needs standards, criteria and laws that will offer the life abundant. Religion will be preached at him in vain if society will not offer him justice, mercy and peace.

So much for the plain man. Now a final word about the creative spirits whom we earlier dismissed as self-sufficient. What does religion offer them? A warning that their ivory towers and laboratories will avail them nothing if they are indifferent to the fate of man, if they do not cautiously calculate the effects of their work on society. They will be defiled in the climate of opinion which the masses will generate; they will be debased by the passions of the mart. They will be crushed by a hostile world unprepared to appreciate truth, beauty and goodness. It were well to remember that Greece, despite its unmatched philosophy and art, perished because its greatest sons were forever moving in the narrow realm of an arrogant, albeit cultured, aristocracy, oblivious of the plain man. Judaism survived because the Isaiahs and Jeremiahs and Hillels burnt out their hearts in anguish over the miseries of humanity, the maladjustments of society. To them the goal of life was not only the contemplation and self-expression of the few *aristoi,* but the health, longevity, joy, peace and wisdom of the nation, and of humanity.

FELIX A. LEVY

Felix A. Levy is a native of New York City. Graduating in 1904 from the College of the City of New York, he did graduate work in Columbia University, the Jewish Theological Seminary of America, and Hebrew Union College, where he was made a rabbi in 1907. Ten years later he took the Ph.D. degree at the University of Chicago. After a brief rabbinate in Rochester, New York, he was called in 1908 to Emanuel Congregation, Chicago, where he has since carried on an unbroken ministry. His strong educational interest is evidenced by his membership on the Board of Governors of Hebrew Union College, the Jewish Board of Education, and his chairmanship of the Board of the College of Jewish Studies.

He has been lecturer of the Jewish Chautauqua Society, associate editor of the *B'nai B'rith News,* delegate to and vice-president of the World Conference of Liberal Judaism, and a distinguished leader of the Central Conference of American Rabbis, the national organization of Reform Rabbis. Of this influential group he is at present the national president. Always a scholar, he has in the midst of his numerous parish and other duties found time to write. He is a frequent contributor to many well-known and important Jewish journals, and his list of published works includes the following: *Moses Mendelssohn's Ideals of Religion,* 1929; *The Task of Reform Judaism,* 1930; *Judaism and Modern Thought,* 1931; and *Reform Judaism and God,* 1935. He has just completed the task of editing a four-volume work on the life and writings of H. G. Enclow.

The reader may with confidence accept Rabbi Levy's statement of the goal of religion as representative of Reform Judaism at its best.

XVII

REFORM JUDAISM

By FELIX A. LEVY

I WRITE as a Jewish liberal in religion. Yet it must not be thought that the Jewish brand of progressivism is the same as the Christian. While liberalism is an attitude and not a philosophy, and Jew and Gentile alike can agree on how they are to regard tradition, dogma and authority, the Jewish liberal has a far less radical pruning of doctrine to perform than has his Christian confrere. In a sense Judaism, by its very nature, is free in spirit, for it does not recognize any *status quo* as permanent or desirable, but as essentially subject to the possibility of change. Not being creed but life, it was organic or organismic rather than ideal — not a system of dogma but a means of expression of the consciousness of a people and of its desire to live. Reform differs from the older form in this regard particularly — that it is more willing to initiate changes, even revolutionary ones undreamed of by conservative theology. Judaism is liberal in that it makes no extraordinary demands upon faith. The cleavage between that and knowledge is not so great as in the daughter religion. Belief, to use the terminology of the newer dispensation, was never the supreme test of faith or the condition of salvation.

Salvation then does not depend upon a man's acceptance of what he might consider absurd or impossible, whether it be the Sinaitic theophany or the virgin birth, but upon conduct. From the ethical monotheism of the Bible through rabbinism and its modern successors, the good life has been stressed as the prerequisite of salvation here and hereafter.

Yet for all this emphasis on upright living and the performance of meritorious deeds that reflect man's obedience to the
divine behest, the Torah, Judaism must not be thought of as
ethical culture. It was ethnic as well. Surrender to the
supramundane, awe in the presence of the holy, exaltation
of the personality suffused with a glow from on high are
never wanting. God as central to thought and action is testimony to this awareness of the divine. He revealed himself
and gave man his law for life through the Torah, which includes belief and morals, as well as piety and legal ordinance.
The Torah is peculiarly Jewish and is the people's distin-
guishing mark. Nay, Torah could be called Judaism or
Jewish religion.

Torah is Israel's national possession though certain ethical
elements in it belonged to all people, that is, were universally
binding. It was the charter of Israel's peculiarity or individuality, the agreement which national experience, as it were,
drew up between the Jew and his God. From the time of
Jehovah's choice of Abraham to "be a blessing," the real
beginning of Jewish history, an intimate bond existed be-
tween the two contracting parties, affirming on the one hand
Israel's selection of God and the Lord's election of a people.
This original acceptance of the Kingdom, or better, the
Kingship of God, the descendants of the patriarchs all rati-
fied whether they were the early children of Israel, the later
Hellenistic Jews, the subsequent protagonists of Torah in
Palestine or Babylon, or the more recent dwellers along the
Rhine and Tiber that preferred death to acceptance of a
Messiah who they felt was untrue to the Jewish ideal of a
redeemer. For the Jew in every age and clime only God
ruled and his reign was righteousness and love in his city on
earth.

The Jewish religion is the spiritual expression of the inner life of the Jewish nation. The remarkable phenomenon of a people dedicating itself to God and to the moral life in his name, is one of the inexplicable riddles of mankind's story and on a par with the enigma of this folk's persistence. For according to all known laws of the historic and social sciences, the landless, stateless and wandering group must long ago have disappeared. The presence of the Jew is still a miracle. That a whole nation should choose as its role to serve the Eternal and to suffer if necessary in and for that service is a unique manifestation. To be devoted to an ideal, to make material comfort subsidiary to faithfulness to conscience and the "vision splendid" is spirituality. The aim of Jewish national life as interpreted by prophet and legalist was the recognition and acceptance of the Kingship of God by the people as a whole, and the object of personal life was the individual's submission to the yoke of heaven. This, however, did not mean that Jew or Judaism was occupied with the other world and neglected this. Jewish experiences were not unusual. Slavery, war, conquest, depressions, exploitation, persecution, disability are the lot of all peoples — but the interpretation of these as caused by God, who functioned in righteousness and love, is passing strange. It implies purpose in history and creation, the recognition of a unitary spiritual principle at work in the universe. Above all the din of national clashes and personal debate, Israel stoutly asserted that man lives most richly by spirit.

There is nothing in this outlook that the liberal cannot accept. Nay, reform Judaism may be said to have recovered this kernel of the best Jewish thought, the normative, by breaking through the shell of ceremonialism and exaggerated legalism that encased it. Not that reform has abolished the law — that would be Paulinism — even as it has not exchanged the Israel of the flesh for the Israel of the spirit of the same apostle. It has as a movement saved itself from this danger, though these tendencies which distinguish Christianity have not been absent. Jewish spirituality, while it resembles other types, has its distinctive features, chief among which is that the Jewish people is the vehicle for expression of its spiritual message — a will to live as an organic unit with a definite religious end in view. Despite this ethnic feature of being born into the fold, anyone outside who feels a kinship with Jewish thought and believes in the teaching of Judaism is welcomed as a proselyte and is received into the corporate group. People and religion cannot be separated; the concepts merge. The Jewish watchword is "Hear, O Israel" — not man — "The Lord our God, the Lord is One."

Israel was and is, in Hosea's words, God's affianced, forever, in righteousness and in steadfastness. Whatever Israel might do, however fickle and untrue it might become, nothing could break the plighted relationship. Sin was punished and the Bible records the list of Israel's defections and subsequent sufferings therefor. The individual too stood in a similar relation to his Maker. When the reform Jew then, as over against the secular nationalist, who would make of Judaism a culture or a civilization, insists upon the primacy of the spiritual, religious and ethical elements, he is in the straight line of his people's tradition and evolution. Reform has tried to recover the prophetic spirit and outlook. While religion for us was never creed exclusively and did embrace what today are regarded as national elements — law, language, social organization — nevertheless the theocratic element was central. The whole Talmudic legislation (the law with which Christianity makes from one point of view a correct contrast, as over against Christian stress on belief, and — due to a mistranslation of Torah — a false contrast as being the totality of Jewish life, leaving no room for spontaneity, mysticism and spiritual experience) had for its object the " religionizing " of the Jew. The Torah might be a national product, yet it had universal aspects: as law it was specifically Jewish, as ethics and religion (in our latter-day sense) it was universal, for all of man.

There is no inherent antithesis, though there is polarity, between the universal and particular features of Jewish thought. When one is exaggerated at the expense of the other, or one of these elements is completely disregarded, we get aberrations — such as a purely secular nationalism divorced from all religious interest or a purely theological formulation of Judaism cut off from the factor of a Jewish people. Reform runs the peril of the second and Zionism that of the first limitation. Much of our quarreling and our incorrect thinking comes from the fact that Judaism has these two aspects of nation and faith and that our vocabulary is too inexact to describe precisely the nature of Judaism. Israel is unique in this double character of its nature. Logic cannot resolve whatever ideological contradiction appears to exist between the two tendencies, but life does. At least Jewish life had and still has room for both these trends — the preservation of the nation and the mission of losing identity in one human family acknowledging God as King.

Normative Judaism never attempted to separate the two. Reform, in so far as it broke from traditional concepts and patterns, did abrogate the idea that Israel was a nation. It tried to reduce the Jewish people to a church, which stood at the side of the other churches in the state, the various worshipers being alike in everything that concerned their life —

language, laws, customs of the country — and differing only in theological expression. In attempting this leveling down, the liberal movement was motivated by two considerations: first, a desire for citizenship and participation in the activities of the state, hitherto denied the Jew, on a par with all other patriots — a doctrine preached by the egalitarian movements of the last century; and second, a conviction that Judaism by virtue of its uncompromising monotheism, with its pure and exalted conception of the Godhead, its moral imperative, its human brotherhood ideal, was the simplest and the best religion for humanity. Whatever separatism might still cling to the Jew was to be condoned on the score that such aloofness enabled him to teach his doctrine to a thirsty world ready to accept the Fatherhood of God and the Brotherhood of Man. Jewish life was only religious and religion was narrowed to subscription to a theological formula very much like the Protestant model.

Reform overlooked the fact that Judaism, as religion, was coextensive with all of life. The Hebrew language is part of the religious heritage of the Jew, it is the holy tongue; the Land of Palestine is sacred and bound up with every religious aspiration and many a theological implication; the people is holy and can never disembody its universal ideal from the Israel of the flesh. Isaiah was a staunch nationalist despite his vision of a world redeemed (let it not be forgotten, through Zion); Akiba, who died for his God, was a patriot-martyr or believed himself to be such. It is an *a posteriori* rationalization that would look upon the loss of the land as a blessing in disguise, and that would on the score of an ethical mission erase specifically Jewish traces. If Jewish life is not to be departmentalized, the old Jewish values must be reinstituted.

It may seem strange for a reform Jew to begin this exposition with what seems to be a devastating criticism of the movement to which he belongs. I do so for two reasons: first, because this estimate gives me a chance for presentation of a historic background; and second, because the major current, at least so it seems to the writer, of the progressive movement diverted particularly out of Judaism's national channels again has returned to this main stream. While the question of the compatibility of nationalism with our religious pretensions has long been debated, though now increasingly less so, the line of cleavage between reform and other expressions of Judaism in the modern world hardly breaks along that plane. There are other factors which reform has contributed to the general Jewish outlook, which to me are of far greater significance and which mark it not simply as sterile negation but positive affirmation. For this it must receive credit.

Reform has emphasized religion as direct, emotional experience. Contradictory as this may seem to be in an intellectual movement, the pioneers of Jewish liberalism were deeply pious men with mystic yearnings and they sought their God by direct communion rather than by meticulous observance of precept and ordinance, and attempted to do his will by an appeal to a universal standard of conduct as discoverable by the personality rather than as dictated by a book. In a sense, liberalism tried to preserve the spontaneity of the prophet by means of direct intuition and the ever present sense of the divine nearness that overwhelms the religious consciousness. Many a bit of discipline no longer valid was relegated to the limbo of forgotten and useless rites; the inertia of custom was replaced by a momentum that rendered Judaism truly dynamic, and the fear of altering the past was swept away by the new broom of nineteenth century learning. Liberalism made Judaism modern in its thought, clothed the old concepts whenever necessary in new garb, sloughed off the dead branches from the living tree, giving it access to the sunlight and air of modernity. The services were estheticized; the prayer book was revised, its vocabulary about God, Israel, and other leading ideas was winnowed. There was a ruthlessness, a fanaticism and yet a consistency about the early reformers. They were going to acclimatize Judaism and Jew to the nineteenth century environment, ethical, political and social, and they performed this task with the frantic zeal of a crusader in a great cause. Their enthusiasm sometimes got the better of them, for instance in their complete obliteration from the prayer book of the references to the hope of the restoration of Palestine as the Jewish homeland — for was not Germany or France their native country, and was not Berlin or Washington their Jerusalem? The Messiah was no longer expected, and his advent was changed to the coming of a Messianic era, a general period of good will among men, the coming of which age liberal Judaism was to hasten. Resurrection of the body was supplanted by a belief in the immortality of the soul. The Jewish mission was exalted, the God idea purified to agree with the absolute of Hegel or the idea of deity in Kant. Hebrew as the language of prayer gave way to the vernacular and the sermon was reintroduced and given all-important place in the service. The job of reconstruction was thorough, yet never thought of as final. The influence of Protestant theology is clearly discernible. In Catholic countries reform was slow in starting and to this day has made little headway.

The protagonists thought they saved Jew and Judaism and to some extent they prevented apostasy and desertion.

Their efforts at spiritualization certainly met with some degree of success. One has but to look at the growth of liberalism, its importance in Jewish life, its influence upon its own followers and those in other wings of Judaism to become convinced of the immeasurable good it has brought. It made its synthesis with the new age; it enabled the Jew without any reservation to become companion with the non-Jew in their common tasks; it recognized the right to make changes which it called progress, probably correctly. Our prayer book, for all its omissions of Zion, of out-of-date concepts and practices in Bible and later literature, is a monumental tribute to the liberals' theistic outlook and deeply ingrained yearning for thanksgiving, adoration, and the quest for courage and solace that comes from communion with the Source of All. The pious Jew cannot but be touched to his very depths of being by our beautiful liturgy.

All human efforts are tinged with failure and there are the inevitable relaxations that follow in the wake of all great upsurgings of the human spirit. Ardor cannot last forever; man cannot for long breathe the pure air of rationalism or even of undiluted religiosity. The giants always existed in " those days " and Titans are succeeded by men of lesser stature. The movement was taken for granted and threatened to become orthodoxy. Time revealed its weaknesses as well as the frailties of human nature with which the original zealot fails to reckon. Reform made the all too common mistake of looking upon men as intelligent, and when the first fire died down, while the warmth remained and is still here, the flames no longer burn as brightly as they once did. To some, destruction of the past and its institutions was synonymous with liberalism. Criticism was not supplemented by reconstruction. What was once thought of as a method, to wit, the study of the evolution of Judaism, revelatory of its human origins and vicissitudes, became a principle, so that almost any change dependent upon the whim of the individual leader was possible. Thus the Sabbath has not only lost its original sanctity, but its exchange for a Sunday day of rest has been called for by some leaders. Some rabbis and congregations completely disregard it as they do some of our holy days and the dietary laws on the score of expediency or of obsoleteness. Despite conferences of rabbis and laymen, there is no source of authority. The Bible, Talmud and codes are no longer binding since they are of human origin, and human wisdom in the person of anyone who can get a following abolishes institutions and practices by whim. If ethics or even religiosity is supreme, Hebrew, rituals, ceremonials, the solidarity of all the Jewish people are incidents in the Jewish career, and are relegated to a secondary position or completely dispensed with.

Liberalism always runs the peril of having no authoritarian command, and, even if it had one, of having no way of enforcing its demands. This is due, of course, to the fact that it is not a platform but a mode of approach. Though articles of faith, minimal always, as to what constitutes reform Judaism were drafted by synods and by rabbinical councils, they never received complete acceptance. Many do what is right in their own eyes and justify it on the ground of liberalism. Those who adhere to what has become the classic expression of American reform make of this pronouncement issued by the rabbinical conference at Pittsburgh in 1885 a more or less binding creed; in other words, an orthodoxy. I give a brief summary of this manifesto which, however, was never officially accepted as authoritative:

(1) Judaism has the highest conception of the God idea.

(2) Despite the Bible's high moral and religious value, it is the product of its own age.

(3) Mosaic legislation was a system of preparatory training and much of it is no longer adapted to modern times and sentiment.

(4) Many Mosaic and rabbinic laws, such as those on diet, priestly purity, etc., are obsolete and obstructive of modern spiritual elevation.

(5) Israel is no longer a nation, but a religious community. Its aim is not a return to Palestine but the establishment of the kingdom of truth, justice, and peace among men.

(6) Judaism is a reasonable, progressive religion. Its mission is to spread monotheistic and moral truth in which aim the daughter religions can help.

(7) The soul is immortal. Bodily resurrection is rejected as well as hell and paradise with their punishment and reward.

(8) We Jews must help to solve the important questions of " social justice " in our modern society.

This document reflects the spirit of its own day, the liberal's naïve faith. A reader of it a half century later is impressed by its humanitarian spirit even though he be annoyed by its pomposity, cocksureness and high sounding verbiage. Much water has run under the bridge since that time and the liberal movement now has its sectaries and its divisions. Many, perhaps the majority, of rabbis feel that the time has come for a restatement of our position, while others would not touch what has become to them a sacrosanct charter. The old authority of divine revelation resident in the Torah now reposes in the Pittsburgh platform. This statement is eloquent for what it says as well as for what it does not say. It rejects the nationality of Israel, fails to admit the national character of its religion, of its holy days and ritual. It contains moral and religious generalizations, which are superb for all their generality, and makes Judaism a rational religion. That religion is more psychological than it knows, that Judaism as universalism may not be incompatible with its particularism and the nationalistic aims, that ceremonies such as the dietary laws may have value in our own day — of survival, of discipline, of uniting a people — never seems to have occurred to the framers of 1885. They were the victims of the humanitarian, cosmopolitan, hopeful — almost to the point of millenarianism around the corner — spirit of their age.

Since the 'nineties, Zionism has made its impress upon our people and our thought. Today Palestine is a reality and a grim necessity for some of us. Democracy is threatened by dictatorship, and the gospel of human fraternity winces before the onslaughts of theories of racial supremacies. Jews receive scant courtesy even in some so-called liberal circles, who would deny them the little place in the sun that Palestine gives and shut the doors of immigration in their faces, so they cannot escape the hells which Jews find now in some countries. Even the liberal Christians, with few exceptions, cherish the secret longing that the Jew will transfer his allegiance from God to Jesus. If the Jew is to live, whether it be just to continue or for the purpose of fulfilling a mission, no means to achieve this end can be neglected. For many liberals of today, Palestine offers a chance to save a remnant of our people that may be doomed elsewhere. The old antipathy of reform Judaism to Zionism is gone except in the case of a few die-hards whose Judaism is compressed into the formula of anti-nationalism. The reform leaders who are sympathetic to Palestine and to the re-establishment of a Jewish homeland and a rebuilding of Jewish culture nearly all interpret their Zionism in religious terms. Their hope is that the new life will develop along religious lines and so strengthen us in our missionary task. Our very working together for the Zion homeland solidifies our ranks. Palestine can be the sign of Jewish unity.

Reform has felt the need of greater ceremonialism. The comparatively colorless ritual has been enriched by the introduction of some of the old observances into the synagogue and the home for their symbolic and esthetic values. By the performance of such rites identity with Israel past and present is achieved. Holy days and Sabbath have been made more meaningful, and the old purely rational attitude that only ethics or religious emotion matters have largely disappeared. Music in the traditional mode is more and more insisted upon. A glance at the publications of the official reform groups — the Rabbis' Manual, the Seder Service for Passover, and The Book of Private Prayers — shows clearly this tendency. The responses, of which there is a large collection dealing with questions of conduct and attitude on a great variety of questions, all show a conservative trend. Education of adults and children in the history, thought and language of their people is receiving more and more attention. Reform, while not yielding its universal aims or its claims to a mission, is striving to fortify its Jewish line of defense.

This is not true of all rabbis and congregations. Some of these still adhere to the old program and present drab pictures of Jewish life, being simply Jewish ethical societies or lecture forums where anything specifically Jewish is resisted lest it sully pure universalism. A few congregations have no Sabbath, but instead Sunday services, and these groups are indistinguishable from Christian denominations whom they would resemble. These " assimilatory " groups take their Judaism most lightly. They identify assimilation with colorless anonymity. Occasionally one meets a humanistic group. This latest phase of religious thinking has won few adherents and seems to be waning. Reform Judaism is strongly theistic and very slight inroads have been made upon its theocentric concept of life.

Reform is making its adjustments to life and by its very nature can do so. Its adherents are becoming more deeply Jewish or at least aware of the new Jewishness in the particularistic sense of the word. " Catholic Israel " has not rejected us and we feel ourselves integral to it. The solidarity of Israel that the liberal movement once threatened to undermine by secession is no longer menaced. Jewish life in Reform may not be as diverse in its many specific manifestations as it is for Orthodoxy, but the Jewish note is there and is being developed more and more. Its quality in the two factions is identical with the following difference.

The old Judaism provided for every phase of human life, a proof that it was concerned with this world. Reform broke sharply with the traditional legislation, the legal aspect of Torah, and made the Talmudic dictum of " The law of the land is law," originally uttered to apply to purely religious matters, a basic principle. Thus marriage and divorce, religious concerns of the older interpretations, are accepted by the liberal as regulatable by the state. Marriages forbidden by Jewish law between consanguineous and affinitive relations do not coincide with those prohibited by the state and some inconsistencies arise in practice. Yet the liberal Jew is not the only one who has conflict between his loyalty to the state and to his religion.

This indecision is of grave concern. What are we to do with our Torah as law? As ethics it is still valid, as civil law it yields sovereignty to the state. The very fact that we can question its authority shows that we can no longer regard it as divine, for if we did we should have no doubts as to its force. Yet the law is part of Jewish life or rather gives Jewish life its tang. What are we to do and where is the source of our authority for liberal Judaism?

It is probably true that for most of us, the source of authority resides in the great principles of our faith and in the Jewish people, or perhaps better, in the mutual interaction of the two, ideals and nation. That is Jewish which agrees with basic Jewish thought and has been or is accepted by the Jewish group. Such has been the case in the past, as the chronicles of our assimilating of foreign elements and making them Jewish prove; so it must be now and in the future. If sanction and authority are no longer divine but human, not the single person but the group must be ultimately decisive.

Perhaps too little has been said of salvation, goal and the like. Jews do not think in these terms. To the Jew, duty, loyalty to the tradition of his fathers, looms largest upon his horizon. While the object of all religion in a sense is salvation, and Judaism like its sister faiths feels that through salvation man gains happiness, these are incidents. The Jewish faith teaches that trust and confidence in God will bring man all that he needs and all that he wants. God's grace comes to everyone and his favor rests upon all. To do his will is man's happiness.

CONCLUSION

SEVENTEEN eminent men representing seventeen fairly distinct points of view within religion have expressed their own convictions with reference to religion's goal, and its means of attainment. Can any generalizations be made on the basis of these statements? The subjective element must of necessity enter strongly into one's attempt to summarize and generalize. What follows represents only the impression that the editor of the collection has received from his repeated rereading and study of the work of each man.

Has anything strikingly new been disclosed? Does anything startling emerge from their study? The answer is no. The editor had a pretty well defined idea of what he would find. He has found about as he expected, but his present ideas with reference to the various groups now rest on the basis not of general impressions from widely scattered books but from concise statements on a single theme.

If one asks, first of all, whether there are any differences in the goal as here represented, the answer is yes, in the degree to which it is this-worldly or other-worldly. It is absurd to represent any religion as totally concerned with the life beyond the grave. Certainly no one who wrote for this book is without a lively sense of the present value of religion. Fundamentalism, sometimes charged with other-worldliness, if properly represented by Dr. Riley, is certainly concerned with the here and now. Salvation of the soul is the ultimate goal, but the spiritual fruitage is that " the Divinely indwelt man is a better man, a happier man, and a greater man." That the writer means not in some after-life is clear from his illustrations. The Roman Catholic writer has least to say about the this-worldly values of religion, salvation being for him also the ultimate goal, but his constant reference to the moral order and the necessity of deliberate choice of one's directions clearly imply present values.

Those which here give most attention to the after-life are Spiritualism, Theosophy with its successive incarnations and world periods, Fundamentalism, Roman Catholicism, Mormonism, Orthodox Protestantism, and Orthodox Judaism. On the other hand, Humanism is completely this-worldly and knows nothing of any other. Dominantly this-worldly though without denial of an ongoing life are Dr. Tittle, Dr. Ames, Dr. Goldman, Dr. Levy and Dr. Bridges.

If any one impression stands out above the others it is the fact that even those usually regarded as other-worldly give such meager attention to the life beyond. Likewise that on the whole so few deal with the negative aspect of salvation, namely eternal loss. In most cases, even in Orthodox Protestantism as represented here, there seems to be some reluctance to deal with the negative side of the question, although one of the editor's questions deliberately concerned itself with that. One other outstanding impression is the infrequency of the appearance of the term salvation as expressing religion's goal. The word seems not to be used so readily as in other years. It is used freely only by Dr. Riley and Father Sheen. Both Dr. Bridges and Dr. Ames use the term, but in both cases defining it somewhat differently from the traditional usage. Others use it clearly in a sense somewhat differing from its historic meaning, but without defining it closely. Yet in the question list the term was used specifically and a definition of it was sought.

Salvation from sin, one of the most commonly expressed

functions of religion in Evangelical Christianity, finds emphasis only in Dr. Riley and Father Sheen in the usual way. Even Dr. Foulkes has comparatively little to say about it. To Father Sheen and perhaps, by implication, Bishop Stewart, though his emphasis is different, the offsetting by baptism of the entail of guilt resulting from the fall of man is one important function of religion. The term sin, however, or its equivalent and the aid of religion in overcoming it or securing forgiveness for it is found running through most of the chapters. And sin, for most of the writers, is ethically conceived rather than ritualistically or ceremonially. Some define it specifically. Dr. Bridges, for example, thinks of it as " siding with the animal nature common to us with other creatures and foregoing the painful and perpetual effort to make our differential human nature dominant over it." Dr. Homrighausen says " it consists in a selfish independence and autonomy on man's part, which takes the things of God and uses them for egocentric purposes." Religion seems to be conceived of by all as a support of moral living.

While some stress particularly the individual aspect of religion none fails to state that it has also social implications. Those who stress most strongly the social factor are the humanist, the Jewish writers (all three of them, for Judaism was ever highly social in its faith), the ethical culturist, the liberal Protestant, the Mormon and the sacramentarian. Here, if anywhere, a different selection of writers might have made a notable difference. For example, one might have chosen a representative of the sacramentarian point of view who would have been much less social in his emphasis than Bishop Stewart. In the case of Roman Catholicism a representative might have been chosen who would have laid very much greater stress on the social aspects of his faith. Obviously no one man can represent every variety of viewpoint in a great church.

With Humanism, of course, the social emphasis is basic. There is only man and his control of his world upon which man himself may depend. Alone he is lost. Only in co-operatively striving for the salvation of all through the mastery of the physical and social forces of his world is there any possibility of salvation or self-realization for himself. There is a close correlation between the degree of this-worldliness of the ideal and the emphasis upon the social importance of religion manifested in the various chapters.

When one turns from the statement of the nature of the goal to the means by which it is to be attained the differences are no less pronounced, but they fall out in quite a different way. Here is found all the difference between the Barthian view, as represented by Dr. Homrighausen who theoretically rests everything upon God who must take the initiative in man's salvation, and Humanism which recognizes no force outside man himself upon which he may depend in his endeavor to reach the goal. Differentiated on this basis horizontally, not vertically, one finds some such classification as the following: Beginning with the sheer self-effort system of Humanism as represented by Dr. Dietrich there follow the points of view represented by Dr. Goldman, Dr. Bridges, Mr. Barwise, Dr. Ames, Dr. Levy, Dr. Tittle, Mr. Warrington, Dr. Widtsoe, Dr. Jung, Mr. Gilmore, Mr. Fillmore, Bishop Stewart, Dr. Foulkes, Dr. Riley, Father Sheen, and Dr. Homrighausen. Here again it ought to be said that this is only one person's classification and may be open to criticism. Let anyone who will, try to make such a horizontal scale. Of course, even in the more extreme case of Barthianism man can respond or not as he wills, so the human element of will is not absent even there. The important thing is that the human will does not suffice. God or Christ or some other aid must enter in to make possible the attainment of the goal. Who can say in this scale just where the balance lies between the human and the extrahuman factor in the process in any given case? Obviously the cleavage is by no means along denominational lines, nor even along the lines of Christian or non-Christian faiths.

Many other interesting comparisons might be made and will be made. The implications deriving from such comparisons — what will they be? One general conclusion to which the editor himself has come is that among them all there is vastly more ground of genuine agreement than difference. He cherishes the hope that this attempt to place them side by side may in the long run contribute to a better understanding among the various points of view and help to draw them into a closer fellowship of effort in the achievement of their common ends.

APPENDIX

The following are the questions and suggestions which the editor submitted to each of the contributors to this volume.

WHAT is it, in your opinion, that religion offers to men, individually? Socially?

If as in historic Christianity your answer is *salvation* or *includes* salvation, just what does the term salvation connote to you as a religious leader in the twentieth century? Not according to some historic creedal statement, but as you yourself think of it and preach or teach it to present-day individuals or groups? What is the essential difference between one who is "saved" and one who is not? Are the "not saved" lost? If so what does "lost" mean? Is salvation an individual matter or is it social, or is it both? Can there be a "saved" society which includes "unsaved" individuals? Or do these terms have meaning for today? If they do not have meaning, what terms stand for the peculiar ideas or values which they once connoted?

If salvation is only one phase of what religion offers, what else does it do for men? It may be suggested that others when asked this have replied variously: It gives meaning and purpose to life; it furnishes a moral ideal and moral dynamic; it gives a basis for hope; it affords comfort; it helps explain the inequalities and injustices of the present life and it brings assurance of a recompense hereafter; it offers a possibility of complete self-realization, etc. — the list is by no means exhaustive. Which of these — whether one or more or all, or what others if not these — expresses your own belief as religion's major contribution to human life?

If salvation does answer for you the first question, how is

it to be attained? Through sheer self-effort unaided by anything outside the self? Through Christ? But in what
sense? How does salvation come through Christ? Does
Christ do something for man which man cannot do for himself? Various answers have been given here: By ransoming
him from the evil one; by satisfying the justice of God or by
upholding the government of God by taking upon himself
humanity's guilt; by the force and beauty of his life showing men how to find the Father God — again the list is
merely suggestive. How do you think of it yourself?

If salvation is only *included* among the values which religion mediates to man, how are the other things which it
offers made available?

An able critic of this project objects that too much emphasis has been put upon *salvation*. He thinks that it is a
word which has lost its usefulness for the present generation.
But, I replied, it is found all through the New Testament
and in Christian hymnology. Ought it not to be given new
content and meaning? He held that it is actually dropping
out of the hymnology and will gradually disappear from our
hymns. He wasn't quite certain what to say about the New
Testament. But he thought that in attempting even to rein-
terpret the word we were creating difficulties greater than
would be the case if we were to drop it and use language
better suited to the modern view of religion. What do you
think?

I pointed out that I thought I had in my questions above
left room for the person who does not make use of the term
at all. To such the questions reduce simply to this: What
is it that religion offers man, and how are these values mediated to him? That is really the heart of this whole inquiry.
What is the goal of religion and how is it to be attained?

INDEX